Living Spirituality

Living Spirituality

Contemporary Australians Search for the Meaning of Life

Compiled
with an introduction
by
Christine McColl

First published in 1989 by
Greenhouse Publications Pty Ltd
122-126 Ormond Road
Elwood Victoria 3184 Australia

© Christine McColl 1989

Typeset by Trade Graphics
Printed in Australia by
The Book Printer, Maryborough, Victoria
Cover and book Design Sharon Carr, Graphic Divine

McColl, Christine.
 Living spirituality.

 Includes index.
 ISBN 0 86436 265 X.

 1. Spiritual life. I. Title.

291.4

Acknowledgements

I would like to thank all those who gave of their time and talked so freely with me about their spirituality. Although not all their stories are in this book, each was important in deepening my understanding of the ways in which contemporary Australians pursue spiritual development.

Contents

Introduction

This is a book about the search for meaning in the lives of contemporary Australians. It presents the stories of the inner worlds and outer experiences of particular sorts of people: those whose commitment to spiritual development is far greater than that of the average nominally religious, agnostic or atheist person, but who are not ordained — a traditional indicator of spiritual fervour. The widespread existence of such people is fairly recent, and significant. It demonstrates the eclectic quality of our current spiritual state, and reflects numerous factors: changes in mainstream Christian denominations, including both a decline in their influence and attempts radically to modify their forms; the erosion of secular rationalism; the influx of Eastern and other culturally innovative forms of spirituality; feminism; the belief in personal responsibility for one's health and growth on all levels; affluence and the frontiers it reveals.

I use the word 'spiritual' to describe any activity aimed at deepening the individual's awareness of spirit, soul, self, truth, reality. 'God' is a word that some traditions use for this quality of being, 'shunyata' others, the 'tao' others again. Whatever the concept, what is being described in all teachings is a level of being, to be found both within and without, that is different from the one we experience in our ordinary day to day living, and the mundane consciousness associated with that. Absorbed in that state, the individual feels joy, oneness with all life and a deep sense of meaning; living from a knowledge of that state, s/he has a purpose and an inner integration often lacking in the modern psyche. The search for that level of existence may give to life a quality of rightness, almost as if there were some grid in our psyches which needs this connection to feel whole. Religion and spirituality are not identical. The term 'religion' generally refers to a particular system of faith and worship; in Western societies religions are generally linked to institutions, and their expression may be distorted by the inflexibility, intolerance and dogmatism to which such structures are prone. Religions are made by people, but the essence from which they draw is the spiritual: that essence exists regardless of the institution, and may be tapped without its aid.

These are statements of belief that run counter to the secular rationalism that still characterises much of Western culture today. To articulate this belief more clearly, I believe that this ultimate ground of being exists and can be contacted by the individual. The search for that ground, and the refining of being that such a search both brings about and entails, constitutes the process of spiritual development.

Spiritual autobiography is an ancient genre, but one not commonly encountered in Australia. In compiling these accounts, I have had several aims. The most fundamental has been to explore the way in which spiritual development takes place in contemporary Australia. What compels individuals to undertake a spiritual search, and what problems do they encounter on their journeys? How do they resolve them, what do they actually gain from the process, and how are their lives, and ours, affected by the results? We tend to think of Australia as a materialistic, hedonistic, post-Christian and secular society. So our cultural cringe becomes spiritual too, and we believe that we need to make long sojourns into other cultures — Eastern, African, Aboriginal, Egyptian — to encounter real opportunities for spiritual growth. Our reading reflects this belief. Whatever our spiritual direction — Christian, Eastern, New Age — the literature that inspires us is frequently drawn from other cultures, other places, other times. So our bookshelves abound with stories of medieval mystics, healers in America, yogis in the Himalayas, sorcerers in Mexico. We are inspired, but left with the question, 'How can I, here in suburbia, with my house, car, job and family, emulate these models?' What we want is perceived to exist remote from our lives, which leaves us frustrated and restless. Yet, as we confront environmental catastrophes and the possibility of nuclear war, it's all the more important that we develop inner, spiritual resources. Peace of mind is harder and harder to find, and yet, without the inner strength it brings, it's more difficult to deal constructively with the threats to the survival of humanity that abound today.

The literature on religion and spirituality in Australia does little to answer these questions about spiritual developments, for they are pitched at a level of experience it does not seek to address. The bulk of the literature is orientated to the macro[1]: the history and politics of religious institutions, or to the micro[2]: behaviour — whether or not the individual attends church, believes in God, prays regularly, has been baptised etc. This material does set the context in which the journeys recounted in this book have taken place. It describes firstly, the decline in influence of the traditional Christian denominations: fewer people today affiliate themselves with a particular denomination, attend church regularly or profess a belief in God than did fifty years ago; fewer children go to Sunday School and adolescents socialise far less frequently at church groups which were widespread until the sixties; civil celebrants conduct many marriages, and decisions on such crucial moral issues as homosexuality, abortion, divorce and birth control tend to be made by the individual, often with little regard for the teachings of the church. Secondly, this material describes changes that have taken place within the traditional denominations: Vatican 11 and its effect on the Catholic Church, the growth of an ecumenical spirit, the rise of fundamentalist movements, new theological understandings. However, in between the macro[1] and the micro[2], in the context this material sets, real people are pursuing spiritual development. Their journeys would be facilitated if they had role models within our own culture. To provide such role models, and to examine their experiences, has been one of my aims.

A second and related aim has been to question some of our Western preconceptions of Eastern religions. People in Australia are becoming involved with Eastern traditions for the same reason as are millions all over the world. Their search for meaning is not satisfied by the traditional churches, and Eastern religions, made familiar by jet travel and mass market paperbacks, seem to offer a workable pathway for spiritual development. Identity, community and purpose, associated benefits of such involvement, are deep and unmet needs in our society and do not contradict the genuinely spiritual quality of the Eastern tradition. However, the controversies surrounding, for example, the Reverend Sun Myung Moon (leader of the Moonies) and Bhagwan Shree Rajneesh[3], have left in the popular consciousness a fairly negative image of Eastern religions. Media coverage of these movements is more likely to be directed towards an exposure of a power-hungry guru, dependent and brainwashed followers and families ripped asunder in a trail of exploitation, than towards an open-minded discussion of the powerful force for transformation inherent in Eastern thought. Ideas which touch the human psyche at its deepest and most vulnerable level will always be able to wreack havoc as great as their potential for good and a discernment is important in spiritual choices, as in any other. So there is a truth in the problems, and as well there is the truth that many people's lives are profoundly changed for the better by their involvement with Eastern teachings. Personal experiences of the achievement of Eastern spirituality are conveyed in some of the accounts in this book.

Finally, these accounts can be seen as a 'progress-report' on the human potential movement that has swept the West since the late sixties. Leaving aside all questions of its political significance for good or bad, the fact remains that people involved in this movement can and do make changes in their personal and spiritual lives that would have been unthinkable in the fifties. They go to self-development courses, such as Forum, Insight and Self-Transformation; they practise Tai-chi, rebirthing and meditation; they learn how to assert themselves and resolve conflict; they study self-hypnosis and bio-feedback. These activities are not confined to an educated and affluent elite. Even the most suburban of bookstores now stocks literature on such once obscure subjects as kundalini, dream power and tapping the unconscious. Much journalistic coverage of these subjects has been cynical, focussing on their flakier aspects and expressing an old and particularly Australian suspicion of being had, which throws up a barrier which restricts as much as it shelters. Less cynical reports have tended to apply a reductionist framework to the behaviour of participants: their educational and class backgrounds are noted, and their need for intimacy, community and an immediate, intense experiential validation of concepts is discussed. Amidst the analysis, what is obscured is the genuine potential for human transformation of this movement. To demonstrate this has been another of my aims.

Choice of Subjects

My fundamental criteria were that the people I interviewed be stable and mature, with fairly well established work and relationship patterns. These criteria, I felt, would make it harder for the charge of 'escapism' or 'dependence', sometimes levelled at those who take spirituality seriously, to stick. Particularly with Eastern religious the cliché of 'drop-out' is often, quite erroneously, invoked. Since I wanted to examine the spirituality of ordinary people, I deliberately excluded ordained members of any tradition: nuns, priests, ministers, sannyasin, acharyas[4]. Although four of the sixteen people in the book have spent some time in such roles, all had left them years before my interview. In pursuit of the more typical Australia, I excluded professional psychotherapists, since, although many of these have a strong spiritual commitment, it is something that their work expects them to develop. In terms of occupation they fall into the following categories: administration (4), teaching (2), community or-ganisation/social work (3), semi-professional (2), scientist, butcher, reporter, osteopath and naturopath, one each. Their ages, at the time of interview, ranged from 29 to 57 with an average age of 44; ten of the sixteen are either married or in stable long-term relationships, six are parents and two were expecting mothers/fathers.

Half of those I interviewed have been involved primarily with Christian denominations and half with newer religious movements, a broad term I shall use to describe Eastern teachings, the human potential movement and other recently formed groups. Although, in terms of adherents in the community, this considerably over-represents the second category, it helps to redress an imbalance of inquiry, which has generally been focussed on established denominations. It is unusual for followers of alternative and more traditional pathways to be brought together like this. My doing so reflects partly my aims, and partly my belief that, at some level, all seekers ask the same questions and reach the same destination; thus it helps to legitimise the alternative. Although the concept of 'representativeness' is of limited value when one is discussing an area as internal and evolving as a spiritual journey, nevertheless, out of a sense that different traditions do generate different issues, and that it is important for many to have a voice, I have used it as a criterion in seeking subjects. Thus, within each of these major categories, I have sought to include both large and small denominations/traditions/movements. Of the Christians, four are Catholic, two Anglican, one Salvation Army, and one fundamentalist. In the alternative spectrum, I have included people who have been involved with Indian paths, Buddhism, the human potential movement, feminist spirituality and some smaller eclectic groups. Most of those interviewed have pursued their journeys within the framework of one particular tradition. Several, however, have been more eclectic, and even in the former group, many have, at times, sought outside the tradition for techniques to deal with particular issues. This raises the important issue of 'spiritual smorgasbording' (sampling different pathways rather than making a wholehearted commitment to one), to which I'll return later. Finally, a sense of my own inability to cross profound cultural barriers has meant that I've chosen to exclude some significant strands in contemporary Australian spirituality, notably the experience of Aboriginals and non-Anglo-Saxon migrants, and therefore of Muslims, one of the fastest growing faiths in Australia today. I hope that one day each of these groups will choose to tell its own story.

Although most people whom I approached were remarkably happy to cooperate with a strange voice on the telephone asking them to recount their spiritual autobiographies, I did encounter hesitations and reserves which, in themselves, throw some light on the pursuit of spirituality today. Some felt their journeys were too private to share; some felt that being included in the book would give them some kind of spiritual status they were reluctant to claim; some felt that their journeys were still very much in process and therefore difficult to describe. Some followers of newer religious movements, sensitive to past media harassment, were afraid that an interview would lead to another hostile piece of sensational journalism. People whose connection with a teacher had been profoundly important were sometimes inhibited by loyalty and the fear of antagonising a figure of considerable psycho-spiritual power, from discussing all aspects of their relationship with the teacher, especially if these were controversial (sexual relationship between teacher and student, for example). These factors prevented some from sharing their journeys. There were other more general constraints when I considered whom to interview. Reserved and laconic Australians are not accustomed to talking about spirituality and some I knew, of deep faith and substantial spiritual attainment, would not have found it easy to conceptualise their journeys. Others were simply born into a tradition, and in their lives deepened their sense of it with little struggle. Their journeys, though profound, had not the episode needed to create a story.

Nevertheless, enough spoke, and spoke well, to produce the stories in the book. Each account is based on a lengthy interview in which the subject, prompted at times by me, related his/her spiritual autobiography. Although I had no predetermined set of questions, in general I probed people about their pre-adult spirituality; their mentors/teachers; their involvement with a particular tradition and the benefits and difficulties associated with that; crucial experiences, crises/turning points/stepping stones; their current spiritual practice; the way in which their spirituality affected their work, relationships, handling of crises and attitude to politics. I wanted people to tell their stories, not recount their beliefs, therefore the stories are experiential, not philosophical. Where necessary, I've included a brief account of a movement's ideas at the start of the interview. Other than editing necessary for coherence, clarity and grammar, the stories are presented in the speakers' own words.

The Archetypal Journey

To help answer my basic questions about the process of spiritual development in contemporary Australia, I've used the framework of the archetypal journey, as described by Joseph Campbell in *The Hero with a Thousand Faces*[5], to analyse the experiences recounted here. Joseph Campbell has examined myths and legends from all over the world to show that the story of the hero/heroine recurs with a frequency that suggests it reflects a deep need in both the individual psyche and society. In the images of the East, in the narratives of the Greeks, in the legends of the Bible, the same story is retold. A hero/heroine, becoming restless and dissatisfied with mundane life, sets out on a journey in search, although s/he may not know it at the time, of spiritual renewal. The journey is long and arduous, and on the way the traveller must deal with challenges and obstacles: turbulent rivers, icy peaks, monsters and daemons, distracting temptations and false paths. Sometimes a helper, magical, human or animal, assists the seeker on the way. Ultimately the hero/heroine triumphs over all hindrances, and reaches a source of power and spiritual regeneration. Transformed, by this and by the labours of the journey, s/he returns home enriched, to share his/her illuminated self. This return and sharing is as profoundly regenerating for the community as the journey has been for the individual.

This archetypal pattern, which occurs in other cultures and at other times, is also found in the stories of contemporary Australians pursuing a spiritual path. To none of them, incidentally, did I describe the myth at the time of interview. In fact, I found it remarkable that the stories should reflect the archetype to the extent that they do. What I have done in examining the stories is to discuss the way in which each element of the archetype manifests itself in people's lives. Thus, I've looked at 'the call' — the initial urge to embark on a spiritual journey; the role of helpers, whatever form they take; challenges/issues faced by the modern seeker; the goal, and transformation, and the return — practising spirituality in the community. Analysing the accounts within this framework has enabled me to bring out what seekers have in common, without losing the sense that each journey is unique. Each individual's search is enriched by being linked with the mythical, and the spiritual journey provides a useful framework for other seekers to clarify their experiences.

The Archetypal Journey

The Call

'The familiar life horizon has been outgrown; the old concepts, ideals and emotional patterns no longer fit; the time for the passing of a threshold is at hand.'[6]
What compels people to put energy into such an inner process as spiritual development in a culture orientated to external accomplishments and the accumulation of possessions? The call came differently to different individuals. Several of those involved in Christian denominations were born into families of considerable spiritual intensity. So the seeds of their journeys lie, to some extent, in

the rich spiritual ground of their childhood. They were strong enough to withstand the adolescent questioning, the disapproval of peers and the secular rationalism which destroyed the childhood faith of many of those interviewed. Dissatisfaction with a materialistic way of life (Melville), the search for deeper answers to questions of meaning and value (Cleary), and life's origins (Bewlay), and personal crisis (Vernon) set others onto their journeys. Those who became ordained did so for diverse motives: out of a general desire to focus on the centre (Cain); from a vague and, in retrospect, difficult to understand attraction to the religious way of life (Truman), and from a sense of special purpose and the need to serve (Rainbow). Both Cain and Truman, who set out on the path to ordination in the Catholic Church in their late teens, commented that their decisions were made at a time of youth and inexperience. Being born into a tradition did not mean that people followed it unquestioningly: in later life many became rebels against, or innovators within, or in some other way marginal to, the mainstream; generally in pursuit of a purer and more real way of practice than they felt the institution offered.

The majority of those involved in newer religious movements had a religious upbringing, sometimes of considerable fervour, but lost their faith when exposed to the spiritually corrosive factors listed above. This loss of faith was a gradual slide into indifference for some and a shattering disillusionment for others. Thus, none was seriously involved with a traditional denomination when they began their journeys. For some, that journey was undertaken in response to an inner longing, felt since childhood, for something, often initially poorly articulated and ill understood, more than an ordinary life offered: an answer to fundamental questions about the universe, a knowing of the ultimate (King, Cooper). Personal crisis/illness, family worries, profound dissatisfaction with the rat-race — sent others looking (Nelson, Maxwell, Nicholas). Others were caught up in the counter culture's radical critique of institutions: having dropped out from the mainstream, they had energy and interest available to pursue alternatives (Stockford, Bourke). Nevertheless, in contrast to the stereotype, only a minority of those involved with newer religious movements came to them via this route. Most people experienced their longing or their crisis while living a settled way of life.

Reviewing these stories reminds me of the old story of the priest who told an inquirer that people came to his temple for many reasons — for help in crisis, for luck in business, for explanations of life's mysteries, for empowering rituals they could practise. Which, asked the inquirer, is the right reason to come? All are right, said the priest, for God draws people to Him in many ways. As long as they have turned to Him, He will take care of the rest. Albeit in the language of a particular tradition, this story conveys the truth of the archetype: however the call comes, it leads people to embark on the same journey. It is the destination and the process of reaching it which shape the seeker far more than the initial reasons for leaving, a point often obscured by reductionist sociological/psychological analyses of the spiritual.

Assistance
Traditionally on the journey the hero/heroine receives assistance from someone or something — a wise being, a magical animal, a vision. The contemporary equivalents are the outer — teacher/guru/mentor and the inner — wisdom/intuition/dreams/guidance, of which s/he is an expression. How important were these for the seeker?

The role of a guru is particularly relevant for those involved with Eastern traditions, since some, though not all, of these deem spiritual development to be impossible without one. This view is not a comfortable one for those raised in an ostensibly egalitarian culture which hacks at tall poppies, values self-reliant individualism, and, at a deeper level, has great difficulty with the idea that an individual may have attained a state of spiritual perfection that is qualitatively, and not just quantitatively different from the norm. Nevertheless, in many Eastern teachings where enlightenment, total spiritual transformation is, in theory, achievable in this lifetime (as opposed to the after death attainment of Christianity), this belief is held as a matter of fact. 'Guru' is a Sanskrit term meaning literally, from darkness into light. The guru is generally held to be highly developed, sometimes enlightened. Having attained this state, s/he can accelerate the disciple's spiritual development, by direct guidance, sometimes using powers such as clairvoyance acquired by lengthy spiritual practice, and by other more subtle psycho-spiritual means involving working with energy. Commitment to the guru connects the individual with the power of the spiritual lineage s/he represents and guru devotion, as well as opening the seeker's heart, may calm and purify his/her mind, opening it to deeper transpersonal realms. Ultimately, however, the guru without is recognised to be a manifestation of the wisdom within and his/her deepest function to connect the seeker with that inner depth. Thus a guru is seen as a figure of immensely more power than a teacher, and it is this power which makes him/her so crucial for spiritual development.

Four of the five involved with Eastern teachings had a guru for some, if not most, of the journey they described. John Cooper, a Buddhist and the one exception, although he had a teacher, Robert Aitkin a Western Zen master, felt that Aitkin was as much a friend as a teacher, and that in general people who claimed to be gurus took themselves far too seriously. Three of the gurus were Asian and one, though immersed in an Eastern tradition, Rumanian by birth. One of the gurus was a woman, Swami

Chidvilasananda the head of the Siddha Yoga movement, and the rest were men.

People's relationships with their gurus were as complex and diverse, as troubled and ecstatic, as ordinary relationships can be. Some had not been looking for a guru, but were drawn into a relationship by the strength of their immediate reaction to them. Nelson describes falling overwhelmingly in love with Swami Chidvilasananda, at first sight, and Stockford felt a profound inner connection with 'Baba' the leader of the Ananda Marga movement. At the other extreme, Bourke, a Tibetan Buddhist who was also not looking, at first found the teacher who was to become his guru to be quite ordinary. His relationship with Lama Yeshe evolved over years, and was as much based on Lama's skill in expounding teachings as on his spiritual-emotional reaction to him. All felt respect and awe for their gurus. Fear had for some time inhibited Nelson, Bourke and Stockford from forming a close external relationship with their gurus; however each, to some extent, worked on their anxieties and developed a relationship in which they felt freer to express themselves. King, on the other hand, felt at first so unintimidated by her guru that she was able to respond to his request that she work for him by stipulating the conditions under which she would do so. The processes by which gurus exerted their effect on their devotees/students varied enormously. King felt that she had learnt to accept with joy whatever life offered by dealing with the bewildering array of situations to which her guru exposed her. Bourke received extensive formal teachings, tantric initiations which connected him with the power of the guru's spiritual lineage, and the opportunity to work for his guru in positions which strengthened him personally and spiritually. Nelson received from her guru 'shaktipat', an Indian term meaning transmission or spiritual energy: the process initiated a movement of spiritual energies in her body that generated both ecstatic states of spiritual bliss and intense fear and anger as old patterns of negativity were cleared out. Stockford had very little personal contact with her guru, but felt inspired by her sense of inner connection with him, and guided by the philosophy and practices of the movement he'd created.

None of the gurus encouraged dependent behaviour in their followers. Both Nelson and King's gurus sent them away from their ashrams back to their home countries, where, the guru perceived, their duty and path lay. Neither Stockford nor Bourke even had the opportunity to spend much time with their gurus: the former because her guru lived in India, and was for several years in gaol, the latter because his guru travelled constantly around the world. Although all in general followed their guru's advice and suggestions, their trust was not blind credulity. It came from observing in their own and their friend's lives the positive consequences of listening to the teacher. None was asked to act in ways discordant with their values and interests, and Bourke felt that he had scope not to do what he was asked, should it be difficult for some reason. All had surrendered some autonomy by virtue of their acknowledgement of a guru, but this was a process voluntarily undertaken and bringing in exchange a sense of spiritual progress and a greater ability to function in the ordinary world. Overall, their relationships with their gurus gave to these seekers a connection, which they felt was incredibly valuable, with individuals embodying that state of higher consciousness which they all hoped one day to realise themselves.

Most others, whatever their paths, had teachers or mentors, rather than gurus. Schoolteachers, university chaplains, therapists, co-workers, friends, spouses, re-treat/course directors were some of the people from whom individuals received spiritual assistance, in connections which could be as brief as a weekend, or as long-lasting

as a lifetime. Finding a teacher was not always easy.
Vernon described years of looking before she encountered,
virtually by chance, someone who could guide her
spiritually. All these people were a source of new ideas,
feedback, deeper self-awareness, support in times of crisis
and, in general, of community, a feeling for the seeker
that others had directed their lives to the same ends.
The emotional charge around these figures, although it
could be strong, was far less than that around a guru,
and their influence on people's lives operated in far more
circumscribed domains. Only one person interviewed
described a bad experience with a teacher, in this case a
woman whose behaviour seemed to bear little relationship
to the ideals of the movement she purported to represent.
Interestingly, this incident took place within a small
organisation without an established tradition, one of the
contexts in which such events may be likely to occur[7].

Several mentioned guidance/assistance from a realm
classically described as the spiritual. King, hospitalised
for years in her adolescence, received a visit from a
vision, a little old lady whom she'd never seen before
and never saw again, who told her how to deal with the
excruciating pain she was experiencing. Maxwell recounts
a long conversation he had with a 'wise presence', about all
aspects of his life from current trauma to the directions his
practice as an osteopath should take. For some, this deeper
realm was manifested in dreams and other expressions of
the unconscious. A dream catalysed a major shift in life
direction for Melville. Others mentioned guidance from
their intuition, and several had changed work/life paths
substantially on that basis. Maxwell, previously a highly
stressed executive, took up osteopathy. King took her
family with her to the USA in order to train as a yoga
teacher. Both Bewlay and Cleary felt a sense of divine
intervention in their acquisition of the jobs they wanted.

Challenges

Traditionally on the path the hero/heroine must confront obstacles. The challenges, albeit symbolic representations of the psyche, may be represented as external — deep gorges, endless deserts, daemons — or they may be inner qualities — sloth, doubt, greed — which threaten the pilgrim's journey. What are the contemporary equivalents of the trials of the myth?

Some obstacles people encounter seem straight from the myth. Inertia, getting started and staying motivated, particularly when one is working from books alone, (Maxwell,Cooper) was dealt with by the individual connecting with a teacher or group whose energy inspired movement. The opposite problem, speed, racing at the spiritual path with an ego-inspired Western 'go for it — enlightenment or bust' attitude was mentioned by one Buddhist I interviewed. The advice of a teacher slowed him down. The classic loneliness of the pilgrim was an obstacle for Cain, who left her support group, her 'root people', the Dominican Order, to follow her own path. Work and spiritual activities for Cleary and King left them no time to pursue deep one to one relationships. Several were more distant from their families as a consequence of their journeys, either because their families disapproved of or could not comprehend their spiritual paths (Nelson, Nicholas), or because they'd felt it appropriate to distance themselves from them to enjoy greater freedom (Maxwell, Stockford). Simple physical threat to life and limb was encountered by Melville, working in the slums of Chile, and Stockford, captured by Vietnamese soldiers in Kampuchea while on a mission of service for Ananda Marga. Having trust and faith, keeping going in the face of difficulties, the ancient problem of Job, suffering and yet believing, was mentioned specifically by Cleary, and yet I had a sense of it as an underlying issue in many of the stories.

Since a spiritual journey involves letting go of familiar concepts, values and identities, fear is a perennial issue on the path. Truman, pondering whether or not to leave the priesthood, was afraid not just of financial insecurity but of the risk of actually loving another human being in an intimate relationship. The spiritual choices Goodman and Cain had made left them with little surplus income, if not impoverished. Cain described working with her unconscious to deal with the fear of being penniless; ultimately she realised she had to live out her belief that she was being cared for. Another source of fear lies in unconscious material, the release of which is encouraged by the practices of some traditions, and by therapeutic self-exploration, which may come to be necessary for further progress. Both Nelson and Maxwell experienced intense panic as unconscious material erupted in the course of their spiritual practices. Both finally reached an understanding that such material came from lifetimes of trauma, and its release was a purification. Alcock had to contact the fear and helplessness he had experienced during a long repressed childhood trauma before he could deepen his being and therefore his relationship with God. Even ecstacy can be frightening, when it comes unexpectedly, as Nelson describes. People dealt with their fears by contacting friends/teachers/gurus for advice and support, by coming to an understanding of what was going on (which could entail internalising a conceptual system quite different from that of the West), and, ultimately, by learning how to live with the fear, however bizarre the catalyst (Nelson).

Doubt and questioning were important aspects of many people's journeys, and, in general, because they did not degenerate into a narrow cynicism, were trials which deepened rather than imperilled an individual's search. Doubts in some cases were manifested as challenges to the structures and practices of the institution with which the individual was involved, and in some cases as questions of belief. For example, several evolved different concepts of the ultimate in a process that sometimes involved many years of questioning. Truman, Alcock and Maxwell all moved from childhood concepts of a remote and punitive God to a perception of the ultimate as profoundly benign, and immanent as well as external. Vernon, Rainbow, Stockford and to some extent Goodman all came to reconceptualise the ultimate in feminine terms, referring to the Goddess rather than God, and feeling a quite different connection flowing from what is more than a mere linguistic shift. It's worth emphasising that doubt, sometimes seen to indicate a problem with faith is not necessarily so. In Buddhist teachings, students are encouraged to doubt, and not to believe until their own experiences validate what they are taught. From a Christian perspective, Alcock offers the view that God is big enough to be able to handle all doubts and heresies. In fact, a mature faith contains doubt and can tolerate uncertainties and ambiguities. For sceptical, educated and questioning minds in the late twentieth century, doubt may well be an intrinsic part of the journey. Certainly to acknowledge doubt truthfully is a more constructive way of working with those energies than a false certainty.

In the myth, the hero/heroine sometimes meets obstacles in the form of distracting temptations: riches, the offer of power, sensual pleasures. S/he must learn that these are not the real goal of the journey. These archetypal themes recur in some of the stories. Involvement in the world of psychic powers was a stage that several went through. However, they recognised, ultimately, that although spiritual practices may enhance these abilities, they are not its aim (Cooper, Nicolas). Cain, Truman and Rainbow all let go of the security and power of established clerical roles in their institutions to follow their own paths. Vernon came to the realisation that allowing oneself to be vulnerable and powerless, open to the uncertainties of life, was crucial for spiritual growth. Nicholas and Rainbow both described letting go, as their journeys evolved, of one of the contemporary equivalents of power: the belief that they were special, and had a particular mission in life.

The hero/heroine in the myth may become lost on false paths, or trapped in dark caves, symbolic expressions of being on the wrong track. Our knowledge of the psyche provides the contemporary equivalents of these dead ends. One problem is the use of spiritual teachings to justify not dealing with sensitive emotional issues. Continual spiritual development may need to be based on continual emotional development, as Maxwell describes. Alcock gives an example of this. In his period of fundamentalist Christianity, major aspects of his personality were either repressed or projected onto God or an out-group, the result being a narrow and distorted spirituality. The same problem may also be found in some people involved with Eastern teachings, where non-attachment and non-reactiveness are the ideals, and emotions, particularly anger and desire, are labelled as negative. A premature and over zealous application of these teachings may make it harder for the seeker to acknowledge very real and powerful energies within and create a shallow spiritual attainment, unstable because based on repression. Stockford, involved in the Indian Ananda Marga movement, recounts a fifteen-year struggle to find a way of life and practice that met both her needs for transcendence and her need for relationship. It is worth stressing, in this context, that for many seekers, contacting and dealing with the energies of anger and desire (which does not mean blindly acting them out) and strengthening the ego are developmental tasks without which further spiritual progress will not take place.[8] Another problem associated with the repression of emotion is that it may limit one's concept of the ultimate, as well as making one less able to relate to people. For Alcock, therapy allowed him to experience his vulnerability and powerlessness, and thus to have a sense of the God who heals and saves. Therapy freed him from the blocks in his personality which he had developed to deal with childhood trauma, and so allowed him to relate to God with his feelings as well as his mind. Several others (Cain, Maxwell, Vernon) had had contact, in different ways and with different intensities, with therapy, and had found that broader ways of being spiritual were opened up as they uncovered new ways to be human. Another misuse of spiritual ideals is to invoke them in support of a neurotic lack of self-acceptance. One's main spiritual line becomes, 'I'm not okay now, but if I follow these techniques, eventually I will be'. Judgement, rather than compassion, is levelled at the imperfect self. King came to see that her spirituality had reinforced her hatred of herself, and had given her techniques she could use to avoid looking at the murky areas of her psyche. When she allowed herself to feel the despair, fear and anger that she had blocked for a lifetime, she contacted a well of suppressed positive feelings, and arrived at a self-acceptance that was profoundly healing. In all those ways a particular misinterpretation of spiritual teachings had led people into directions from which they needed ultimately to return for further progress.

A different sort of challenge is that encountered by the seeker in his/her relationship with an institution, church, movement or group. In the history of both Eastern and Western spirituality, the place of the institution, and its role in facilitating or impeding the individual's access to the ultimate has been a perennial issue. Both the mythical hero/heroine and the contemporary seeker, as we have seen, are likely to have a helper of some sort. For some, much of that assistance has been channelled through an institution, for although, in the myth, the pilgrim travels alone, in our society any number of organisations compete for a place on the seeker's journey. Most of those interviewed, (possibly partly by virtue of my selection criteria) were or had been strongly committed to an institution, although there are exceptions: Maxwell, for example, and Cooper; the latter felt it important for his spirituality that he not be too locked into any structure. The rewards of this commitment were community, connection with a tradition, and the security of a path to follow. However in this era of rapid social change, this commitment could bring with it major problems, as individuals struggled to reconcile their evolving personal understanding of spiritual truths with the views of the institution. Melville and Vernon's work of breaking down hierarchy in the Catholic Church and increasing lay participation is one example; Cleary's anti-war and anti-authoritarian stance in the Salvation Army another. Nor were battles with the institution confined to traditional denominations. Stockford's feminism led to intense clashes with the male dominated hierarchy of Ananda Marga.

Exit and innovation were the paths open to seekers at odds with their institution. The three who were once ordained each derobed to pursue a way of life more sustaining to their spiritual development. Cain, a Dominican nun, sought peace and space for contemplation, unavailable to her in a religious order orientated to service, and in turmoil after Vatican 11. Truman, a priest for over twenty years, felt that he could best deepen his connection with God by experiencing in a human relationship the intimacy, love and forgiveness which he felt God offered to all people. How, he wondered, could he exhort his parishioners to love and forgive if he himself could not take that risk? For Rainbow, a minister in first the Congregationalist and then the Uniting Church, women's issues were the catalyst for her departure from the church, a move which, at a deeper level, expressed her sense that her spirituality had outgrown the boundaries the institution had set. King, after two long immersions in highly structured and goal orientated spiritual groups, eventually concluded that the gurus, concepts and techniques characteristic of such groups actually distracted the individual from self-acceptance and living in the moment, the fundamental point of spiritual practice. Cain, Rainbow, and King all went on to work in innovative spiritual roles: Cain as a spiritual director and a facilitator of workshops exploring the link between depth psychology and spirituality; Rainbow as a researcher into and expresser of feminist spirituality; King as a therapist working with people with life-threatening illnesses. Other spiritual innovators were Alcock who, with two friends, founded the Eremos Institute to encourage a deeper exploration of spirituality than is traditional in the church; and Goodman, who for the last ten years has lived in a small Christian community where income sharing and communal prayer and meals are the framework for lives dedicated to service in the local area.

Some women faced particular problems with institutions as feminism became fundamental to their journeys (Vernon, Rainbow, Stockford, Goodman). These women sought changes in the structure, practices and philosophy of both traditional (Catholic, Anglican, Uniting Church) and newer religious movements (Ananda Marga). The issues were fairly similar across the spiritual spectrum. To redress the male monopoly of authority roles, both clerical and lay, women sought more power from and greater access to decision making roles and the right, if not already available, to be ordained. From men, unaware of the restrictions motherhood imposed, women sought changes that would allow them and their children to partake in the rituals of the church. They asked, for example, not to be placed during Mass with bored teenagers behind a glass partition, as was Vernon and to be taught new skills. To remedy the subtle but powerful effects of exclusive language women developed inclusive language and referred to God as the Goddess. More generally, cramped and denied by the hierarchical structures associated with male power, women sought space for their mode of being. They wanted more respect for intuition and experience than for rules and texts, and honour to be accorded to women's ministry; the constant unseen sustaining of the social web by women's nurturing skills.

To address in depth the response of traditional and newer institutions to the feminist critique would require another, and different volume.[9] However, these stories illustrate the intense resistance women could encounter even in a left wing and alternative movement such as Ananda Marga (although left wing political movements have never been noted for their lack of sexism). The support of small women's groups formed within the larger structure, the struggle and the hope for change, enabled several women to stay within an institution about which, in many ways, they felt so deeply critical. One woman, Rainbow, withdrew completely from all established structures to explore women's spirituality — its symbols, rituals, histories and beliefs. Not all women interviewed felt feminism to be important and some men expressed sympathy for the feminist perspective. Nevertheless, enough women felt strongly about women's issues to suggest that coming to terms with feminist spirituality will continue to be crucial to the journeys of more and more women and a major issue for institutions across the spiritual spectrum, (the growing strength of fundamentalist churches with their narrow interpretation of women's role notwithstanding). Such changes within the established churches as the influence of creation spirituality, with its pro-women and pro-ecology values, and the increasing shortage of male clerics, will only quicken this current of change.

The Goal

The archetypal hero/heroine, having met these challenges, reaches the destination. There s/he undergoes a crucial transformative experience, 'an expansion of consciousness, and therewith of being ... illumination, transfiguration, freedom'[10]. S/he is now ready to return home.

The stories, being of people still journeying, do not match the myth at this point. Some stressed that the process of spiritual development was lengthy, gradual and imperceptible, and that far more frequent than the occasional times when one felt a dramatic sense of movement were the long hauls where, only retrospectively one had any awareness of a difference in being. This point is worth emphasising since we live in a culture where our ability to gratify most desires rapidly gives us an expectation of instant results which is quite misleading when applied to spirituality. A few (Nicholas, Vernon) described mystical experiences, characterised, as they classically are, by a sense of ecstatic union with all being. Nevertheless, although these left people with a deep gratitude and a greater feeling of meaning, they were highlights rather than endpoints of their journeys. People still had to wrestle with issues and problems and felt their journeys to be far from complete.

Still, the energy people had put into their spiritual development had borne some fruit, and after years of inner work, most had changed Their values were different: love and helping others, following a spiritual path and, sometimes, working for social justice were more important for them than material/career rewards or living up to the expectations of others. People tended to accept themselves more, partly because this was one aim of the therapy many had experienced, partly because they had come to see themselves as ultimately a manifestation of the divine and partly because they could encounter themselves with the love and compassion they had learned to give to others. Spirituality had deepened the sense of meaning and purpose acquired in youth by many of those born into traditional denominations, and brought those qualities to people without religion. None struck me as sanctimonious or self-righteous: most had a humility and lightness of being. In some cases, with an enhanced awareness of the moment developed by their spiritual practice, people enjoyed life more, feeling it to be ultimately good and themselves to be of significance in it.

Their journeys had given understandings and techniques that helped them to deal with life's crises — day to day minutia or major trauma. Different traditions encouraged different attitudes. The resurrection was a powerful metaphor for some Christians, conveying a faith that, no matter what, life would continue with new birth, new growth. Some, at one level more open and loving, felt a greater ability to be detached from their problems. Nelson, for instance, felt the world had become, in the Hindu metaphor, a play she could observe unaffected. The capacity to accept had grown in Stockford as she learnt to let go and surrender control of events to a God who, she perceived, ordained all for the best. Maxwell had learned to see in all experiences, no matter how thorny, an opportunity to learn and grow. Most were sustained by a sense of a deeper meaning to life than that depicted by the external play of events. The techniques people employed in crisis all helped them to contact a higher source of energy and guidance, and to transform their agitation into calm. These ranged from meditation, prayer and dreamwork through to rituals such as chanting, singing and making offerings, to techniques of positive thinking. A spiritual commitment did not mean that people had easy lives, almost the opposite, as the discussion of challenges brought out. What a spiritual discipline did for people, however, was to empower them, by giving them inner tools with which they could approach their difficulties. In a society where so many feel powerless, this is a valuable outcome.

The Return
Crucial to the journey is that the hero/heroine returns to the community to share what has been learned. The community is regenerated by this return, for it needs constant reminder that there is more to life than the mundanity day to day reality presents. It is not an easy task for the hero/heroine: 'To teach again ... what has been taught correctly and incorrectly learned a thousand thousand times, throughout the millenniums of mankind's prudent folly ... to communicate to people who insist on the exclusive evidence of their senses the message of the all generating void.'[11] How is the drama of the return played out in contemporary society?

Again, since none of our subjects had arrived at the destination, the archetype at this stage does not manifest itself exactly in their stories. Yet all had progressed far enough to feel that they had something to share. It is almost as if, in real life, at some stages the journey and the return take place simultaneously. Although none was at the time of interview paid clerics in any institution, the work of most, voluntary or paid, provided an opportunity to communicate their beliefs. Doing so was generally seen as important. This may reflect the archetypal pattern. The Christian axiom that faith leads to ministry again conveys that there is sometimes more to expounding one's philosphy than the ego's drive to convert. Several were involved, full or part time, in helping professions. Bourke was a publisher of Buddhist books, Cleary was a journalist on religious matters for the ABC, Cooper had been an academic in the Department of Religious Studies at the University of Sydney, and Truman spoke at the funerals of those who'd died without links with the church.

Bewlay door-knocked to spread the doctrines of the fundamentalist group to which he belonged, the Assembly of God. Others had established new organisations to give expression to their beliefs. In Nicholas's Planetary Healing Group people of all nationalities met once a week in a suburban high school to meditate on healing the earth. Melville had helped set up the Festival of Life, to energise lay participation in the church. Alcock helped to found the Eremos Institute, to deepen contemporary Christian spirituality. Vernon, Goodman and Rainbow all worked in women's groups to further feminist spirituality, the first two in the Christian inter-denominational groups of MOW (Movement for the Ordination of Women) and WATAC (Woman and the Australian Church), and the latter in a number of small groups, some of which she had herself set up. Institutional change was the focus for some, maintaining and developing a small organisation the aim for others, and simply making people aware of what was seen as a better way of being the principal endeavour for the rest. Only Bewlay saw those of different beliefs as potentially damned by their ignorance, and this is a basic tenet of his fundamentalist Christianity, which draws a sharp distinction between believers and non-believers. The rest worked from a more ecumenical stance. Many would perhaps have agreed with King's view that absolute acceptance of another human is the greatest gift one can give them. It would be simplistic to say that all sought to convey the same ideas for there are real and deep differences between, for example, the Tibetan Buddhism of Bourke and the New Age philosophies of Maxwell. Nevertheless, the values of love and service, a concept of a universal ground of being to be found within and without, a sense of life as sacramental, and spiritual truths to be found here and now in awareness of being, were convictions that were important to many seekers across the entire spiritual spectrum.

The interviews challenge the view that the spiritually orientated are conservative. They also contradict the view that involvement in Eastern traditions generates an apolitical attitude to a world perceived ultimately as illusory, for several of the subjects turned to politics in pursuit of social change.[12] Such a choice was more common amongst Christians, many of whom were well aware that Christianity was originally a force for radical social transformation, and thus strove to revive that tradition. For one Quaker woman interviewed, a sense of God in everyone and life as sacramental, and of the importance of the individual assuming responsibility for the world, had led to over thirty years of work for Aboriginal rights, the environment and peace. Cleary found in the radical political heritage of the Salvation Army a philosophy that supported his reformist politics and actions, including opposition to the Vietnam war and intense union activism in his workplace. Realising the 'Kingdom' — justice, peace and love — was for Melville the crux of Christianity, and to achieve this she worked for three years amongst the poor and dispossessed of Chile in a situation where political choices had to be made every day. Goodman, with others, had set up training facilities for the unemployed in her local area, recognising that unemployment is the responsibility not just of the individual but of the community. Amongst those involved with alternative traditions, Stockford's story is the most passionate in its political commitment. Her commitment to change at one period was encouraged by Ananda Marga, with its radical and socio-political philosophy, yet later ran foul of the organisation as feminism became of central importance to her. Neither Bourke nor Cooper, the two Buddhists in the book, felt that politics was futile. In fact the latter found in the Buddhist concept of the interdependence of all beings a spiritual justification for political action.[12] It is certainly true that some voiced

serious reservations about politics. Nelson expressed the
Hindu view that the world is just a play, so what does
it matter? Cain felt that many politicians did not live out
the values they espoused, while Bewlay felt that politics
was far less important than the titanic battle between God
and the devil for control of the universe. However, enough
people from diverse paths took politics seriously to suggest
that spirituality and politics may, for some, fuse again in
the future as they have in the past, into a potent force
for change. Clearly spirituality can be used in support
of extremely conservative political and moral positions.
However, Cleary's prediction that environmental values
will bring all religions together as the ecological crisis
worsens suggests a more radical alternative.

Spirituality is a spring that both offers renewal and
needs sustaining, and each person had some form of daily
practice for these ends. Virtually all set aside some time
each day for prayer and/or meditation, to commune with
the ultimate, however they understood its nature. Methods
of prayer and meditation varied in different traditions. For
some, prayer was a stilling technique which offered the
opportunity silently to be with the God within; for others
it was an occasion actively to make requests of God, or
simply to express gratitude. Ways of meditating included
focus on the breath, images and mantras to quieten the
conscious mind and contact the deeper truths beyond.
People gained from these practices interludes of calm,
guidance and inspiration in lives that were often hectic
and demanding. Several observed that meditation/prayer
should not be activities isolated from the rest of life,
rather that the awareness cultivated during those practices
should be maintained at all times. As Cooper stressed,
what is here now is what is spiritual, and losing ourselves
as we constantly do, in memories, fantasies and other
forms of mental chatter, we are cut off from this. Some
had highly disciplined approaches to prayer/meditation.

Others had a less structured style, several because they felt that excessive order distorted the organic flowing quality that true spirituality should possess. To differing extents, individuals benefited from association with an institution. There, common rituals such as chanting and singing, prayer and meditation; exposure to teachings; and the opportunity to feel the ultimate, enhanced as its manifestation often is by group energy, maintained and deepened their spiritual commitment.

Several had found in intimate relationships a way of expressing and enlarging their spirituality. For some this was a choice to follow what was perceived as a more difficult path. Maxwell felt that opening his heart in a family situation was more spiritually challenging for him than a disciplined life of spiritual austerities. Bourke, though he operated more efficiently when alone, found it spiritually valuable to have to consider the viewpoint of his partner in their shared life. Truman left the priesthood to find a deeper understanding of God in the experience of marriage. Others simply said that in relationships they could make choices to love, and thus constantly express their spiritual values. Of the six people in the book neither married nor in stable de facto situations, one (Rainbow) had fairly recently separated from a long-term partner. Of the other five, two (Cleary, King) felt that their spiritual and work activities allowed them no time for intimate one to one relationships, although King after an unhappy marriage, was almost ready to be vulnerable again. Cleary had been through a period of excruciating loneliness, but was sustained by his belief that, if the centre was right, the peripheries would take care of themselves. The remaining three (Cain, Bewlay, Goodman), although open in general to the prospect of marriage, were comfortable with their celibate and single status. Cain and Goodman had many of their intimacy needs met by friends and community, and Bewlay, a member of a small and closely knit Assembly of

God church, felt that God had ordained his current single status the better to use him for His work.

Although each person interviewed had substantial areas of work competence, the choice to pursue spirituality and an associated way of life had left many less affluent than they might otherwise have been. Many, in pursuit of a quieter and less hectic way of being, or time for intense spiritual practice, had chosen to work part time, or to have interludes of not working (Maxwell, Cooper, Rainbow, Cain). Others had, for years, worked extremely hard for a spiritual institution, in a voluntary or fairly lowly paid capacity (Goodman, Alcock, Melville, Stockford, Bourke). None had embraced the values of radical poverty, though simplicity was a consciously chosen value for some and fewer than half were in the process of buying their own homes. Many had decided to make spiritual growth, not material gain, the paramount goal in their lives, and to accept the material losses, if any, thus entailed. A deep belief that guidance from the ultimate would resolve life crises helped to sustain this choice.

The Processes of Spiritual Development

To conclude this exploration of the way in which the archetypal quest is lived out in our society, it remains to clarify the way in which the activities seekers describe bring about spiritual development. This is not easy, as the processes of spiritual development, operating as they do in a realm of the psyche that is susceptible neither to conceptual analysis nor to quantification, intrinsically elude precise description. Nevertheless, it is possible to talk about the sorts of things people do, and the ways in which they might achieve their effect, and thus gain at least a rough idea of the processes involved.

A seeker strives to develop a sense of the self as no longer separate from, but rather of the same stuff as, and thus interdependent with, all life. What unites the self within with all others is that they are an expression of the same ultimate reality. This common ground is shared by all in the book with the exception of Bewlay, whose fundamentalist Christianity dualistically views God as external to humanity. Even so the processes he uses to deepen his connection with his God are not dissimilar to those used by the rest. There are three fundamental ways in which people worked on their spirituality. Different individuals placed different emphases on each. Morality is the first of these. By this I mean not wowserism or sexual repression, stereotypes too easily associated with any link between spirituality and morality, but simply a way of life based on restraint and self-discipline. Such a morality, in itself based on a view of the self as not separate, contributes to spiritual development in that it fosters a peaceful state of mind and the self-control needed for spiritual practices. Secondly, by reading, contemplation, and listening to teachings, lectures and other presentations of ideas, the seeker comes to understand the concepts of spirituality. And thirdly, by such techniques as prayer, meditation, chanting and singing, group worship and guru devotion, the individual enters into a different state of consciousness where spiritual truths may become intuitively obvious as s/he has a direct experience of the reality of the ultimate.[13]

Clearly each of these may actually subvert the process of spiritual development. Morality may degenerate into self-righteous intolerance. Concepts received from others may stifle the truth of one's own experience or lead one into a maze of intellectual and spiritual confusion. The experience of different states of consciousness may function as an escape, or render a person unstable, or generate truths which are not integrated with the rest of the psyche. Furthermore, as the history of religion demonstrates, an institution may monopolise these techniques and impose them on others so that spirituality becomes an agent of power and intolerance, and the paths available to the individual choked with the received wisdom of the past. Equally clearly, many other activities may generate states of mind and understanding which lead to spiritual development. Much therapy, by deepening an individual's self-awareness, may have this effect, and particular schools of therapy may have a strong transpersonal orientation. Sport, work, raising a family — anything done with a sense of decency and inner focus — will lead to some spiritual development, for the spiritual part of our psyches exists and may be nourished whether or not we are conscious of it. Life itself, without any particular effort on the seeker's part, may generate experiences that deepen one's spirituality, as the high percentage of people in the community who report spontaneous mystical experiences suggests. Nevertheless, if we are to speak of conscious ways of spiritual development, these, and a variety of techniques associated with them, are what the people in this book have used.

Our Spiritual Landscape Redefined

This review of the processes of spiritual development in contemporary Australia suggests that it might be more fruitful to look at ourselves differently. Rather than focussing on the ways in which our society does not foster spirituality — its materialism, its hedonism, its secular rationalism — we can look at the opportunities available to us here, opportunities which are, perhaps, historically unique. We are healthier, more affluent and more literate, and we live longer than our ancestors or our contemporaries in non-Western societies. Women, although still the objects of much prejudice and restriction, have somewhat more freedom than was available to them in the past. Moreover, although bigotry is still to be found, we live in an era of unprecedented religious tolerance, a situation we take for granted, forgetting that such freedom was largely unavailable to our ancestors, and is still not the right of many of our contemporaries. As well as these advantages we have available to us an immense choice of spiritual traditions, some of which are illustrated in this book. We value an individual's expression of his/her particular character and destiny, and we allow, indeed encourage, innovation, both personal and organisational, more than many other societies. Although there are substantial class based differences in life chances, we have almost unlimited opportunities to pursue our own particular spiritual path, whether that entails rigidly adhering to fundamentalism, Eastern or Western, to liberal Christianity, to New Age teachings or an eclectic mixture of the lot. Any opportunity brings with it risks. The seeker may become confused, make false starts, become trapped in some of the dead ends I've described. S/he may become disenchanted with some of the more patently absurd manifestations of spiritual innovation or, at the other extreme, with the arid emptiness of a rigid institution. These are all real and serious issues. Nevertheless they arise by virtue of our opportunities, and should not cloud these, lest we fall into the deeper trap of 'it's too hard, if not impossible here'.

What we need to realise is that our spiritual landscape will never resemble that of other cultures or other times. Our image of other cultures is of a place where a dominant spiritual tradition enriches but does not oppress, where the perfect teacher is easily found by the ardent student, where time and place can comfortably be found for practice and retreat, where myth and legend give to everyday life a numinous depth. This image is a romantic ideal. Nevertheless, other cultures have offered opportunities for spiritual development that are different from those to be found in our society, notably a living and confident tradition and easier access to good teachers. However, these opportunities were available to people who were often sicker, poorer, less literate and less free than we are, and were largely unavailable to women in any form. In any case, whatever the choices available to others, our spiritual landscape can only be one of the late twentieth century. As such, it reveals a variety of spiritual movements, traditional and eclectic, thriving in a culture most of whose values are secular. Barring a major shift in the political arena, bringing to dominance right wing fundamentalist forces and associated spiritual intolerance, this spiritual pluralism will continue to prevail. This pluralism is richly exemplified in the stories presented here. Aboriginal spirituality, our awareness of which has been deepened by the Bicentenary, will contribute to this landscape of diversity. Australia is no more likely to generate a major new spiritual tradition comparable to Christianity or Buddhism than is any other culture exposed to a ferment of teachings and valuing change and innovation. What is distinctively Australian — the symbols, proximity to Asia, the different strengths of different Christian denominations, a style more low key and laconic than that of America — is probably less important in shaping our spiritual landscape than the opportunities shared by all Western industrialised states. Their spiritual geography, no less than ours, is likely to remain pluralist and unique.

In this landscape of diversity, Eastern religions are likely to have a permanent place. The forms of Eastern religion existing in Australia are multifarious and to explore the history and problems of each tradition represented here would take another and quite different volume. I have simply wanted to convey that the stereotypes often associated with these traditions bear little relationship to the experiences of seekers immersed in a spirituality that is patterned in ways unfamiliar to us. It is worth citing here, as a further comment on the stereotype, the observation of two American scholars, Anthony and

Robbins[14]. They believe the brainwashing metaphor often invoked to explain the behaviour of followers of these movements, is a social weapon which provides a rationale for persecuting unpopular social movements. Influence, they note, takes place in all organisations from the Boy Scouts to Rotary, and few of the followers of Eastern religions live in such situations of tight information control as did the American prisoners-of-war in Korea, whose experiences gave rise to the concept of 'brainwashing'. It is also worth noting that the desire for an immediate experience of the ultimate, and the valuing of right-brain phenomenon are to be found not just in Eastern religious movements but in fundamentalist Christian groups which, at first glance, seem to inhabit the other end of the spiritual spectrum. In newer religious movements there is much talk of intuition, healing and psychic powers; in fundamentalist groups of speaking in tongues, prophecy, healing and miracles. Both groups are likely to find in the most trivial of daily events a manifestation of the grace/will of the guru/God, and to believe that on such grace/will depends the success of any endeavour. So both traditions tap a widespread longing for a type of spirituality not to be found in the mainstream denominations (although charismatic renewal movements within these clearly aim to cater for these needs). Education, social background and one's ability to maintain a fundamentalist stance in a pluralistic society are some of the factors which stream the seeker into these different spiritual channels.

Eastern traditions will change as they become entrenched in the West, just as Christianity has changed as it has spread to Asia, Africa and Latin America. In many societies in which they originated, contemplative traditions have been crushed by hostile regimes (China, Tibet, Kampuchea); in others (Sri Lanka, Burma) political upheaval has made access by Western students difficult. The 1984 stipulation that Commonwealth citizens could no longer live indefinitely and visa-free in India[15] has meant that Western students cannot spend years absorbing Hindu and Tibetan traditions (the latter represented by the one hundred thousand Tibetans living in exile in India). Moreover, in the late eighties, fewer people are prepared to spend years of their lives in Asia. So fewer of those involved in Eastern teachings will have had lengthy periods of contact with particular traditions in their native lands. However, they may well approach Eastern religions with more critical discernment than did those caught up in the idealistic turn to the East in the sixties and seventies. At the same time, a generation of Westerners matured in different Eastern paths by fifteen years of study is emerging, and will provide both a community of wise elders, important in any tradition, and a source of lay teachers.

In this situation, structural and cultural adaptations are likely to become important for each tradition. Such questions as the development of practices, liturgy and images that are appropriate in the local context, and the use of English instead of Sanskrit/Tibetan/Pali/Sino-Japanese (to cite the Asian languages most frequently to be found in Eastern religions), may well be more important to seekers who've spent little time in the East, and perhaps also to those of an older generation secure enough to contemplate change. Another issue is that of democratising structures, one that is more germane to large hierarchical movements than to smaller more confederate ones. Although hierarchies are as likely to entrench themselves in 'democratised' Eastern structures as they are in their Western counterparts, nevertheless widespread participation in decision making and open channels for the expression of grievances may act as a check on the excesses of teachers and gurus. Generating forms of community, particularly in the cities, that give seekers the opportunity for intense practice without demanding that they become ordained for life, is another challenge which some traditions are beginning to take up. And Eastern religions, no less than Christian religions, must enlarge themselves until women feel that every aspect of their experience is honoured as much as that of men's.

It should not be assumed that change will come any more easily in these traditions than it has in mainstream denominations. Stockford's story shows that even an innovative and politically radical Indian movement can resist change tenaciously. Nor should it be assumed that changes will 'adulterate' the essence of these teachings. The changes that will be made will be those necessary for each tradition to grow local roots without which no amount of 'purity' could prevent a withering away of exotic specimens. However much the institutions change, at the core level Eastern traditions address questions relevant to us all. Our chance to pursue spiritual development in the framework they provide is one of the unique spiritual opportunities available in the West today.

The human potential movement, too, will permanently enrich our spiritual landscape. It is true that many large corporations now use its techniques to increase employee satisfaction, and thereby productivity. It is true that believers in the oft-repeated human potential axiom that 'you create your own reality' generally avoid discussing the way in which class, sex and race shape that creation and, at a deeper level, of the influence such spiritually potent factors as grace and karma may exert on the individual's struggle for autonomy. And it is true that many participants in human potential courses are exposed to a smattering of over simplified ideas and techniques. The human potential movement has flourished in the environment of late twentieth-century capitalism, and has taken on its hues. It is used for profit, to express middle-class values, is mass produced and over optimistic to the point of hubris. However, none of this should blind us to the fact that, as so many of these interviews show, the ideas and techniques of the human potential movement have touched the lives of people of all classes and spiritual persuasions, and touched them for the better. Access to the inner realm, tools for making positive changes in our lives, a belief in the individual's ability to grow are the gifts of the human potential movement. It is surely time that the corrosive journalistic cynicism about this movement is replaced by an open-minded examination of what is, for all its imperfections, an innovative and healing social force.

Finally, the Christian denominations, for all that they have lost ground this century, still possess a numerical dominance and a role as articulators of our basically Judeo-Christian values that ensure them a place of significance in the evolving spiritual landscape. It would be erroneous to conclude from stories of the mostly radical Christians in this book that the churches are in a ferment of change. Most denominations, as is the nature of any long established hierarchy, are dominated by conservative thinkers and tend to resist, if not actively stifle, movements for change. Indeed, in an era of heightening class polarisation, rapid social change and insecurity at the prospect of nuclear war and environmental crises, a move to the conservative and familiar is to be expected. One of the fastest growing movements in Australia today, fundamentalism, is overtly and profoundly conservative, as judged by its attitude to women, moral issues such as abortion and homosexuality, and its literal interpretations of the Bible. Nevertheless, the church does not exist in a vacuum, and within all major denominations pockets of innovation can be found which attempt constructively to deal with wider social change. The role of the laity and of women, new ways of practising and deepening one's spirituality, politics and justice, new forms of liturgy and community, and ecumenism are all issues of crucial relevance to some contemporary Christians. Where new answers to some of these questions are put into practice we find the innovations many of the stories illustrate.

To foresee the future for the mainstream denominations would require another sort of book. However, one could speculate that the degree to which the Christian churches, no less than newer religious movements, deal constructively with these issues will determine the extent to which they remain spiritually relevant to a large section of the community.

Where does all this leave the individual seeker? You are a woman whose children are grown up, who has sharpened your intellect with a part time degree, and now looks for something deeper. You are an electrician whose frequent intuitive flashes have made you aware that there is something more to life than material phenomena. You are the partner of an addict, drawn to spirituality by Al-Anon and AA's belief that faith in a higher power is essential for healing. You are a teacher whose personal development courses in schools have led you to therapy and meditation retreats, and to the communal ecstacies of rebirthing weekends. You exist in a thousand more forms, but whoever you are, you wonder where to start, or how to go on, as you look at the bewildering array of options available in today's spiritual marketplace.

Perhaps the deepest message of these stories is that you can only follow your own path, whether it leads you to Christianity, to a newer religious movement or to the wilds of eclecticism. In this era, spiritual smorgasbording may be a quite appropriate response, or indeed the ultimate expression of your journey. Ultimately, no one but yourself can save you from closed mind scepticism or too open gullibility, or from a surrender that is dependence or a resistance that is the ego's attachment to its autonomy. No one can steer you from the trap of spiritual materialism[16], or prevent you from squashing the living flow of your own spirituality with the weight of received truths. Conversely, none but a higher intelligence can judge whether or not an experience is spiritually fruitful. Support from friends, community and teachers is valuable, but in the end what will best guide you is your own inner wisdom, the clarity and intelligence of perception that is intrinsic to the mind, albeit often blurred by the voices of others. To cultivate this inner wisdom, in all the ways the seekers in this book demonstrate, is to tune into the voice within. It is that inner intelligence which will both guide you to the next step and give you a taste of the ultimate, of which it is but an expression.

---

1 See the books listed in the bibliography under Spirituality in Australia: entries 1, 4, 5, 9

2 Mol, Hans *The Faith of Australians* (Allen and Unwin, Sydney, 1985)

3 Milne, Hugh *Bhagwan, the God that Failed* (Sphere Books, London, 1987)

4 'sannyasin' and 'acharya': Eastern terms for those who have taken robes

5 Campbell, Joseph *The Hero with a Thousand Faces*, Second Edition (Princeton University Press, New Jersey, 1971)

6 ibid p51

7 Anthony, Dick, Ecker, Bruce and Wilber, Ken *Spiritual Choice: the Problem of Recognizing Authentic Paths to Inner Transformation* (Paragon House, New York, 1987) It is suggested here that abuse of power is more likely to be found in leaders of groups without an established tradition or lineage.

8 Wilber, Ken, Engler, Jack and Brown, Daniel P. *Transformations of Consciousness* (Shambhala Publications, Boston 1986) See Jack Engler's essay.

9 See, for an exploration of this subject in an Australian context: Franklin, Margaret Ann (ed): *The Force of the Feminine* (Allen and Unwin, Sydney, 1986) and Franklin, Margaret Ann and Jones, Ruth Sturmey, (ed): *Opening the Cage* (Allen and Unwin, Sydney, 1987)

10 Campbell, op.cit., p246

11   ibid., p218

12   For essays by socially involved Buddhists, see Eppsteiner, Fred (ed): *The Path of Compassion: Writings on Socially Engaged Buddhism* (Parallax Press, Berkely, 1988)

13   Service, which is important for several seekers, is a form of 'right action', which flows from morality.

14   Anthony, Dick and Robbins, Thomas *New Religions, Families and 'Brainwashing'* in Robbins T. and Anthony D. (ed): *In Gods We Trust: New Patterns of Religious Pluralism in America* (Transaction, New Brunswick, 1981)

15   Until 1984, citizens of Commonwealth countries could live in India indefinitely, without a visa. Now, like people from the rest of the world, they must apply for a visa. Maximum stay is six months.

16   Spiritual materialism describes the tendency of the ego to aggrandise itself by spiritual accomplishments. See *Cutting Through Spiritual Materialism* (Chogyam, Trungpa, Shambhala, Colorado, 1973)

Kerry Nelson

'I would feel this tangible energy in my heart chakra. It would whirl, and I would feel the most immense love and bliss. My whole being would be absorbed into that sometimes light, always love, always a feeling of absolute ecstacy.'

Kerry Nelson was born in 1943. Illness and family crisis revived her childhood interest in spirituality, and she went to a meditation course run by a Siddha Yoga ashram. She quickly found that the mantra she learned there brought her peace and blissful transpersonal experiences. Soon afterwards, she attended programmes where Swami Chidvilasananda, the head of the Siddha Yoga movement, spoke. Although Kerry was not looking for a guru, she fell overwhelmingly in love with Swami Chidvilasananda. A six months 'spiritual honeymoon', during which Kerry constantly experienced spiritual ecstasy, was followed by a long period of turmoil as she had to deal with the fear and anger that spiritual practices released in her. This is a beautiful story of spiritual development patterned in a tradition of guru devotion unfamiliar to the West.

Siddha Yoga means, literally, the yoga (i.e. oneness with the self, God) that is received by the grace of a Siddha, a perfectly realised master. It is a Hindu tradition, emphasising the role of the guru as a transmitter of spiritual energy to the disciple, a process which in turn awakens the disciple's own subtle spiritual energies. 'Bhakti', devotion to the guru as the embodiment of the Absolute, which is also one's own true nature, is a fundamental practice of Siddha Yoga.

Siddha Yoga was brought to the West in the seventies by Swami Muktananda, then head of the tradition. It spread rapidly, and today there are Siddha Yoga ashrams and centres in more than twenty countries. Ganeshpuri, eighty kilometres north-east of Bombay, is the main ashram in India. Swami Chidvilasananda is now the head of the tradition, a position to which she was appointed by Swami Muktananda before his death in 1982.

Kerry Nelson was raised in Melbourne in a Roman Catholic family. She was an ardent Catholic until her marriage at the age of nineteen.

As soon as we were married my husband went headlong into Eastern religion — couldn't tolerate Catholicism at all. I was terribly influenced by him. I dropped all my practices totally. While he contemplated, and read a great deal, I had absolutely nothing. I did nothing. Before that, I had been going to church and having moments of meditation. They've never formally taught meditation in the Catholic Church but I don't think I've ever stopped meditating. Moments when I was quiet, I'd have strange experiences where I was witnessing myself. My mind would get quieter and quieter, and all of a sudden I would have the sense of not being myself. Sometimes quite powerful experiences would leave me very scared. When I started anticipating them, I would block them, put on music, because I had such a fear of them. They have never left me, never. But I had no formal religion to support me, and it left a big blank in my life.

I looked to lots of other things to fill in that blank,

but I was never satisfied. Everything made me miserable. I would think I would be happy if I had something else, and something else would come, and I would be miserable. I was utterly materialistic. I was looking at my family, my job, my house. I would get different jobs, we would move to different houses. We've moved eleven times. I'd renovate houses endlessly but I could find no satisfaction in anything. Gordon tried to interest me in Eastern religions, and I'd read a bit, but I felt no attraction to them at all.

When I was about twenty-eight, bad things started happening in my life. My health became very poor and I suffered a lot of pain. I had a chronic illness, systemic lupus erythematosus[1]. It affects the connective tissue. My knees and ankles went, and I couldn't walk. I had endless operations, and none of them worked. I started looking at Gordon's spiritual books, mainly the Eastern ones. I'd pick them up and skim them, and think, 'There's something there. I'll get to that, but I'm not ready, not yet.' The children were taking all my energy. I had three girls, all little at that time, and, not being able to walk, it was heavy going!

Then, the next catastrophe in my life. My beloved, beautiful eldest daughter went wild when she hit thirteen. She dressed up in punk gear, she ran away, she took to drugs, to alcohol, petty thieving — everything possible that an adolescent could do. It was devastating because it was totally out of keeping with our life, and the lives of our friends. We took it very badly. Nothing we did would stop this girl going crazy. I'd sit up all Saturday night beside myself with anxiety and terror at what she was doing. This continued and got worse over several years; it took my last energy and enthusiasm. I knew I needed some help to get through.

The last straw came when my youngest daughter, Emma, had an accident. She was hit on the head with a ball. She had brain injury and suffered epilepsy. That was it. I felt I could take no more. I was very depressed, and I needed support. I knew then that I had to meditate. I had read in magazines that meditation was beneficial, and I knew I had to do something.

Just at that time an article on Siddha Yoga appeared in the *Australian*. Gordon saw it and thought it would be good for me as they didn't seem to be too rigid about the way people sat. (I find it hard to sit cross-legged.) So he rang to ask about a 'Learn to Meditate'[2] course. They didn't have anything going at the time but they had a little centre that was offering a course several months away in January. That was great, because it was closer to home, and it felt less intimidating.

That was November but it was almost as if my sadhana[3] had started from the phone call. I picked up books that Gordon had had for years, and I was rigid with interest in them. Practices like 'japa'[4] made me think 'Wow, this is wonderful'. I didn't do them, I didn't understand them, but just reading about them made me feel great. I was just dying for the meditation course to start. The books were all Paul Brunton[5]. Gordon was very involved with Paul Brunton, his works and his group. Over the past fifteen years he had written to him and visited him several times in Switzerland. I was on the fringes of that. I think I got a lot of grace from him as Paul Brunton gave it to Gordon, and it filtered through to me.

When I went to the meditation course, I was well and truly ready for it. I don't think it was a terribly good course but the moment I heard the mantra[6], that was it for me. I don't remember a single word that anyone said. It was the traditional cliché in Siddha Yoga — I heard it, and felt that all my Christmases had come at once. Not only did they present the mantra to me, but they said I could take it home and use it! I felt at last I had something to hang on to, something tangible and real that was there to help me.

I took to japa with great gusto. The next day, I took
four little children to the beach. I remember walking up
and down thinking, 'Wow, I could do something, I could
say this mantra'. I said it, and said it, and said it, and the
more I said it, the better I felt. Nothing happened, I just felt
good. That was just the first day. I started to read *The Inner
Reality* by Paul Brunton, and I felt very enthusiastic about
his practices. He said that we should meditate every day, so
I thought, 'this is it, the big thing — meditation is going to
start'. I didn't realise at the time that I'd been meditating
all my life. In the course we were told that it is best to sit on
the floor. Funnily enough, that was the biggest stumbling
block, having to sit on the floor cross-legged. It sounded
an affectation. But I did it.

So I went to a quiet spot. I sat cross-legged, and I started
to say the mantra, and I immediately started to have an
experience. I was suffused with white light. I didn't know
what was happening at the time, but I suppose, when I look
back, I had been building up to this. I immediately jumped
up and ran downstairs saying, 'Gordon, Gordon, what
have you done to me, what's happening to me?' He could
guide me at the time, and tell me what was happening,
because he'd read so much about it. He was enthusiastic
and terribly happy. He explained that this was a spiritual
experience. So I felt slightly reassured, but disbelieving
about it happening instantly. But that was my sadhana
at that time. My early sadhana was that I got everything
instantly.

I took to meditation with incredible enthusiasm. I
decided to work out exercises for myself. I tried to
concentrate my mind totally on nothing. I did mantra
squares, then I put my concentration inside them, and my
thoughts outside them. The room where I was meditating
was next to the kitchen, and I could hear the fridge.
Initially, I thought the noise of the fridge was distracting.
Then I found it helpful. If I could focus on the noise

I wouldn't think. Actually, I had read somewhere that Buddhists put new people under a waterfall for the same reasons. I didn't know that at the time, but I latched onto this fridge noise. It was wonderful as it really helped my meditation. I'd start to meditate, and I always felt good and full of grace. It doesn't sound very dramatic, but from the depth of my depression and misery, to sit down and feel none of that misery, but feel good, was splendid for me.

For a fortnight I did that. Then, I bought a tape of the mantra and I started to play it for about fifteen minutes just before I'd meditate. While I was listening to the tape, I would focus my mind on the letters of the mantra, so that no thoughts could intrude. I was totally, absolutely focussed on the mantra. One night, as I was meditating like this, I received shaktipat[7]. I was suffused with grace, with God, with golden light. I felt completely elevated, uplifted, full of immense ecstasy and bliss. I called Gordon, and said: 'What have you done to me, what's happened to me?' He was totally dumbfounded, but I still thought he had done something to me. I said: 'Did you go out for your walk in the bush?' He said, 'Yes.' I asked: 'When you were out there, what did you do to me?' He replied: 'I did nothing to you. I don't know anything about this.' He had not read anything about shaktipat, so he didn't know what had happened. I stayed in that state almost all night. I would go and walk and talk, and I would go back and sit in meditation. I didn't matter, I couldn't shake it. I sat like that, in this wonderful state, for hours. I didn't talk to anyone about the experience, but I didn't feel frightened by it. It was too wonderful to feel frightened about. I knew it was connected to a much higher consciousness.

Some weeks after that, this guru person that they talked about came to Sydney. I thought it was a great coincidence, but obviously it wasn't. They talked about her at the meditation centre and I thought perhaps I would go to see her. I enrolled in the Intensive[8]. I thought, if I'm going to do the Intensive, I'd better go and check her out first at an evening programme. I had a very negative feeling about gurus, I didn't want one, I didn't even think of one. I felt she was a bit of an intrusion into these wonderful experiences I was having. I went to the programme out of curiosity, mainly to get my money's worth out of the Intensive. The Intensive cost $200, and we couldn't really afford it. I thought, if I'm going to pay that much money, I'd better get used to her first. I was totally mercenary!

As soon as she walked into the room, I had the most amazing reaction to her. My hair stood on end, my body rippled with expectation and delight, and I totally fell in love with her. I don't remember a single word she said, just my own inner reaction to her. She gave a talk, and then there was a meditation with her. It was a wonderful meditation. There were tiny blue lights[9] twinkling and suffusing me, I felt superb. Going home, I couldn't shake this wonderful experience of love, and divinity, and bliss.

The next day, I was driving around, feeling that nothing could ever touch me, speeding down the road going to work, thinking life was so superb. It was a scintillating feeling, everything was wonderful. Thinking, I could do anything, I could do everything. I was a very timid person, I could never express myself properly, but suddenly I was doing it, with gusto, and enjoying it. But I was also feeling detached from it. I went to the public programme again the next night. I couldn't stay away. One night I couldn't go to the programme, because Gordon was working and the children were at home. I did something I'd never done before in my life — I left my children unattended. I trekked out to an unknown place about fifteen kilometres away. I ended up completely lost and missed the programme, but my desire to be with her was so great that I had tried to be there.

During the Intensive, she touched me very gently[10], and stroked my head. On the second day, all I could think of was the most total, overwhelming and unbelievable love. It wasn't directed to her, it was just directed towards everything. I thought how can anyone feel this love, can it be really happening? At that time, I was too timid to go to darshan[11]. I wouldn't go up to her. I would sit in the hall during the breaks, I wouldn't go out for a tea or coffee, I would look at her. But I was still too timid to actually go up formally and pranaam[12] to her. I was just too frightened of her, of her position more than anything. I'd moved into the ashram to do the Intensive, and when I went home on Sunday night, Gordon said: 'You're glimmering with blue light, it's pouring out all over you, I can see it glittering from you.'

For the next couple of weeks, I couldn't come out of meditation. I'd try to go shopping, and I'd sit in the seats around the shopping centre totally drugged and heavy with this bliss of meditation. Whatever I did I was suffused with total meditation. I just couldn't function. I could talk, and do everything, but the meditation was very powerful. I was bursting with it. I thought this was the best thing anyone could ever do. I felt uplifted, and absolutely connected with this higher consciousness, and with the guru. I only had to look at her picture and I'd fall into bliss. So pictures started appearing all round the house. I had no mental commitment to her, just an inner commitment. I didn't think of her as my guru, just as someone I loved to look at.

My spiritual experiences started getting much more intense. It was the norm to have them every time I meditated. I would go to the ashram and meditate, and I would just suffuse, and my body would levitate. I'd go to school — I was a school librarian — and I'd have meditated and chanted all the way in. By the time I got there, I literally could not put my feet on the ground. My physical body was always about half an inch off the ground. I literally floated on air for the first two hours in that library. It was amazing. I wouldn't know what was going on, but they were sublime experiences. I felt very close to God. I felt that with one blink I would become God. I thought this was normal, everyone was doing this. Everyone had the mantra, and this was what happened.

Gordon had never had a meditation experience. He started getting very intense, and borrowing books from the library on Buddhism and contemplation. He started practising all sorts of things in a desperate attempt to meditate, and to hang on to Paul Brunton. I took him to a programme at the little centre, and he was disgusted. All this chanting and singing. It wasn't what he perceived Paul Brunton to be advocating. His was a much more English, stiff upper lip style of spiritual practice. You did these things quietly, by yourself, behind closed doors, and didn't talk about them. You certainly didn't sing about it, or display it, or do puja[13]. It was merely his closed perception of meditation. So he wouldn't go back for a while. I had to fight that, because I thought he was the last word in sprirituality. I had to believe there was something there for me even if he disapproved of it. It was terribly difficult for me to do that. But when he started seeing that I was experiencing all the sorts of things the saints had experienced, he was terribly supportive and enthusiastic. But he also felt a bit forlorn about it all, wondering why he had been left behind. He still feels that, to this day. He still has never had a spiritual experience, though he is the most spiritual person I know and the most committed, loving and good person.

I started reading books about Siddha Yoga, and I wanted to go to Ganeshpuri. We went, taking our youngest child as we thought her brain injury might be healed there. We had read in a Siddha magazine that Baba could deny you nothing if you asked for it in his samadhi shrine[14]. We thought that we had nothing to lose, so we took her. In fact, she was very hostile. She was nine, and she thought it would be boring. So we bribed her by telling her that we would buy her a television computer game in Singapore.

We had the most harrowing trip. All sorts of catastrophes — there were floods, the taxi broke down, and it took us eight hours to get there from the airport. We went straight into an Intensive with the guru. She touched me again, several times. That was a great start to that trip. I was in very deep, constant meditation.

After having a very intense inner connection with her, but never having been to darshan, I had gone to Ganeshpuri wanting to make an external connection with the guru. After reading all about Baba, and his books[15], all the Satsang books and *Play of Consciousness*, I had no doubt this was for me. And of course, I sat there demanding an external relationship with her, and she wouldn't give it to me. I wanted her to acknowledge me as a person. I wanted her to talk to me. I wanted to have her as a friend. In my experience, when I made a commitment to a person, they would generally be friendly back to me. They would talk to me, and we would have a nice external relationship. I was prepared to say, 'Okay, you're my guru, now start connecting with me on this external level'. It was a misunderstanding of the role of a guru. I'd only had one set of experiences with people, and I was applying them to the guru-disciple relationship, wanting it to be the same.

It was a very intimate group of about one hundred and fifty people. Often the darshans were only twenty or fifty people. I was close to her all the time. The more I internally demanded attention, the more she would turn away and not give it to me. This caused a great crisis inside me. I started to feel puzzled and hurt and unsure of myself. I thought that Siddha Yoga is wrong, she is not my guru, I'm in the wrong place. Surely if she were my guru, she would give me more attention. She would acknowledge me.

The crisis came after I'd been there about two and a half weeks. We'd been given a video to watch on Saturday night, of the guru laughing and being friendly to people. I just sat there disgusted, and thought that it was all just a pretence. So I stormed off in a big rage, thinking I didn't belong in Ganeshpuri at all. Then, the very next morning, the talk was by a Swami who read a letter written by Swami Nityananda. Part of it was: if you're climbing a mountain, you come to chasms. When you come to one that looks too deep or too hard to cross, you can either turn around and go back, in which case you won't get to the top of the hill, or you can chance it and have faith — jump across the chasm and get to the top of the hill. 'In sadhana', he said, 'it's exactly the same. You come to a chasm in your sadhana, and you can either give it up and say it is too hard, and go home and say, this is not for me. Or you can jump over it, and have a leap of faith, and say, I don't understand, but I accept.' The timing was wonderful. It was exactly what I wanted. I sat right in front of her, which I was usually too frightened to do. I started to cry, because it was exactly how I felt. This crisis had come from her, whether she was my guru, or whether she wasn't. I formally accepted her inside, in front of her, even though I didn't tell her.

We went from that programme into lunch. I was sitting in the dining hall cross-legged meditating and waiting for lunch to come, and she came through like a whirlwind. As she was leaving, she threw a mala[16] into my lap. It was a rudraksha[17] wrist mala with silver on it. It was the one mala that I had really wanted, but we couldn't afford it. It was a most amazing gift too, because it had her perfume impregnated into the rudraksha beads themselves. I only had to put it to my nose, or just hold it, and the smell just wafted. That afternoon, I arrived at darshan late from my seva[18]. Everyone was there, and there was total silence. Because of my physical deformities, I can't pranaam properly, and I always try to do it with a group of people. Usually, I'd have just snuck into the back and sat down. But this time, in front of everyone, I went up to her and pranaamed, as a formal acknowledgement. And so she had acknowledged me, and I had acknowledged her formally, though neither of us had spoken a word.

Six weeks after we came home from Ganeshpuri I started having the ultimate spiritual experiences. It's difficult to describe them. Since shaktipat, I've always felt the kundalini[19] energy going through all my chakras[20], and coming out of the sahasrara[21]. I would feel this tangible energy in my heart chakra. It would whirl, and I would feel the most immense love and bliss. My whole being would be absorbed in that sometimes light, always love, always a feeling of absolute ecstasy. I would love everyone to go out, so I could go into the meditation room and just be absorbed into this wonderful ecstasy — totally and absolutely lose myself. I would start to meditate after dinner and I would stay there till 2 or 3 am. I think I was in samadhi[22] some of the time. I hate to say that, because it sounds pretentious, but I was. I felt the difference between me and God was a fine line. I wish I had known then that these experiences were not going to last, and that they were as profound as they were, because, though I appreciated them, I didn't appreciate them as much as I do now.

These experiences lasted for six months, then they stopped, within a week. I'd always felt very frightened of Gordon's sadhana, and I'd always tried to push him away from it. I hated to share the guru with him, I felt jealous and resentful when he came anywhere near her. This was always going on, and I was trying to keep him away from anything that my conscience would allow me to. But my conscience wouldn't allow me to do that very much, because I felt in my mind he had a right to this. It was my emotions speaking. I've never told anyone this, except the guru. I feel ashamed of this, but that's the way I felt. So what happened was that he got a very loving letter from the guru giving him a present, just flower petals, and giving him a name[23]. I didn't have a name. I freaked out. I thought that she must like him more than me. She couldn't love us both, she could only love him, or me. So she had chosen him, and that was it. My mind blocked the experiences. So they totally disappeared, in the course of a weekend.

And having had those sublime experiences, and now having them taken away from me, I went mad. Absolute panic and fear at night. I thought that all I could do was commit suicide. I had to restrain myself from doing so. I was in total fear. I'd find myself walking around the bush in the middle of the night, not knowing what I was doing or where I was. It was as much as I could do to say the mantra, and even to do that brought fear and terror to me. I couldn't look at a picture of the guru without the most intense terror overtaking me. I didn't know what was going on. I knew that kundalini was involved. I knew that it was partly samskaras[24] coming up, and that there was some connection with Gordon that I didn't understand. All I knew was that I needed help. All I could do was go to Ganeshpuri to ask her what was happening to me. Within a couple of weeks I went.

She arrived a week after I got there. I was quite unable to go up to her and tell her what had happened. I was intimidated, and overwhelmed by the people round her. Looking back, it seems ridiculous, but it was so. I tried to steel myself to ask for a private darshan, but I couldn't. She was watching me intensely all the time, but she was so ferocious with me. She'd look at me, but never with a smile. I kept thinking, 'What have I done?' People would say, 'You turned your back and walked in there, and she was watching you'. It was a cat and mouse game. One day, she walked around giving things out to people, and she just ignored me and gave to the next person.

I didn't know how to take that. I went home in disarray. Only when I was leaving did I go up to her, and ask her to bless the mala I had. She asked about my family. I thought,

'You knew all along how I was, and you treated me like this. You knew what I was going through, and you did this to me.'

I came home. The sense of panic and terror had dampened down to a tolerable level. It would come up when I started to meditate, but I could stand it, I could half control it. I would have experiences, but whenever I saw Gordon, or thought about him, they would wipe totally. But how could I do sadhana without seeing or thinking of my husband? It became a nightmare, intolerable. I started to treat him very badly. It was not his fault that I was suffering, but in a sense I was blaming him. I became a monster — I would criticise him, ridicule him, attack him. The more I did it, the nicer he was which made me feel even worse. If he'd given me something back, I could have handled it, but because he was so nice to me, it became really difficult.

The tension at home became unbearable. I would go walking by myself at night in the bush, and have these wonderful experiences of peace, and God, and meditation, and I'd come home, and it would all be wiped. I tried not to talk to Gordon about it, it hurt him an awful lot, because he had done nothing to justify it. In fact I didn't talk about it to anyone. In the end, I decided that the only thing I could do was to leave. I couldn't live like this any longer. So I resigned from my job, and wrote to the guru and told her everything. I told her that I had felt too intimidated to talk to her in Ganeshpuri. I said that the only solution I could see, for my sadhana's sake, was to leave my husband. After posting the letter, somehow the blocks I was experiencing were slightly released, and I began to feel good again.

Two weeks later, she telephoned the ashram and said that on no account was I to leave my husband. Everything was all right and I was just to do my sadhana. I accepted what the guru said. Not only did she tell me to do that, but I felt as if she had come into my home. Funnily

enough, about four days before that phone call, Gordon
and Emma had left for Ganeshpuri, so I was at home by
myself with the two older girls. The guru gave me grace —
it was as though she was always present. She was certainly
meditating on me. I'd wake up in the middle of the night,
feeling incredibly strange, as if she was with me and I was
with her. She was pouring grace into me, and I was in a
very high spiritual state for those six weeks until Gordon
came home.

When Gordon came home, the experience faded, but
I was determined, somehow, to try to live with this.
My sadhana became my only interest in life, my total
preoccupation. I saw the role I had as my dharma[25]. I
performed my functions as seva, as an offering to God. I
had to try to include Gordon in it somehow. It became
liveable, but my experiences dampened down.

In September 1985, my daughter and I went to
Ganeshpuri for three months. One morning, I went up to
the guru in darshan, and told her that I still had a problem
with my husband, that I still felt jealous. I asked her for
help.

We had a discussion and she said that I should talk to a
particular Swami about it. He said that I was psychotic, and
that I should give up sadhana, go into psychotherapy, and
when I was okay again I could go back to it. That devastated
me, so I wrote to the guru, and told her that it had been
no help whatsoever. I gave her this letter in darshan, and
the next day one of her Swamis knocked on the door and
told me that the guru wanted to speak to me.

A private darshan was arranged — best clothes, buy a
coconut[26] — an elaborate production. She talked a lot
about my daughter, about her illness. She said that she
would be healed — she had looked at her future. I had to
do nothing with her but look after her. In fact, I was just her
caretaker. She was concerned only about the medication
she was taking, its side effects. Then she said it was my

sadhana and my seva and my dharma to look after my children, and that I would have to stay with them, and my husband. She wouldn't talk about this jealousy thing with Gordon. She didn't say it would resolve itself. She kept laughing and saying, 'You worry too much'. She was very loving. She put a scarf around my neck, and she kept stroking my head. She was implying more than saying, 'It's alright, your sadhana is well, don't worry'. She did not mention the Swami's statement about psychotherapy, and I forgot. Your mind doesn't function too much when you're having a conversation with her.

Just after that, we came home. I had to work to pay for the trip as we'd run out of money. I worked for nine months in an accountant's office in the city, which drained me. Gordon went to see the guru, it was his turn. While he was away, I went to see a psychic person. The first thing she said was, 'There's a man in your life'. All I could think of was that everywhere I go everyone makes a fuss of my husband and ignores me — even my guru, even in my sadhana. Now I go and have a reading for myself, and the first thing she says is, there's a man in your life! It's not Gordon, he doesn't choose that, it's what happens.

She said, 'You are peas in a pod'. She explained the whole thing. 'You are the same soul, you are the same person. You are both totally at the same level. You are like Siamese twins.' Our sadhanas are the same. We chose to do it this way, because we had a chance of it being our last incarnation. With the double sadhana, we have double input into this one. We can do it, if we do it together. If we were to split up and go our separate ways, both our sadhanas would die. Our whole incarnation would be wasted, and we'd have to go back. She explained this out of the blue, off the top of her head. She didn't know what the guru had said. The guru had known this, but didn't tell me. She had just said, 'Stay together'.

I accepted what the psychic said, because it made sense

of my total experience with Gordon. He is the other part of me. We are the same person, we think the same, we breathe the same, we do sadhana the same — we are totally connected. I'd always felt this. Understanding it has helped a great deal. We can joke about it now. It hasn't got rid of the jealousy totally, but it's almost gone now. Gordon is still blocking off my meditation experiences — it's like a reflex. I start to go into meditation and, 'Oh, no, you can't do that', I come out of it, and it's irritating. But I recognise that this is just a reflex. It's also my ego fighting back. I was getting too close[27], so the ego was blocking it. I see it as a major obstacle in my sadhana, but I have to resolve it by myself. It's resolved a lot by my including Gordon in my love for my guru, worshipping Gordon as God. It's a ploy I use, and it helps my relationship with him. I've been extremely hard on him, blaming him for all this. Of course, he's blameless. He would have done anything to help me through it, even given up his own sadhana. He's a very sacrificing sort of person ... it's almost a burden to have someone like that.

Things have settled down a lot now. I have occasional moments, weeks in my sadhana where I get a lot of fear and panic coming through, but I understand that as being part of my kundalini activity. Sometimes I'm almost frightened to say the mantra, because the kundalini shakti[28] starts whirring away inside me. Sometimes it brings up ecstatic bliss, and sometimes desperate fear. It's just whatever I have stored. I have endless nights where kundalini activity whirls and burns through my body. It concentrates in a particular chakra, and I can feel it whirling. Sometimes when it does that in the stomach particularly, pain and fear come out, and I know that it's a very old samskara. I will attach the fear to whatever I happen to be concentrating on at that time. I will say, 'I am frightened because of x,' but in fact I'm not. I'm getting samskaras coming through from this intense kundalini activity. It makes me upset, but I accept it as part of the ups and downs of sadhana. It's taken a long time to be able to recognise this, and to look back, and to think, 'well, that's really all that's happening,' and to accept it.

Sometimes I can't even say the mantra, because the kundalini burns me so much that when I start to say it, I hear a lot of nada[29], or noises, in my head. I hear bells ringing, and conches blowing and drums beating. They're the noises of the Arati[30]. It all becomes a little too much when I try to sleep at night. It's a joke in the family. Sometimes when I look miserable, Gordon asks, 'Is the Arati in full blast?'

My first six months of total God and bliss was a spiritual honeymoon. Because it was so wonderful, I could never give up sadhana, no matter how difficult and gross and intense it becomes. Sometimes I feel I can't stand it. It hurts so much, it's so painful, so hard — I feel so frightened and negative. But I have to grit my teeth and get through it because if I don't get through it this time, I will only have to come back and get through it in my next lifetime. I just have to stop and remember how wonderful it really is, and it keeps me plugging away.

I remember one private darshan when the guru told me I couldn't stay with her in Ganeshpuri, that it was my duty to go home. As much as I wanted to be around her, I wasn't allowed to be. Then she asked if I lived close to the ashram. I told her I live a long way away. She suggested that we move closer to the ashram. We had wanted to move to a smaller house. So we decided that if we were going to move, we may as well move next door to the ashram, which was why we bought this house, and not something else on the Peninsula.

The move hasn't been as good as I thought it would be. I thought being close to the ashram would be wonderful, and would outweigh having to move into a grotty neighbourhood. In fact, I don't think on balance it has. We've all missed the big house and the space and the trees and the ambience of the Peninsula. Also, living near the ashram, we have observed all its politics and that's not been very edifying.

However, being here allows us to do our sadhana at the level we want while still keeping the family together. Gordon likes to watch the Sunday night movie with the children as a family activity. It's our dharma to do it. We can zip over to the ashram, watch the guru on the video, and come back and sit down with the family. They're all brushing their teeth, and getting ready while we're at the ashram. We can go to the chant on a Saturday night, and come straight back home. Saptahs[31] you can go to as much as you like. So we can combine our family life, our dharma as parents and as householders, and our wanting to live a spiritual life, as long as I am very careful not to get too involved with the squabbles.

I'll stay in this area, because my daughter was fortunate in being accepted by a nearby private school. Because of her illness, she has to be driven to school. When we were in Mount Eliza, she went to school at Mornington, which was miles away, so we were constantly driving her backwards and forwards. Here, though she's taken to school, she can walk home. So that's a great physical load off me, not to have to do all that driving. So while she's at school, we'll stay here.

When I move, I would like very much just to be with the guru. It would be my total focus. As much as she will allow it, because she doesn't allow me to do that very much. She questions me whenever I go near her. 'Should you really be here? Shouldn't you be with your family?' She knows where my interest really lies, and she won't allow that. I would still like to be with Gordon, but I don't think he would take to it too readily. He dislikes institutions, ashrams. He refuses ever to live in one. He finds the regimentation appalling. He goes along with it, but would not be happy inside. I don't mind it at all. I'm far more docile than he is. Because you see, she anaesthetises me. I'm with her a couple of days, and the grace, the shakti — they're cliché words, I'm trying to find other ones, but I don't know what to use — descend on me. I feel this bliss with her, and it pervades everything. I walk around, and it doesn't matter what I do, I'm in such a great state. So who cares about regimentation.

I do some seva now, but not a lot. I feel my main seva is here with the children. I meditate regularly. We get up at 5.30 every morning. Gordon wouldn't miss meditation, literally if the house was on fire. I use the mantra, but sometimes it's too intense. I hate not using it, I feel like something's missing, but if things get too painful, I don't. I do all my work around the house as an offering. I try to do it as my dharma, not as a job.

We see friends occasionally, when it's necessary. We have no recreational social life — only the ashram. We rarely go out anywhere else. My mother lives in Brisbane. She is a little disgusted, thinks our preoccupation is an aberration, and hopes I'll grow out of it. Gordon's parents also think it's an aberration, and hope that we won't be too rampant when they're around. They don't like coming here, and wherever they sit, they put their backs to the pictures of the guru. But recently, they've done a 'Learn to Meditate' course, and they're a little more tolerant of it.

I'm totally focussed on the guru. In the past, whenever I've gone to Ganeshpuri, though I've never met Baba, I've felt fairly connected with him. I've actually seen him in visions, and he's been in my dreams. But the last time I was there, that had gone completely. I went to greet the guru when I first arrived. I trampled on all the darshan girls[32] and lobbed myself at her feet. I looked up at her, and she looked down at me. Her face seemed to expand — her cheeks went out — I dissolved into her totally. I looked at her, and I started to talk, and talk, and talk. I don't know what I said, it was just to stay there. When I felt I was looking and dissolving into her, she was pulling me into her. So we had a spiritual embrace. It was as if she had filled the whole ashram for me. I couldn't find Baba at all. It was all her, everywhere. Her in the flowers, her in the samadhi shrine. She filled the ashram, and she filled me with herself — in photos of her I'd see me, in photos of me I'd see her. It was just her.

An immense change has taken place in me since I started doing sadhana. It was as if, before, I had a hood over my head. I didn't have a clue what life was about. I was just buffeted, and wanting, and not knowing why on earth I felt so unhappy. Mundane existence was too mundane. It was empty, I was miserable and unsatisfied. Sadhana, or spiritual life, suddenly made life wonderful. It's incredibly intense, and focussed, as if the hood has gone and I can suddenly see everything. There's a reason for living, there's love. Though the intensity is very high, it's also very low, and I experience the swings of the pendulum between those extremes. Still, there's an intensity and a light and a depth that there wasn't in life before. I feel I can handle any misfortune that comes my way. I can be detached from almost anything. It's just simply a play, a happening, and who cares anyway. Before, I was a victim of everything. Now it feels as though nothing can touch me.

---

1 SLE: a chronic, usually fatal disease, characterised by pathological changes in the vascular system, leading to narrowing of the arteries and impairment of function in whatever organ is affected. Marked constitutional symptoms include fever and arthritis.

2 'Learn to Meditate' courses are run regularly at Siddha Yoga ashrams. They consist usually of 4 evening classes in which the practice and theory of meditation are explained.

3 sadhana: spiritual discipline, a life based on a spiritual discipline.

4 japa: the practice of repeating mantras, silently or aloud. A form of meditation.

5 Paul Brunton: an English author who, via his works, introduced many readers to Eastern religions.

6 mantra: sacred words/sounds, invested with the power to transform the individual who repeats them. In Siddha Yoga, the chief mantra used is: 'Om Namah Shivahya,' — 'I honour Shiva,' Shiva denotes the inner self.

7 shaktipat: in Siddha Yoga, spiritual awakening, the transmission of spiritual power from guru to disciple. It is often associated with strong movements of kundalini energy and hence with intense experiences.

8 Intensive: a two-day workshop, consisting of talks, videos, chanting and meditation, aimed at transmitting the guru's grace to the disciple.

9 Blue lights are significant in that Swami Muktananda has experienced visions of a blue pearl whilst in deep meditation, and many meditators in this tradition experience a vision of blue light in meditation.

10 During Intensives, if the guru is present, s/he touches everyone present on the head, while they are meditating: shaktipat, the guru's grace, may be transmitted by this touch.

11 darshan: literally, seeing a saint or sacred idol, which bestows blessing.

12 pranaaming: bowing down — either on knees and hands, or flat on the ground. A gesture of great respect.

13 puja: ceremonial worship.

14 Baba: term of affection for saint. Swami Muktananda was/is often referred to as Baba. Samadhi describes a state of meditative union with the Absolute. Baba's samadhi shrine is where Swami Muktananda's body is buried.

15 Swami Muktananda wrote many books, including *Play of Consciousness* — his spiritual autobiography, and the Satsang books, (Satsang — meeting of devotees to hear scriptures, chant or sit in the presence of a guru). The Satsang books are collections of questions and answers to Swami Muktananda.

16 mala: string of prayer beads, similar to rosary.

17 rudraksha: dried seeds from which prayer beads are made.

18 seva: work done for the guru. All residents of Siddha Yoga ashrams do several hours seva per day, as a spiritual practice that also maintains

the ashram. Types of seva at Ganeshpuri range from polishing marble courtyards at 3 am, to chopping vegetables or helping to administer the ashram.

19 kundalini energy: in Siddha Yoga, the personal aspect of the creative force of the universe, which lies coiled like a serpent at the base of the spine. Spiritual practice leads to a movement of this energy up through the subtle energy channels of the body, with accompanying experiences that range from ecstatic to horrific, as the energy encounters and clears blocks.

20 chakras: subtle energy centres of the body.

21 sahasrara: the topmost spiritual centre/chakra, located in the crown of the head, said to be the seat of Shiva and symbolised by a thousand petalled lotus.

22 samadhi: complete absorption into the Self; meditative union with the Absolute.

23 Students of Siddha Yoga, as in other spiritual disciplines, may ask for a spiritual name, which is given to them by the guru.

24 samskaras: past impressions — i.e. feelings, memories, personality characteristics from past lives.

25 dharma: duty, action which is moral, right, appropriate.

26 A coconut is given to the guru as a symbol of the ego, which needs to be cracked apart to find the sweet inner essence, i.e. the absolute within.

27 'too close' i.e. too near to transcending the ego.

28 shakti: in the Siddha Yoga tradition, the divine cosmic energy which projects, maintains and dissolves the universe.

29 nada: divine music/sounds; sounds heard during advanced stages of meditation.

30 arati: a ritual of worship, involving waving lights, incense to the guru. Accompanied in Siddha Yoga by drums, conch shells, harmonium.

31 saptah: long chant, held on special occasions. Generally continuing for one to four days.

32 darshan girls: women who sit at the guru's feet, receive the presents from people in the darshan line, and help regulate access to the guru.

Colin Alcock

'If you can't experience yourself as unloved, then you won't meet the God who loves. If I couldn't experience myself as a person who feared, then I couldn't experience the God who meets and overcomes my fears. So my psychological disintegration meant that my God was tiny.'

Colin Alcock was born in 1950, and is the executive director of the Eremos Institute, a Christian group which encourages a deeper and wider exploration of spirituality than is traditional in the church. Converted to fundamentalism by a Billy Graham Crusade in 1959, Colin perceptively describes his sense of the psychological dynamics of this expression of Christianity, and the experiences which led him to what he feels is a broader and more mature faith. Colin entered therapy at the age of thirty-five to explore the childhood origins of his inability to trust others, and to accept his own body. What he learned there enabled him to relate to God from a deeper and wider sense of himself. Colin's story reveals much about the way in which personality affects spirituality, and his discussion of the Eremos Institute describes an innovation within the Anglican Church.

My recollections of my childhood are few and scattered. That's because I experienced a major trauma when I was seven, and the repression of that led to the loss of many memories. I was a fairly happy child. My parents were loving, but my father was withheld emotionally. My mother had come over from Canada as a war bride, so she was living in a totally new environment, without the support of family or friends. She found that difficult to a degree that none of us comprehended. She went by the books on how to raise children, which in my case involved the theory that you leave the child crying in bed until feed time. It's an attempt to train and discipline the child. So, by the time I met this trauma at seven, I was unprepared for it, having already learned to suppress my emotions and operate in different ways.

When I was seven, a fellow offered to give me a free bicycle if I went down to the bush and cycled around the track a number of times. As it turned out, his intentions weren't honourable, and he tied me up and sexually abused me in a violent way. I had no clear memories of that experience until three years ago. Until then, I could not account for why my childhood after that time appeared to me to be very unhappy. I seemed to be aware of a frightening underworld of experience. I'd lost my innocence, and yet I was having to live while never acknowledging the depth and the pain of that new reality. That led to a split in me. There was the side that knew too much, and experienced great fear, and a sense of abandonment, and pain, and betrayal, and the other side that was trying to function in a family which wasn't able to handle emotion.

I was extremely unhappy at school. What I tended to do was to align myself with friends who were bigger and tougher than I was. I suspect I was trying to ensure my own protection, but that meant that the friends I chose were not only bigger and tougher but also nastier and less considerate. Again, until recently, I could never work out why I chose friends like that. It wasn't all seeking protection. There were a couple of very good friendships, and I think the ability to form close friendships with males came out of this sense of being introduced to an underworld. It gave me an awareness of deeper things. I didn't like school at all. In my third and fourth year of high school a friend and I used to wag school to go to Bronte Beach, to the domain or for a ferry ride. My family had no idea about this so I must have been practised in deception. I see that now as a survival mechanism, but again it was a sign of a split in my character.

At the end of the fifties, when I was about nine, the Billy Graham Crusade came to Australia for the first time. I underwent a conversion to fundamentalist Christianity, although I didn't understand it then as such. I felt a sense of guilt about who I was, and then a profound sense of relief following my so-called reception of Jesus Christ into my heart. My parents had not been strong Christians until then, but my mother went forward at the Crusade, and my father became a Christian a few weeks later. The fundamentalist Christianity we embraced was puritanical in its approach to the Bible and faith, but it did allow for the expression of emotion. However, all the emotions were expressed towards God. The problem is that emotion that functions in that way is often sentimental. Sentimentality is emotion that isn't aware of the context in which it is operating, or of the sources from which it is drawn. For example, I could feel great love towards a heavenly father as a replacement for my inability to feel love for an earthly father. That can be a useful phase for people to go through, provided it's seen and understood as a phase. But often that doesn't happen. It tends to be accepted in the church, and, sadly enough, the notion that we can't love God unless we are loving our neighbour is lost. So often you see families that are unhappy and relating poorly, but this is not made a focus for their Christian life.

What our conversion meant for our family was that everything became religious, everything had a religious significance. I experienced this as a terrible tyranny. God became the disciplinarian. Before that, God was the one who had abandoned me, who wasn't there when I was attacked. God was the one who held me responsible for the attack. I understood myself to be guilty. I shouldn't have gone into the park, I was disobeying my parent's instructions, and God had punished me. So the disciplinarian God that came into my life in a more manifest way in 1959 fitted into that stereotype. It suited my needs and it suited the needs of the family. Unfortunately, that concept of God just reinforced the lack of relationship in our family.

I had my first girlfriend when I was thirteen. That was a wonderful experience of sexual awakening and vitality. That first girlfriend lasted only a couple of weeks, and then I met *the* girlfriend, the one who was going to bring me total fulfilment. That lasted for about eight months, and again it was an extraordinary experience of fun, intimacy, exploration and excitement. Before that, my father had decided to go into the ministry. He had been an accountant in a big electrical firm, so he went into the ministry in his mid-thirties. Both my parents experienced that as a great relief. It involved a radical change for them. For example, my father was treasurer of the local RSL. We used to go up to watch people playing the pokies, and occasionally we'd get to pull the handle ourselves. The Christianity my parents adopted said that you could not be a Christian and go to the RSL to drink, gamble and smoke. So my father gave all those things up.

My father was invited to a seaside parish in Sydney. There I met the local fellowship, all young kids about my age, fifteen and sixteen, and all very religious. I underwent another radical conversion, similar to that of my parents.

I became a strict Christian with all the legalism and the puritanism that involved. Getting involved with girls and nicking off from school was 'backsliding', not at all consistent with the fellowship, so I turned my back on relationships with women and became a misogynist. I became one of the leading lights in the fellowship, very dogmatic, severe and literalist. Again I was split apart. Before this I had been experiencing the depths and the emotional range of the other side, but then I did a back flip into this severe kind of religion that involved the suppression of real emotion.

It wasn't hard to make the switch. I did feel myself to be split apart, but fundamentalist religion caters for that. They say that we all sin, and, provided we repent and are deeply sorry for what we do, we can all be forgiven. It's a false version of the victorious Christian life. As far as I can make out now, the victorious Christian life is meant to be a virtually perfect life where you are totally familiar with the words of God, you believe all the right things and you act in the right way.

It's very literalist and very superficial, but it's an ideal for which the fundamentalist will strive. It's an ideal that sees sin as the desperate enemy, out there to pull you down. Now, if you are split apart, if there is no integration between spirit and emotion, body and spirit, will and emotion, will and beliefs, if all these things are separated out and everything is compartmentalised, then reality can be shut out. You can shut out the fact that you've got a lousy relationship with your kids — fundamentalist homes are renowned for child abuse. Fundamentalists are frequently involved in corporate crime and the kind of thing recently exposed about American television religion. Those things are perfectly predictable, because the religion supports the split personality. Also, they have an elevated and fearful view of the devil, so that misdemeanours can be attributed to the power of Satan. They know about the power of the devil, because they are always being oppressed by it.

There was a split in our family because my father moved into Charismatic Renewal. Charismatics are like Pentecostalists. They emphasise the work of the Holy Spirit in the individual, the gifts and manifestations of the spirit — speaking in tongues, healing and spontaneous prophecy. My father experienced that as a liberation from the shackles of rigid fundamentalism, but I was still in that, and I saw him as betraying the faith and moving off into something weird. Really, what he was doing, and what the Charismatics have been doing, was making people more aware of their experience. It was a deeper way of addressing the lack of integration in their lives. So my father and mother went on that path, and I differed, and there was a clash. In the end it suited us all for me to take up a scholarship and go to university to do an arts course.

In my first year I met a university chaplain, Bruce Wilson, who seemed to stand for something deeper. This puzzled me, but I liked the fellow, and was drawn to him. At the end of that first year, I still maintained a rigid approach to Christianity, but things were starting to be undermined. I was beginning to be exposed to a wider world, and, although I wasn't very sure about it, I could see there were other things for me. My second year was the radical one, one of the best years of my life. I moved out of home and into an Anglican college. Being away from the immediate influence of my family was like a breath of fresh air. I soon became very critical of the kind of Christianity that I experienced in the college. I remember one day I was feeling quite low, and a guy from a fundamentalist student group called the 'Navigators' met me on the stairs. He asked how I was and when I told him that I was feeling pretty awful he said, 'There's sunshine in my heart, brother,' and patted me on the back and moved off. I was furious at his lack of concern. This was what triumphant Christian living was all about — ignoring the neighbour and charging off with a satisfied self.

I experienced wonderful friendships in those years — even now, I am very close to three of those people from college days. But it was also a time of experimenting and of radical change. I threw overboard all my taboos. That had good and bad consequences. When you live a life with such dichotomies, the process of merely reacting against it is going to sustain them. It will not lead, initially, to integration but to a moving from one extreme to the other. But I did experience this time as an enormous release. I met the woman whom I was later to marry, and, as a result of my friendship with the chaplain I became more involved in university life. In 1973 I coedited the student newspaper, *Tharunka*, with a Marxist. So we had a Christian–Marxist editorial team, and again that represented part of my growing awareness of other ways of looking at things.

I remained a Christian because of the sensible approach to Christianity I found in Bruce Wilson. I was also introduced to Paul Tillich, the German theologian. In them I encountered an adult approach to Christianity, one that said we cannot grow as Christians unless we are growing as people. As we mature, our approach to God and faith needs to mature. A mature faith is one that is less certain, more open, one that pays attention to the needs of people and the world we live in. It's a faith that is more interested in the products of human creativity, and one that takes account of the knowledge generated by the social and the natural sciences. A mature faith doesn't see a huge split between God and the world. It sees God intimately involved in all that is happening, but also as above and beyond, and in that sense not totally identified with the sensory world.

I never felt frightened by leaving the certainties of fundamentalist Christianity. The tyranny of that religion was so great that I experienced the opportunity to doubt as a pleasure. Unless we doubt, we can't grow. The image I have now of God is that He is big enough to cope with all that we bring, doubts, questions or heresies. So I'm not desperately worried if what I happen to be thinking at the moment might be regarded as heretical. I see that as one point in time, provided I continue to search for images and formulations that meet the interpretive needs of my experience.

My new vision of Christianity wasn't sufficient to overcome my radical psychological splits. My attempt to address that problem would come later. Also, there were more than two Colins stalking around. There was the Colin who edited *Tharunka*, who was different from the Colin who was president of the Evangelical Union, and the Colin who attended the Student Christian Movement nights, and the Colin who got drunk with the English honours students, and the Colin who tore around on the motorbike and the Colin at the college. All these were parts of myself that needed expression, but there wasn't a centre. In some senses, my friendship with the chaplain provided a centre for me. He accepted who I was, and realised where I came from, and could see in me the promise to move on from there. That was a source of security for me.

I ended up dropping out of my honours year and driving taxis. After that, I started a Bachelor of Divinity at Sydney University, as an attempt to articulate my new vision of Christianity. Since I was nine, I had wanted to be a missionary, and I was planning to be a minister after the degree. I spent five years doing an honours degree in divinity. During that time, I consolidated my understanding of Christianity, and developed a much more commonsense approach, one that was truer to my experience. The most important work I did was to look at the philosophy of science. I saw in the methodology of scientists an approach that involved courage, risk, experimentation, doubt, a love for truth and a quest to be honest, and a peer community which would assess whatever you produced. I thought the ingredients of the scientific method were appropriate for a

Christian approach to love.

I decided not to go to Moore College, the acceptable place to go if you were going into the ministry in Sydney. I had seen how Moore College had locked my father into an evangelical fundamentalism, and I knew that it would be an unhelpful step for me. When it came to searching out whether ordination was possible, I found that the examining chaplains wanted me to do two years at Moore College. I'd already completed five years at Sydney University. They didn't think I was suitable material for the ministry. One of the people on the panel accused me of being a pornographer and a communist. Communist because I'd supported the move to establish a Department of Political Economy within Sydney University. Pornographer because I was on a small committee that had produced a broadsheet with a small cartoon of a couple having sex on a table and exchanging money. It was a satire on the false values of our society. It was a ridiculous charge, and I expect the person who made it would not want to stand by it today. But I got the impression that the committee would not be interested in promoting my vocation within the diocesan structures. It wasn't a big shock. I had been a little naive expecting that the diocese would accept someone with my approach to things, but I was disappointed.

I then worked in a bookshop for nine months. I became assistant manager within a couple of months, and was promised a successful career within the retail book trade. But I knew that most of my interests weren't being fulfilled there. So I took a job with the national Anglican Church newspaper, *Church Scene*. I became the Sydney journalist, and then the Sydney editor. That involved me in looking at the church in New South Wales and Queensland, in particular. I began to see that things weren't very good, and became convinced that my place was as a lay person with some theological training.

I saw the terrible gap between the church and society in Australia. This is partly to do with the fundamentalism and anti-life stance that's taken in the church. This is in stark contrast to the experience of ordinary Australians, who enjoy life and who see the church as puritanical and wowserish. When you say you are a Christian, people expect you to be straight, boring, and immature. Usually they are right. I don't think the church encourages people to explore the depths of human experience, and to meet God at those depths. If it did, you would find that people in the church were mature, had weathered all the storms, and come out with a sense of trust and hope and vision. Ralph Waldo Emerson says that we believe only as deeply as we live. In the church, people have not been encouraged to live deeply, and therefore they don't believe deeply. In our church, for example, the notion of headship is strong: the man is the boss and the woman in the end submits to his decision. The tragedy of that is that it gives the man and the woman roles, and you can't have a successful marriage where the couple is locked up like that. Marriage, and in fact all relationships, require flexibility and compromise. That requires courage, hope and a sense of commitment. It's hard work, but it's very rewarding when it works. The doctrines espoused in the church put the brakes on meeting at that level, so people can't experience the true intimacy marriage can provide. That's a model of what happens in relationships between parents and children, and in relationships outside marriage, between women and women and men and men, and men and women. The brakes are put on at every stage. I would like to see Christianity offering a radical critique of those patterns, and exploring new ways of relating. But what has happened is that other radical movements have forged ahead here — feminism, for example. The church ought to be at the forefront of the feminist vision, but most of the time they fight a rearguard action against it.

As I reported what was going on in the church, I became more and more unhappy about it. My concern to work for change came when Bruce Wilson and Don Meadows and myself started thinking about Eremos. It was Bruce's vision, and in the context of the friendship between the three of us, Don and I responded to it. In 1982 the Eremos Institute was established. Eremos is the New Testament Greek word for desert. There was a lot of sense in taking that name. The desert was a biblical and historical location for the church. It's also an Australian location. You could push that a little further, and say that the secularised cities of Australia are a bit of a spiritual desert.

Eremos has always had a vision of deepening Christian spirituality, of pushing the boundaries out and exploring them. The way I interpret those original aims now is that we work to help Christians and others to live more fully in the context of society. It's an attempt to bridge the gap between church and society, and also to encourage the church along an adventurous exploratory path which affirms the way of God in the world.

I was working with the Anglican paper when Eremos started. I reduced my work with the paper gradually and ended up the third year working full time for Eremos. I've been full time ever since. We get our support through membership. Everything we run has to pay for itself. Our budget is about $60000 a year, and we have 850 members from different denominations throughout Australia. The majority are Anglican. The hierarchy of the church accepted Eremos, and many of the bishops are members and friends. In my Sydney diocese, the Archbishop agreed to be patron, and one of the assistant bishops was on our advisory panel. They gave us substantial support by lending their name to what we were doing. They see a place for Eremos. They probably do not agree with much of what we do, but they see that we reach people that other organisations may not contact. We are extending the frontiers, and there is only so much support you can expect from institutions if you are doing that. In this diocese, there hasn't been a good acceptance of Eremos by the clergy, but in other dioceses it's not been too bad. Our main support is lay people. That's because we are trying to relate the Christian faith to ordinary human experience.

The need to establish some sense of what prayer might be was deeply felt by all of us at Eremos. I knew what prayer used to mean, but it hadn't meant that for many years. Prayer had meant praise and thanksgiving, and also a middle-class pious routine where you formulated certain requests after reading a Bible passage and took them to God. In the chaos of the new life that I was leading at university and after, I found prayer to be meaningless. I had a sense of God, but no sense of where the connections were, and how to nourish them. We also wanted to explore devotional life and piety. There were very straight rules about how Christians ought to conduct themselves — what clothes they ought to wear, how long their hair ought to be, what was and wasn't appropriate for them to say. All of these were, to some extent, expressions of the middle-class nature of the Western Christianity we had inherited. Many of us felt that to be an inadequate way of expressing the fullness of life.

We began to explore Christian meditation, and the uses of silence and solitude. They began to be fundamental to our understanding of how we nurture our connections between God and the self, God and others. On our retreat weekends, we have a mixture of silence and solitude, walking and chatting along the beach. At meal times we eat as well, and we have some wine. There is an affirmation of life, within the context of exploring the depths of the self. There, we meet the depths of each other, and the depths of God. We use various forms of meditation, from mantras and guided imagery to meditation that uses touch or the senses to meditation on the Bible. Our approach is that not everyone is going to be drawn to each style. We want to find ways that suit, and when those ways are no longer suitable we look for others. So there is a basic flexibility, so Christians can begin to see that there are many different ways of being Christian. Each person's way always needs to be consistent with his or her personality. I define spirituality as personality in response to God, so people's personalities are quite fundamental to how they are going to experience and relate to God. We are all brought up with images of God formed in childhood and adolescence by our experiences with church and Sunday School. Some of those images are distorted and unhelpful, and some of them are only there embryonically, and need to be expanded. Retreats provide people with an opportunity to explore all this, and to share with each other. Through meditation, silence and solitude, and by chatting socially, they can start to see new possibilities.

We run courses on spirituality. These courses will always address people's personal formation, which includes the impact of history and society, as well as psychological factors. We run retreats, and we train retreat leaders. We publish the Eremos newsletter four times a year, and occasionally write essays for it. We run seminars, conferences and workshops, using psycho-drama, prayer and meditation. We are starting a new group for women with a history of incest or childhood sexual assault. We also have a bookshop, and we provide discussion material for small groups. I do some counselling with the Anglican Counselling Centre. A lot of the things that I do are similar to what parish clergy would do, except that my parishioners, if you like, are dispersed all over Australia and I don't have much contact with many of them.

One of our limitations is that most of our members are middle or upper middle class. We have very few working-class members. I'm not sure what we can do about that. It's remained a dilemma for me, although I've not felt a great urgency about it. I'm concerned, for example, about Aboriginal issues in our society. One of the things I am doing under the Eremos banner is organising for some Aboriginal people to go to South America to meet with indigenous people and to share their experience of the 1988 Bicentenary. In 1992, there will be a celebration of five hundred years of colonisation in South America and the Caribbean, so there will be an exchange on that issue. I see that as very important. It's not a ministry to middle-class white Australia, which is basically what Eremos is doing, but an attempt to use the power that we have to make it possible for growth and vision to develop among the Aboriginal people. They are already developing those qualities, but it's a way of lending some of our resources to make that more possible.

Three years ago, at the age of thirty-three, I began therapy. The pressure to do it came from the original attack, when I was seven. Anyone who undergoes severe crisis, sexual abuse, incest or intense emotional abuse, will feel its impact later in life. It may mean, for example, an inability to trust, and therefore an inability to give and to make deep personal connections. Then there is the darker side, the repeating of patterns. Fortunately I haven't wanted to attack other people sexually, but there were implications for me in terms of a highly distorted understanding of sexuality and an inability to accept my body.

I had primal therapy, with the Anglican Counselling Centre. That type of therapy involves allowing oneself to re-experience as fully as possible all the emotions associated with a trauma. The first in-depth session I had rekindled my memories of that experience in the bush. I had never recalled it to that extent, and I had never relived it. In the course of a year of consistent primal therapy, I re-experienced that event many many times, going through all the different feelings involved: helplessness, hopelessness, anger, sadness, loss, abandonment. That put me in touch with other experiences I had had when I was a bit younger, which weren't quite so formative, but which had shaped the way I responded to the attack — my mother neglecting me or not responding to me.

I don't think I would have gone into the therapy unless my understanding of God had changed. A few years earlier, I had begun to see that God was a God of grace and love, not a God of fear and guilt and judgement. I began to see that this God could be approached by me and was accepting of me, no matter what. That brought enormous relief, and in a sense it prepared me for acknowledging what was in my past. That was the beginning of my radical integration. I began to become a person who could once again feel. I had been avoiding any experience that hooked into a sense of helplessness, or, if I did have such experiences, I suppressed the feeling. If I had allowed that feeling to surface, it would have put me in touch with the primal feeling of helplessness, which would have reminded me of the trauma. I had learnt to defend myself against the trauma and its implications. So any experience of helplessness was a threat, which meant that I was an inadequate person when it came to an experience where I was required to act with a sense of power. This has intimate bearings on my spiritual life, because I don't think I can relate fully to God without a deep acknowledgement of my own helplessness. You do not find the God who will help or the God who will comfort because you cannot experience yourself as without comfort. It's too painful. If you can't experience yourself as unloved, then you won't meet the God who loves. If I couldn't experience myself as a person who feared, then I couldn't experience the God who meets and overcomes my fear. So the psychological disintegration meant that my God was very tiny.

Unfortunately I think that is the case for many people. Many of us have suffered deeply in the past, and have lived our lives attempting to cope with the pain. In the child, the defences against pain are a survival mechanism, but there comes a time when in order to grow we have to let go of those survival mechanisms and face the pain. This is a challenge to our personal maturity as well as to our sense of spirituality and our understanding of God.

Therapy allowed me to relate more deeply to God, with my whole self. It started a long process of experiencing myself not just as mind, but as body and emotion, as capable of making choices that emerged out of a more complete sense of self. It's a long process, which I expect will continue for the rest of my life. I expect life will become fuller, deeper, richer as I go on. That's what the Christian vision is about. Now, I have bouts of therapy when I need it. When a crisis emerges and I get an inkling that things aren't right, I go back to the counsellor and work on it for a few sessions. It's usually not as traumatic as that original event, which is a great relief.

I see myself as fundamentally Christian and ecumenical. I like the Anglican tradition for its richness and its liberal understanding, its generosity of spirit and its diversity. My friend Don Meadows says that the great strength of the Anglican Church is its 'wishy-washiness'. That's what I'm talking about when I say liberal, generous spirit. I enjoy its liturgy and its traditions. I am part of that tradition. I speak from within it, but I can operate in other traditions and in ecumenical contexts too, quite happily. But I always return to a tradition that I am familiar with. We need to have one steady stream running through our experience, and that's it for me.

My spiritual practice now? I jog every morning, and that's part of a centreing pattern. I pray when I need to pray, and there is nothing very regular about that. I wouldn't want to recommend this to anyone — I'm just talking about what I experience. It's still not helpful for me to set aside a regular part of the day for a discipline like reading the Bible and praying. The prayer that I do is much more spontaneous, more a consequence of the moment. When I'm jogging, for example, I'll toss a few things around in my head. I don't think I need to address God and say, will you please pay attention to what I'm thinking, because I know that is happening anyway. I'm seeing God here as a source of creativity and life and love, beyond myself but also within myself and around me. Nowadays I'm aware that there is much more happening to me than I was aware of a few years ago. I can identify my emotions much more easily than ever before.

There is a tradition in the Christian church which says that contemplation is being attentive. I have learned to become much more attentive than I ever was. The ability to be fully present in the moment means that we meet God then, because we encounter what is real and what is true in the moment. As we encounter it, then we respond, and that response is prayer. It's an exchange, an interaction, a relationship. A couple of times a month, I find time for meditation. It's not meditation to relax me, but meditation to put me more deeply in touch with myself. As I do that, I become more in touch with God. My meditation often produces dreamlike material, with all sorts of levels of understanding to it. I'd be overloaded if I did that kind of meditation too regularly. The meditations I do involve breathing, and can involve mantra as well. The mantra meditation is an attempt to clear my head of images. The other type of meditation is one that affirms images, and multiplies them like a dream. In the Christian tradition, there is the Via Positiva and there is the Via Negativa. One tends to multiply images, and one to clear them away. I find both helpful. Sometimes we need to clear away all our images, so we can find some new ones. The ones we have are not helping, and we need to experience a feeling without an image, an emptiness, a space or a desert, and wait.

I can never now separate the questions of a relationship

with God from questions of relationship with others. When the rich man came to Jesus and asked, 'How can I enter the kingdom of heaven?' Jesus didn't say, 'Do some nice pious religious things'. He said, 'Sell up your home.' His challenge to a deeper relationship with God came in terms of an economic choice. My challenge to a deeper relationship with God comes to me in terms of choices that I have to make in my ordinary life. Choices about how I treat others — my wife, my children, my working friends, my neighbours. They are the focus of my relationship with God, and, if that is going to grow, it's because I am addressing these things constantly. I find now that I'm making choices to love, choices which three years ago, before the therapy, I wasn't able to make.

So the main source of my growth is encounter, with others and with self. Encounter with God is all bound up with that. I do address God clearly and openly many times. If I'm going through a period of pain, I don't always go to God first. I know when I'm addressing God with those things, I'm taking them to the ultimate depths. I experience within myself a desire to avoid those depths. I still have some fear of that, an uncertainty about what it's going to mean. So prayer can be a pretty dangerous business, because it's facing reality, and sometimes that hurts. That's why I have a reluctance often to take things to God immediately. There are other aspects of prayer where I feel a great lightness and ease and freedom. I think of times when I pray with my children, and it's a time of fun.

In times of crisis, my spirituality helps insofar as I have come to understand that the only way to live with crises is to experience them fully. If I do that I will come through in one way or the other. I never know in what way but I will end up with some sense of resolution that is linked with my experience of death and resurrection, which is my experience of God in Christ. The most powerful symbol we have in the Christian story is that of the death and resurrection of Christ. Death means the crises. We must experience this death, the sense of loss and sadness, the anger, the rage, the helplessness. That's what Jesus experienced on the cross. He identified himself with the tradition of complaint against God for suffering. So I can no longer be nice and middle class and withheld about my suffering. I take it that it's appropriate to bring to God everything that I'm feeling about this crisis, and I experience that as a death. But my spirituality has given me assurances that whenever I do that, I will experience new birth, new hope, new vision. Something unexpected and surprising is going to be at the end. I know that there is still in me a great resistance to experiencing my crises fully. They are too painful, and I don't want to look at them. That's a very common experience — to defend ourselves against the impact of events. The more we can drop those defences and experience the impact, the more adequately God will meet us where we are.

John Cooper

'It may go back to this feeling that you have
to doubt everything, you have to question
everything, and to avoid patterns.'

Born in 1930, John Cooper tells a story which sheds light
on several generations of spiritual history in Australia:
from the fifties, when the Theosophical Society and various
occult and psychic groups were the main alternative
spiritual options, through the sixties, when John was
present at one of the first Buddhist meditation courses
in Australia, to the seventies, when he helped establish
Sydney's first Zen Buddhist meditation centre and finally
to the eighties when, like so many others, he left the city for
a quieter life in the country. Buddhism and the teachings of
the Indian sage, Krishnamurti, have profoundly influenced
John, and the combination has given him an eclectic
spirituality, a style which reflects his belief that each must
find his own rhythm, 'and just go along from there and see
how it all moves in you'. John sees attachments to gurus,
beliefs and rituals as less important than finding spirituality
in the here and now of everyday life, with an awareness
deepened by the practice of meditation.

Zen Buddhism arose in China in the sixth and seventh
centuries, and spread to Japan in the twelfth century. Its
style is more direct and less symbol laden than that of

other schools of Buddhism, and it values the expression of Buddhist insight, in secular terms, in the arts, manual labour and appreciation of the natural world.

Fundamental to Zen practice is zazen (meditation), aimed at the meditator's realising his/her true nature. Koans, teaching formulations baffling to the logical mind, which point to a truth beyond intellect, are a unique and important aspect of Zen Buddhism.

I was brought up in a very strict Irish Catholic environment in Sydney. I went to Mass almost daily, learned the old Catholic rituals and the Latin Mass almost off by heart, and was very strongly caught up in Catholic sensibilities and culture. When I was still in primary school, I had this great question in my mind: — why is it just for us to receive salvation because Christ died for our sins? Why is it just for us to have benefit without working for it? I was interested in justice and suffering — why are people born ill, and into unpleasant environments? I was almost obsessed with this problem. I could not find the answer. While I was at Christian Brothers College, I was sent into Sydney to buy some art work for one of the teachers. I came across what I would now consider a rather trashy occult magazine. It spoke about reincarnation, and the Indian concept of karma. It made sense to me and I immediately had the feeling that I actually believed it. Nowadays, I am far more agnostic, but at the time — I was about fourteen — I thought it was absolutely true. My thought then was, but this is not Catholicism, I must be a heretic. I accepted this and, to the sadness and horror of my parents, I announced that I was no longer a Catholic.

When I left school, I started to work, trying to find some sort of path in life. My ideals took me in the direction of commercial art and photography until I realised I lacked talent. I spent my time wandering around Sydney looking in secondhand bookshops and going to lectures. I went through a full cycle from Catholicism to total atheism. I was a superior atheist who knew that everything was untrue — there was no God, there was no religion. But then I wasn't very satisfied with that position. It was one of denial and didn't seem to have any logical structure. I was trying to find logical answers in those days. So I became what you could almost call a mellow condescending agnostic saying well, nobody knows — you have your opinion, but nobody knows. But that was not a very comfortable position for me either. Then I started to look into the strange world of spiritualism. I went to trance and flower mediums, and people who picked up vibrations. I was totally unimpressed by this. I felt the phenomena were shaky, that the 'supernatural' sources were rather cheap, but I became interested in the psychological phenomena of people who were moving into other states of consciousness. I also did some work in the occult world, with various Golden Dawn[1] organisations. The rituals were quite powerful, but I always thought it was just a form of theatre. We were building up our imagination and our excitement, and what came out of that we were calling spiritual, or higher phenomena. I had a long relationship, without ever becoming a member, with the Theosophical Society.[2] In the fifties and early sixties, they were the main centre for non-establishment ways of thinking. There was not a great range being offered in those days.

Then I married, and got caught up in a career. I was working in arts administration. I started off working in an art gallery, and I moved from there to the Arts Council of NSW, where I worked my way up to the position of federal administrator. From there I moved to the Australia Council where I was director of its big international and entrepreneurial programmes. I was still asking questions, and I felt that I didn't have a very good academic base for any of this. So I decided to enrol in the University of

New England to do a Bachelor of Arts degree over about fourteen years, taking it slowly. Towards the end I majored in Indian history and religious studies at the University of Sydney. I found that I did fairly well and that I derived great enjoyment from trying to work out what the religious consciousness of mankind had been. After I got my BA, I tutored in the Department of Religious Studies in Sydney, and decided to do my MA. I had originally hoped to work on a comparative study of certain medieval Sanskrit texts to show how yoga had changed over a thousand years. But the professor, Eric Sharpe, indicated that it would be better to work on a topic closer to home. I remembered that in Sydney in the twenties there had been a huge split in the Theosophical Society — they had lost six hundred of their nine hundred members. The story had always been hushed up so I decided that an interesting piece of detective work and research would be to try to work out what had happened. I spent about six years working part time on my MA thesis. I interviewed people who remembered the period and their children, I discovered diaries and went through letters and journals.

The split was over two issues. Firstly, whether the most famous Theosophist in Australia, a man called Charles Webster Leadbeater, was — to quote from their doctrine — a man on the threshold of divinity, an 'Arhat'[3] in Buddhist terms, or whether he was a depraved sexual freak who chased little boys. These two opinions are wide apart. The faithful said that 'this man was too pure to be impure', the argument being of course he's pure, he's an Arhat, and if he's an Arhat he can't be impure. How do you know he's an Arhat? He said he was, and an Arhat can never lie. Circular argument, you see. The evidence was never conclusive, but it did imply that he had some strange theories of how the sexual impulse can be handled. Secondly, others were concerned that the theosophy he taught was different from the theosophy of the prime founder of the movement,

Madame Blavatsky. Now this is most certainly so. Both
in philosophical and psychological terms, it was almost a
complete about-face. But unfortunately many theosophists
had not realised that. They saw the two as being one with
differences of interpretation. But one said there is no God
and the other said there is a God, because I've spoken
to him. Out of that came the very sad saga which led to
the formation of an independent body, the Independent
Theosophical Society, which lasted for thirty years. So in a
city the size of Sydney, there were suddenly two societies.
Later on, there were three, even four.

So, I did that research, and got an MA out of it. It
showed me how much ratbaggery goes on in virtually all
religions. One can look at Christianity, at Buddhism, at
Theosophy, and talk about what's gone wrong, and the
nuts that are in each of them. One of the sad realities is that
the Theosophical Society and other theosophical groups
that were really progressive in the nineteenth century have
become fairly unimportant in the twentieth. One of the
reasons for this has been the members themselves. In
the last century, the society attracted people who were
really looking for answers, whereas in this century it has
become more a group of devotees. Nevertheless, I have
the highest admiration for some theosophists, generally
the maverick ones. And, in that world, there are a great
number of people who are dedicating their lives to spiritual
values. Another change is that while early theosophy was
quite radical — Blavatsky's ideas were very close to those
of Buddhism — later theosophists created a Christianised
form, with gods and devas and god forms, and links to
churches and ceremonials, and all the occult stuff that
Blavatsky rather criticised.

Much of my Buddhism came out of an initial contact
with theosophy, although I do believe that I have avoided
the horrors of some of the occult approaches which you
find, particularly in America. For example Buddhist monks

giving Christianised sermons, with hymns like 'Nearer my Buddha to thee'. The name of Christ has simply been changed to Buddha, and there has been no understanding of the difference between the two teachings. A lot of people have asked me if I am a theosophist. I've always had a problem saying I'm anything, because I have been so strongly influenced by the Hindu and Buddhist understanding that there is no self. But if you pushed me into a corner I would say I was a Buddhist.

About the time I finished my MA, I decided that I'd had enough of working in theatre. I was getting tired of working with the Australia Council. So I decided, at the end of eighty-six, to leave Sydney and become a farmer. I felt that living on a farm would be a much more natural and 'spiritual' way of living. I left the Council at the end of March eighty-seven, and within a month I was offered a job lecturing on Buddhism at Sydney University. I've been teaching there for the last twelve months. That will finish soon and we will then be moving to Bega, where we are building a farm house.

A lot of my adult life was spent in the theatre, working day and night seven days a week with no time at all for anything that you could call spiritual. I was frustrated that I had no time to read the books that were coming out. At one stage I was working from eight in the morning until two the next morning, six days a week and on the seventh day doing all the other work I hadn't done. There was no time at all even to sleep. I was also working in the yoga field. I have been teaching yoga in Sydney for some twenty-five years, often several times a week. I find that yoga is a great advantage in terms of clearing out the body and the emotional nature, although I don't think the techniques taught by the various yoga schools lead to enlightenment. They may lead to deep stages of meditation, they may lead to psychic experiences, they do lead to some form of kundalini[4] arousal, but I'm a bit like Krishnamurti — I don't think you can use a mantra or a meditation technique to go beyond the mind. You are locked in your history, your background, your memories and you can't get beyond them. In yoga I had experiences of what could be called kundalini, when suddenly I felt that an electric light had lit up every cell in my body, and a blazing lot of energy came out. But I've always felt that kundalini is quite different to the consciousness turnabout that occurs in Vipassana[5] meditation. One is, in a sense, psychological, and the other is biological. It is physical, that feeling of great energy. You may be the biggest nut in the world, and yet fanaticism or falling in love may bring it up for you, this great sense of enthusiasm. I think this is in some way linked into the kundalini experience. I was fortunate once to meet one of the great teachers of kundalini in India, Gopi Krishna. He's a remarkable man, a man of great luminosity. He shone, as they say in India. I asked him what brings kundalini on. He laughed, and said that it's a bit like getting pregnant — you know how it starts and after that it's all mysterious. A lot of people believe kundalini is the be all and end all — that the arousal of kundalini is the equivalent of enlightenment. I think they are quite different things.

Possibly the first well known spiritual teacher with whom I made contact with was the Theravadin Buddhist monk, U Thillila,[6] who gave one of the first Vipassana courses here, around 1960. I felt that I must try this and went to sit with him in Leo Berkeley's house where the retreat was being held. The meditation was a very simple technique of just watching the breath move in and out. I found it very deep, although in the beginning it was very painful to sit without any movement, particularly for the two hour stretches they had in those days. I once experienced the feeling that my whole ego was gone, the whole of the mind and the feelings were gone, and there was complete emptiness. It lasted a long time and I was brought out of it by an Alsatian dog licking my face. I was sitting outside

and I realised that the sun had moved by several hours.
I have never meditated before in any long deep sense. In
yoga, you may sit and meditate for half an hour at a time,
but that was nothing like the fifteen hours of the Vipassana
technique. So that was the first time in formal meditation
that something like that had happened to me. I was only
there for two days, because of my work, and it happened
on the second day. For months afterwards, my mind felt
totally open. Things would come in and go out with no
opposition; life was very clear and easy and beautiful.

One of the teachers whose influence on me has been
deepest has been Krishnamurti. He denies that he is a
teacher, or that he has a teaching. But, most certainly, he
does lead you back into your own mind, and into the
exploration of consciousness. I read Krishnamurti, and
listened to tapes of his talks. I had the opportunity of
meeting him in India, and hearing him lecture, and sitting
in small groups with him. I found, from that, at times the
mind would stop, and I could go for one or two days
with hardly a thought. I've always regarded his outlook
as essential for everybody who is on a spiritual path. It
gets you away from so many of the hang-ups — the guru
devotion, the cultism that comes up so readily in people
who go East, or go into a new religious movement.

Buddhism is the school that interests me most of all the
religions. I like the fact that it was started by a man, and
not a god, that it's a fairly rational school of thought, that
it believes in self-effort, that there is not much emphasis
placed on belief, more on practice. One of the areas that
interested me most for many years was Zen Buddhism.
The problem here was that you could read about Zen,
there were lots of books — books by psychoanalysts, books
by D. T. Suzuki[7], and lots of wonderfully enigmatic and
humorous little Zen tales. I felt this is really it but what
does it mean, how do I practise it? I tried to work it out
for myself, but I had great trouble understanding how to

meditate in Zen, maybe because I made it too magical.

I helped start the Sydney Zen group. Lee Davidson, who had worked with me in the yoga field, had spent some time in India and had learned Zen from a Japanese Zen monk in Bodh Gaya, where the Buddha achieved enlightenment. He came back and started to enthuse about it. We used to have monthly sittings with about thirty people. We taught them how to do Zen. I'd give them a bit of yoga to get the body limbered up, and others would talk about meditation. Then we would sit and do it. This became better and better — we were almost a self-organised group. We decided to try and have a sesshin, and intensive meditation session by ourselves, without a roshi[8]. We had the wonderful idea of doing manual labour and sitting at the same time. We would get up at four in the morning and do two hours of sitting, have breakfast, another couple of hours sitting and then go out and dig a creek. You got great physical energy from the sitting and I really like that combination of heavy manual labour and meditation. It lasted for about five days.

We used to play tapes of Robert Aitkin and other roshis from America. There was quite a lot of discussion as to whether we should link up with a roshi. In the end, the group agreed to link with Robert Aitkin, who was the roshi of the Diamond Sangha in Hawaii. He was an extremely fine teacher, a man with a profound knowledge of Zen, and a very fine writer too. We invited him here, and it was agreed that he stay at our house for about a month on his first visit. I didn't have much to do with organising the sesshin; my wife and I were simply his hosts. I went to the first two or three sesshins and lectured on Zen Buddhism with my wife Lee who demonstrated posture. The Sydney Zen group now has a place at Annandale, where they have regular sittings, and they have a place for country sittings too. Robert comes out every year as a roshi.

Robert Aitkin is my meditation master, but it is fairly informal. He has been out here recently four or five times, and I have not done a meditation with him. I've been too busy, I've been too lazy, I've just not had the inclination to do it. I don't know why. It may go back to this feeling I've got that you have to doubt everything, you have to question everything, and to avoid patterns. He has guided me into the depths of Zen Buddhism, where the only way to go was into and beyond the mind, which is what Zen is all about. He has always been a friend, a good and deep friend, and I think there is love between us in the real sense of the word. To me, that is more important than a formalised relationship. I wanted the group to be independent so that students who wanted to work with Robert, including myself, could work with him separately. Others wanted to have the group linked officially to him, and the Diamond Sangha. That's the way it went. I suspect than Zen will take several hundred years to get established in America and Australia. If it maintains its energy, it may start to transform the forms around it. It changed in going to China, it changed in going to Japan, it must change in coming to other countries. It may become less doctrinaire, it may develop forms of ritual that are more in keeping with Western thought, in fact cut ritual back to a minimum. There are so many choices for people who are going into Buddhism: Tibetan, Theravadin, Zen, Mahayana. Of all of these, I think Zen is probably the one which will become most popular in the West, partly because it places a lot less emphasis on ritual.

There are two schools of thought on the question of politics and spirituality in Buddhism. One says that the outside world is unreal — just get on with your practice and forget about it. The other says that we are interpenetrating the whole universe and what we do affects the plants and the stars and the trees, and what the trees do affects us. So we have to be active in politics. I myself tend to favour the latter viewpoint, that we need to be active, and try to improve the environment, get involved

with ecological and anti-nuclear movements. Robert Aitkin
has been very active in ecological green peace groups, and
picketing nuclear centres in Hawaii and on the mainland of
America. That old Indian belief that life is just an illusion
and doesn't matter at all doesn't appeal to me. This is very
real, this is the only world we have, and we need to work
as much as we can to keep it clean.

As you deepen in meditation, you start to realise that
the mind is very large. Krishnamurti says that the mind
is infinite, and I suspect that most of us just live on its
surface. It's not a matter of going down, but of realising
that the depth has been there all the time. Also there
seems to be a picking up externally, when you start to
have a greater sense of the 'nidanas' of Buddhism, the
spokes of the wheel: the way in which one thing flows into
another, what we can call interdependency, or coincidence
carried to an amazing level. This is the important thing in
Buddhism, this sense of interdependency. The individual
is no longer a thing, but a process, an inter-relationship
with the internal and external worlds. As the ego becomes
less, as you become more aware of this, you start to see
what are apparently coincidences happening all the time
around you.

Mahayana must be based on compassion, on the
realisation that interpenetration is a reality. Whatever we
do is affecting ourselves, that everybody is ourself ...
there is no difference. In Theravadin Buddhism, there is
a disjunction between Nirvana[9], up there, and the world
of samsara[10], down here. You try to get from samsara to
Nirvana, the Arhat ideal. In Mahayana, the two are one —
there is no difference between form and space. They are
exactly the same, so until everything is freed nothing is
freed. The Bodhisattva vow is that, 'I will always work for
the salvation of all sentient beings until they precede me
into Nirvana'. Actually all beings already are Nirvana, not
in Nirvana, they are Nirvana.

In Buddhism, any belief structure is regarded as a skilful means to get you to Nirvana, where it can be dropped. So there is not that sense of the dogmatic. I suspect that a lot of the Buddhist statements are true, but I would rather see them in terms of my own understanding. I would not want to have any belief that was there just because I was a member of a certain school. It's all too easy naively to accept religious beliefs. Why do we need to have beliefs? For example, in Zen, essentially it is your own mind, your own meditation problem, and your relationship with a teacher. I'm ignoring the fact that Zen is part of the Buddhist religion in various countries, and they have ritual and monasteries and all that paraphernalia. That is all there, but I think it is ancillary to the essential meditation experience of zazen[11].

I try to be as aware as I can of what is happening in and around me all the time. Zen says it, Krishnamurti says it, theosophy says it, Buddhism says it, Hinduism says it. All we have is the present moment. Time is non-existent, it's a concept in our own minds. We have to actually sense the moment, now. It's spiritual because what is spiritual is not what we construct, not what we put up on high levels up there, but what is. Everything which is, is spiritual. Many of us tend to live in what is not — memories, ambitions for the future, day dreams, fantasies, fanaticisms. I find when I meditate my mind is much clearer, the pressures of society are more easily handled. The problems of life are not solved by meditation, but it reduces the pressure and allows you to handle them more adequately The Zen tradition lets you drop quite a lot of the rubbish of society. The Buddha said that the great problems are desire, craving, ambition — trying to hang on to things, trying to make them better.

Our move to Bega is an attempt to simplify living. I see myself spending half the day working on writing and research, doing my doctoral thesis on Madame Blavatsky, and the other half of the day out in the fields developing the farm. Some time in meditation and yoga, and some time in swimming and skiing up in the mountains — a pleasant bush life. There is a danger in becoming too fanatical, trying to save and change things. Although I applaud the spirit of reformation, it must be done with awareness, humour and balance, or it may make things worse. You have to find your own rhythm, and take it from there. Next year, I'm going to lecture overseas which will be a very intensive time, but that's all right. I'm hoping that, with the farm, I'll have more time for meditation, just sitting and watching the clouds go over, seeing the water rise in the dam.

---

1   Golden Dawn: occult society established in England in the nineteenth century.

2   The Theosophical Society was established in the late nineteenth century, under the leadership of Madame Blavatsky, to synthesise Eastern and Western spirituality into new teachings appropriate for the era.

3   Arhat: a saint, one who has attained enlightenment.

4   kundalini: energy dormant at the base of the spine. When awakened by spiritual practices, it rises through the nervous system to the top of the head, releasing blocks on the way in a process which may lead to experiences of intense pain or bliss.

5   Vipassana: literally (in Pali) insight, intuitive knowledge. A Buddhist meditation technique for developing right mindfulness.

6   The two main traditions in Buddhism are the Theravadin and the Mahayana. Theravadin Buddhism works principally from the original Pali texts, and is the Buddhism of Thailand, Sri Lanka, Burma and Kampuchea. Mahayana Buddhism is the Buddhism of Tibet and China, and has strongly influenced the Buddhism of Japan. One of the main differences between the two is that, in the Mahayana School, the enlightened one compassionately vows not to leave this realm of existence until s/he has attained the enlightenment of all sentient beings.

7   D. T. Suzuki, twentieth-century Japanese philosopher and writer, whose works helped to popularise Zen in the West.

8   roshi: 'old teacher' — name given to a Zen master who gives personal instruction to lay and monastic students.

9   Nirvana: state of supreme enlightenment, beyond intellectual conception, in which ego discriminations are dissolved in union with ultimate reality.

10   samsara: the cycle of birth and death.

11   zazen: Zen sitting/Zen meditation.

Catherine Melville

'Many lay people who are quite competent in other areas of their lives become like little children when they enter church doors. They don't question the status quo, and they accept the norms as gospel, even though the gospel is about questioning the norms.'

Born in 1960, Catherine Melville is a Catholic, and deeply committed to 'the Kingdom': the values of love, faith, justice and truth. To the institution of the church, although sustained by the tradition it embodies, she feels marginal, and is strongly critical of its hierarchical structures, materialist values, and failure to encourage lay participation. Her concern for Third World issues, and a desire to express her faith led her to Chile, where she spent three years working in the slums of Santiago as a lay missionary, giving support and friendship to the poor and dispossessed. On her return to Australia, inner work with her dreams enabled Catherine to let go of the 'shoulds' around going back to Chile, and she allowed the flow of her life to take her to new work and a new relationship. Currently she is working as a writer, and expecting her first child to her husband, Paul.

Catherine Melville was raised in Sydney as a Catholic. She describes her teenage self as, 'A dreamer — heavily steeped in idealism and anti-materialism'. Her story begins when she was a student at the University of New England.

———————————————— ✳ ✳ ✳ ————————————————

At university I took a number of courses on the Third World and development issues. Why did the poor continue to be poor, and the rich to get richer? What could we do? Every time people tried something it ended in failure. I remember one day walking back from the campus thinking of the Lord's Prayer...thy kingdom come, thy will be done, on earth as it is in Heaven. It's the prayer of hope. Jesus promised that if you pray you will receive. It gave me a reason to hope.

I wanted to go to another country, and Chile attracted me probably because it was a Catholic, though non-practising, country. The year after my graduation, I was able to express my faith more explicitly. Because of the possibility of going to Chile, I was advised to do a course at the Pacific Mission Institute in Sydney. The last thing I felt like was another year of study, but it wasn't study in the strict sense of the word. It was more development of me as a person, and discovering that there were other people who had questions similar to my own. It was a year when my faith came out from under the bed, which was where I had kept my Bible when I was at university. I had always had a sneaking suspicion that there was more to Catholicism, and it felt good to find aspects of the church to which I could relate more closely. There was a lot of emphasis on justice, and a faith that was part of life.

It was a very full year, preparing for a modern day mission through discussion, study, anthropology, psychology, prayer and spirituality. There were people from all over the Pacific, going all over the world. It's impossible to train someone to be a missionary, all you can do is make them aware of the complexities of the issues. Through that year, I realised that I needed a little more time in my own church. The mission project wasn't ready to go at the end of the year, so I stayed in Australia doing mission and justice education here. I spoke to people about the reality of mission. To the average Catholic, the mission is a subsidiary company, not fully fledged. They don't realise that the majority of Catholics are in Africa, Asia and Latin America. Given that this means that the bulk of church members are economically poor, the perspective on what it means to be a Catholic will have to change. In Australia, the efforts of Catholics in past generations have been to make themselves successful in the gross society. We succeeded in that and now we're suffering. People are wondering, where have the gospel values gone? Where is the fidelity to the poor, which is what Jesus was on about. I spoke about freedom and justice, and encouraged people to think about these issues.

I went to Chile on a lay missionary project, under the auspices of the Columban priests, a Catholic missionary group. They had always counted on the support of lay people. They had realised that the next step in mission, ideally speaking, was to bring lay people together. So the idea behind the programme was to foster cross-cultural interchange. We were the first — since then Chileans have been sent to Australia to work as missionaries. The aims of the project were to be present, to be together, as a gesture of solidarity on the path. There were two Australians and four Irish.

We were based in Santiago, in a población, a poor area on the outskirts. Santiago is a beautiful city which hides the fact that people live in abject poverty. The military government had been in power since 1973, and poverty was exacerbated by repression. Any sign of protest was squashed. We were living in a simple house but it had running water and electricity. It wasn't real hardship, especially by the local people's standards. I worked with youth and women. Women are the poorest of the poor, and many of them suffer from the 'kick the cat' syndrome. The men were oppressed in their jobs, and took it out on their wives. Chile is a very machismo society, and women don't express their opinions readily. We would bring women together, and encourage them to talk about themselves and their dreams. We taught simple relaxation exercises to encourage them to have some time for themselves. Although they were simple exercises, because there was so little offered, they were powerful.

The continuation of military rule depends on the regime sowing distrust in the people, breeding personal and psychological insecurity. There was a lot of rhetoric about solidarity, giving and commitment, but many people didn't have the security to work together.

I had to face my own mortality, and realise that not all those who were martyred made a difference. I saw a lot of people martyred. Sometimes it really hit home. There were two brothers, I remember, who were killed for their beliefs. One of them wrote a letter to his mother saying that he understood now what being faithful to Jesus meant. He could see Him even in the people who despised what he was doing. He was nineteen years old, and he opted to use the weapons that were crushing him. I think he was used as a dupe. The mother spoke of her hope, and her belief in the resurrected Jesus. I remember admiring her faith but wondering where it came from. I could see how Jesus would choose to be with poor people, yet it seemed so cruel that they continued to be poor. There was that conflict between being poor and discovering the real essence of life, and being poor and it being a travesty and abuse of life. I still feel that conflict.

I didn't always encourage people to take political action. I could see why people didn't want to. The weapon is fear, and at times in Chile I felt more afraid than I have anywhere else in my life. At times I went in protests, at other times I didn't. It has to be a personal decision, because if you are arrested and tortured or killed, you need to believe in what you are doing. So, we would encourage, with caution.

We were there as missionaries and we worked under the Catholic umbrella. It was difficult to be faithful to being a lay person, and not get sucked into the hierarchy. There is no one church, either here or in Chile. Many people are genuinely searching for alternative ways. There are many experiments, amidst the confusion. In the last fifteen years the church in Chile has had to open its doors to social groups and political parties who have found it impossible to meet anywhere other than the church. Its position allows it to offer them accommodation.

I often discussed my faith with others. The cornerstone of my faith is that Jesus came so we could have life, and that Jesus is risen. I believe that the function of the church is to encourage life to the full. Everyone has their own answer to what that means. It's a journey to balance all the forces of life. We have material needs, definitely, but we also have a need for identity and spiritual growth. We have a need to be loved, and to seek our needs actively, to be aware of all the opportunities and promises that life presents. Even while living in oppressive Chile there were opportunities.

In the long run our gift to the people was friendship and love. There is a great generosity amongst the Chileans. Perhaps ironically, the poor, because they are so vulnerable, can afford to be vulnerable. They don't have to build up the defences that rich people use to protect themselves from life.

When I came home after completing my three year contract, two things hit me: the materialism of my friends and the opportunities offered in a society free of fear.

I knew I needed time by myself, so I went up to a small retreat centre in the country near Kempsey. I spent a very gentle three weeks there, listening to myself, doing a little dream work, dancing. Steven Nolan was the priest in charge, and his role was passive, just to listen. It was in

a dream that it became clear to me that my heart wasn't
in returning to Chile, so I started writing the reasons for
and against my going back. I realised I was returning to
Chile because it seemed somehow honourable to do so.
Only in speaking out loud did I realise that I was dreading
going back. From then on, I knew I couldn't return. My
heart wasn't in it. I had learned what I needed to learn,
given what I could give. I would be going back under
sufferance, out of a misguided sense of responsibility. My
first reaction was shame. I had an image of myself as a
woman of my word, and I had broken a promise to return.
In fact, everyone was really understanding, and reassured
me that I didn't have to go back. Their understanding
touched me even more deeply than chastisement would
have.

When the relationship I had been in finished, everything
hit me ... meaninglessness about life, a dark patch, where
am I going? Chile had been my dream, and my identity had
been tied up with it. Once it was gone, I had too many
questions about the church to feel kin with it. I felt angry
at the class struggle in the church, which I had found even
in Chile. I was frustrated at the lack of recognition of the
laity. Many lay people who are quite competent in other
areas of their lives become like little children when they
enter church doors. They don't question the status quo,
and accept the norms as gospel, even though the gospel is
about questioning norms.

I had an intense need to pray. Though I was depressed,
there were times when I felt like letting my soul dance for
a while. There was a real sense that God was with me. It
worries me that it seems that only in the doldrums of life
do we discover that we are spiritual. Even though I know
that God is a God of life, why is it that I, and so many others,
turn to Him only in our lowest moments? The phrase that
kept going through me was, unless a grain of wheat dies,
it remains a single grain. But if it does die, it yields a

rich harvest. Finally I understood that dying is painful, but death is short, and relatively painless, and there was hope, and it was time to go. That saying meant that I had to let go. Everything that had made sense didn't any more, at times it felt as if there was nothing left. I had to realise that, rather than trying to pump meaning into things where there was none. Since returning from Chile, I had put on masses of weight, ten kilos, and I decided to seek harmony with my body. It became a good teacher for me. When I was present to my body, and to the food I put into it, it became a representative of the spiritual, a call to be aware. At that point, I did some rebirthing. When I first arrived back, I had reacted against rebirthing — it seemed to be so individualistic, and I had been so socially orientated. There was no one critical moment in my healing — it was like waves. Spiritual journeying is a continual two steps forward and one step back. At times, I want all the steps to be forward. Now I'm a little more accepting of the pattern of life, and the space I am in. At the moment, it feels very creative. It feels as if I am a giver of life, and life is being given through me. I feel unstoppable, as if I can take on the world.

After the depression, I voted to step out again into the unknown. I decided to finish my job, leave Sydney, pursue a career in writing. Not long after this, I was surprised by the deepening of a relationship with Paul, who had been a friend for a long time. Coming so soon after I had resigned myself to a life of loneliness, it threw me. In the past, the mourning for my relationships had always been long and drawn out. But the grieving after my last separation was short, because I had realised that the grain of wheat had to die. My relationship with Paul continues to be creative, and encourages me to grow. I don't have to lose myself. In fact, I feel that I have gained myself more, and that is a big surprise. Later, I met John Jansen[1] who told me he wanted to write a book. I confessed that one of my desires was to be a ghost writer. We ended up working together and I'm still very involved with that project.

I'm also very involved with a church project called 'Celebration of Life,' in a parish at Wollongong. It came out of a desire to have a mission, but not in the old sense. Rather, we want to encourage people to get more out of their church membership, and not to be complacent with their individualism. The programme contains lots of workshops and drama which I like, and which have often been neglected because they are not 'sacred'. At this stage, I'm spending a few days a week working on a programme for a group that we call the 'animators'. Discussions focus on issues relevant to the church, historically and in the future. There will also be a number of workshops covering themes such as the feminine image of God, meditation and mission today. If people go away thinking that they would like to know more, I would consider the project successful. I would like people to question some of the sacred cows such as why we have to keep going to Mass or whether Catholicism is a religion into which most are born rather than choose to belong. In Chile, people would say, 'I'm very Catholic', and they might be fifty-five years old, and not have been near church since their first communion. Here, people sometimes feel guilty, and say, I'm a bad Catholic because I don't go near the church. The challenge is to let go, let go, and find the sacred in life. That's where religion is, that's where the church is, in being reverent of life, as a manifestation of creation and God. Already, those involved in the 'Celebration of Life' are recognising that it's not just for one night, it's something they can carry all through the week.

I feel more vulnerable, more honest about my limitations. I don't need to assume the role of superior, which I tend to do if I'm feeling under-confident. I don't pretend that 'Celebration of Life' is the answer, but it's an opportunity to find part of the answer, and in that sense it's valuable. Journeying through faith is like speaking. I need to say this sentence before the next one will become clear to me, even though it may not be exactly what I want to say. So, I had to take this step before the next one will become obvious. Being faithful to the moment, to the phase of life through which I'm passing, is what spiritual growth is all about.

I still call myself a Catholic. There are different movements in my life, and one of these days I may not. The tradition, with a big T, keeps me humble, and makes me feel part of the universe. The way I choose to have my membership varies, as does everyone's. To me, the life of the church has always been on the margin. I am on the margin, but the margins have always been part of the church. Catholicism is a tradition that goes back a long way and there is a faithfulness to a community of people, a way of living which suffers and creates. I go to Mass regularly, and I am bonded to the Eucharist, and to many people internationally. I feel that I can live and ask questions. Water needs a vessel from which one can drink and, for me, the church is that vessel. It doesn't mean that I can't bathe in other vessels, or drink from them, but Christianity is the vessel from which I drink, and which I know.

Thy kingdom come, Thy will be done: being an agent of the Kingdom has always been my priority. The Kingdom is justice and truth and life. It's the space Jesus was talking about in which love and faith and justice dwell. You can see instances of it, but never its totality. My commitment is to bringing out that totality. Religion is to faith what marriage is to love — it's an agent. Just as love can exist outside marriage, and not all marriages are based on love, so is it that within the Catholic religion, not all people are faithful, and there is faith outside it too.

What's deepening my spirituality now is my relationship with Paul, and a commitment to being in the moment, rather than waiting for the next. It means going with the

flow rather than looking for something different. In prayer
and meditation I don't feel as judgmental of myself. If I'm
feeling the tension of being the perfect meditator, I admit
it, and I don't *have* to be doing anything just because
that's what the book says. It's more of a dance, that kind
of availability to life. Like everyone, I don't meditate as
much as I want to, but, when I do, I feel that I am in
contact with my soul self. In times of crisis, I am most aware
of my spiritual beliefs. My spirituality doesn't pretend
that it will make everything better, but it is sustaining.
It gets me through because of the realisation that I have
to take this step before the next, and there will be new
life. It gives me hope, and a purpose, even amidst the
purposelessness. My spirituality manifests as my belief in
myself as the vessel through which the Lord flows. Other
people can drink and be nurtured from that. T. S. Eliot said:
'Finding the intersection between time and timelessness is
the occupation of a saint.' For me, it's an invitation to risk
— not that I won't go wrong, because I will. That's the way
I'd like to encourage other people.

---

1 John Jansen: prominent Jungian analyst, involved for several years with
the Community of Living Waters, a transpersonal growth centre in the Blue
Mountains, near Sydney.

2 The Celebration of Life ran for two weeks in a Wollongong parish in
June 88. It was an innovative programme which offered workshops on
such topics as Creation-centred Spirituality, Facing Grief, and Faith and
Change, group-dynamic sessions and life oriented liturgies, with the aim of
encouraging people to 'dream of freedom and broaden their horizons', and
to become more actively involved with the church. No charge was made for
the programme, and childcare facilities and transport were provided.

John Truman

'Was I going to stay in the priesthood, and still not come to terms with having an intimate relationship, and exposing myself to the risk that, when they know what I'm really like, they may not love me back?'

Born in 1942, John Truman tells the story of a Catholic priest living through an era of transition. He gives an incisive picture of the pre-Vatican II Church, from the perspective of a seminarian and parish priest. He then describes the changes Vatican II brought about in his concepts of God, the church, the role of the laity and the validity of many traditional Catholic practices. Eventually a sense of God as immanent and benign, and intimate union with God as the crux of spirituality, led him to leave the priesthood to embark on the challenge of loving another human being in marriage. John Truman's life encapsulates many of the changes in beliefs and practices which have affected not just Catholicism, but Christianity in general over the last three decades. A further exploration of the concepts of community and relationship in the church may be found in Jan Goodman's story.

John Truman was born in Sydney into a 'fairly average, Mass-going, not-eating-meat-on-Friday type Catholic family'. He attended Catholic schools, where he felt an interest in, and was good at, religious studies.

———————————————— ✳ ✳ ✳ ————————————————

Straight after school, I went to the seminary to train for the priesthood. One of the most difficult questions I've ever had to answer is why I became a priest. I couldn't put my finger on any particular thing — it was just a general attraction to that way of life. Besides, I was only fifteen when I made the decision, and sixteen when I went. I really went in to see what it was like — I had to do something. I had spoken to a priest whose job it was to get vocations. He was realistic, and tried to explain what things were like. People used to say it was hard, but I think that was part of the attraction — it was a heroic thing to do. The sacrifices didn't loom all that large because I had no idea what was involved in celibacy. I was definitely not a person of the world. It was seen as part of what you gave up, part of the nobility of it. Going away to a strange place to study was all part of the challenge. It wasn't quite as good as being a missionary, but it was on the way. In the Catholic world, at that time, being a priest was pretty big time and that was probably part of it too. My father definitely wasn't encouraging — he was against it, although he didn't say so at the time. Mum was not pushy, although she's got a lot of kudos from it since, and enjoyed that until the last couple of years.

I went to the seminary in Springwood in 1958. It was still very much a pre-Vatican II church. Everything was cut and dried. The Catholic Church had all the answers, everybody knew their place and where they were going. Training to be a priest was supposed to be on a number of levels. There was the academic training of doing different subjects in philosophy and theology. Then there was the spiritual side. Spirituality was things that you did to be holy. You should do meditation, you should do spiritual reading, you should have a particular examination of yourself, you should go to

Mass. You did all those things, and that meant that you were good. It was something that had to be done, and you did it, and that was the way it was. The spirituality was very much based on the belief that God told the church what was right, and the seminary was the representative of the church. So, by keeping the rules of the seminary, we were really doing what God wanted. Which is a marvellous presumption. It seems so stupid now, but then it seemed to make eminent sense — that was the way to spirituality, and that was how you got to be a priest too.

The other side of the training was physical wellbeing, with a lot of emphasis put on sport and exercise. Part of the socialisation in the seminary which I think was very unhealthy was the law prohibiting what they called particular friendships. I've come to realise since that they were scared to death of homosexuality. I hardly knew what it meant at the time. You never had any firm friends to whom you would confide anything of an intimate or personal nature although you had this marvellous theoretical friendship with everybody. This carried over into the priesthood. Everything was very much on the surface, and everyone had to be happy all the time, because if you weren't happy it meant you didn't like being there, which meant you probably wouldn't like being a priest. If you didn't like it, you could leave if you wanted to. I never wanted to. I shudder to think of it now, but that's what the reality was at the time.

I would have thought that I was maturing spiritually, because I was doing all the right things, and I probably was, slowly ... as the years went on we were given a little more independence ... only a little though ... we could choose our own meditation. But a far greater influence was the negative effect that living in a closed community was having on my human development. We were only let out into the world twice a year — for almost three months over the Christmas holidays and for a fortnight in the middle of the year. There was no contact with women, and no understanding by anybody of what emotions, human development or any kind of warm human relationship were all about. Not being a natural questioner, what should have been my time of adolescence and questioning was a time of conformity. I joke, but only half jokingly, that I had my adolescence and mid-life crisis at the same time.

I was ordained as a priest when I was twenty-two and let loose on the world about a month before my twenty-third birthday, having all the answers to everybody's problems. I was aware that I had a lot of theoretical knowledge, but I was also aware, thankfully, that there was a lot that I didn't know. Because in the seminary, even over seven years, they didn't really teach you very much in the way of practicalities. There was no apprenticeship system — it was a hot house environment where we were taken away from the world, except for holidays, trained and nurtured and given a lot of theoretical knowledge and spirituality, and then let loose to learn as we went along.

I went out with a lot of knowledge, but with a lot of apprehension because I thought I was supposed to be good at certain things. Being a successful priest meant being holy. But it wasn't really to teach or pass on spirituality. It was to be good, and to be able to say Mass, to preach well, to be great with the youth club, to be good with sick people, to be a good administrator, and, being an Australian priest, to be great at sport too. Spirituality was still very much about doing the so-called spiritual exercises. Each day time was spent in meditation, a visit to the blessed sacrament, spiritual reading and saying the divine office. This took half to three quarters of an hour. It was another external formal prayer which was supposed to be doing not only me, but also the church, a lot of good. This is one of the mysteries of life. I tend to be a bit cynical about all that now — I hope it's a healthy cynicism.

I'm sure my idea of God wasn't accurate. It was still

very much the same as it was when I was at school. He was a loving God, who rewarded the good and punished the evil, a God who made laws for us to keep. It was all clear cut. God revealed himself in Jesus. Jesus founded the church, and the church speaks in his name and with his authority. So we know that what the church says is true, and in obeying its laws we have the sure way of pleasing God. There's marvellous security in that, and a real sense of being close to God.

A very significant person in my life was the first parish priest I went to, a man called Mick Kennedy. I still thank God that I went to his parish at Blakehurst. Mick was an alcoholic who'd been sober and in AA for eleven years. He was my saviour in that he had the really marvellous idea that people were more important than laws. That was my first contact with anybody who believed that kind of thing. Mick had come to this knowledge through his own personal life. There were a whole lot of church laws and regulations that I should have picked up in those first years, but because Mick thought they were just a whole lot of hogwash, he never bothered about them, and so I never did. Blakehurst was a great place to live. I was a novelty as they had never had a young priest in the parish before. I was able to cope with my doubts reasonably well because of all the stroking I got from the Catholic community. I had a couple of my mates in nearby parishes who were also priests, and we had a good time. I enjoyed life very much.

After Blakehurst, I went to Lidcombe. By the end of my time there, I'd been a priest for about six years, and I was pretty confident of my ability. I'd been fairly successful and, in spite of Mick Kennedy's influence, I was pretty confident that the church had all the answers, and I knew most of the answers anyway. My spirituality went along similar lines. I thought I was doing the right thing by God, and, because I was doing the right thing by Him, He had to do the right thing by me. Everything was straightforward and cosy and life was pretty good. Strangely enough, it was the time of the church birth control controversy, from Pope Paul VI. But even then, I was a real straight liner.

A person who started to be an influence in my life at Lidcombe, and more so at Rydalmere, my next parish, was a man called Bruce Hawthorne, who had been a classmate of mine through the seminary and who was in a next door parish. He was a thinker and a questioner. He would pose questions, which I would refute straightaway. Then I'd think about them and start to see the sense. Another priest, Alec Nelson, was more of an intellectual than I was. He would come to say Mass at Rydalmere and talk about different ideas; he put a different perspective on things. He made me think that perhaps all this straightforward stuff wasn't so straightforward after all. The effects of Vatican II were filtering through, and questions were coming to my mind.

There was a big change in catechetics, in the way religion was being taught, and that made sense to me. There was talk about an approach coming from our human experience up to God, getting away from the idea of God up there imposing His will. I began to see that the church was not *the* Vatican, or Rome, or the Pope — but a group of people united by their faith, by the spirit. The church has an external structure and a hierarchy, but that's not *the* church. That was pretty new — it's a fairly basic change in your thinking when you're talking about the very nature of the church itself. They started to change all the sacraments — the way we said Mass, our attitude to Mass. I really hadn't thought yet what was behind these changes, because the externals made sense — that people should be taking part, that it be in the language of the people. I was still dealing with my old concept of God although I was strong on the idea of God as love. I hadn't got on to the idea as yet of God's all forgiving love.

In 1972 I took six months long service leave and went

out to the Forbes diocese which covers almost the whole west of NSW. I went there to do relieving work — I was being heroic, you see. A lot of people went on overseas trips but I thought I would do something good. It was completely different, being in the country, even though it was doing the same work in a one man parish. After a couple of months, I liked it, and I asked the bishop if I could stay an extra twelve months. I ended up staying eighteen months out there. Romantically, I like to talk about that as my desert experience. I was away from my ordinary environment, I had a lot of time to myself, and questions about a different approach to religion came up. I started to think more about what the church and the priesthood were all about. It was a time of reflection, but it was also fun. I met a lot of great people — they were a novelty to me, and I was a novelty to them, a young priest from the city.

I returned to Sydney a different person, a lot more self-confident and sure that I was going to be able to do things my way. One external sign was that I decided to give up wearing clerical dress-collar and black suit. I have probably only worn it three or four times since then.

I was about thirty-two when I came back to the Bondi Beach parish. I was stuck with Paddy Cunningham, an elderly parish priest, Irish and authoritarian, who didn't really have much of an idea of the new church that I was interested in. However, soon after I came back to Sydney, a significant event happened in my spirituality. I made a retreat with 'The Movement for a Better World', which had a basis in community spirituality. That Christ had formed a community and believed in people praying together, God's all forgiving nature, and that He loved us first were significant parts of the discussions. I've got a belief now that our spirituality basically depends on our idea of God, our knowledge of God. It was at that retreat that I began to get an idea of God as a person, someone to relate to, as opposed to someone who lays down laws.

It was a time of personal turmoil, not that people would have noticed from the outside. I think my non-existent adolescence was catching up with me, flowing into my mid-life crisis. I was questioning everything, although not my own priesthood — I was still happy in that.

I was becoming more flexible about law, and starting to see what St Paul and Jesus Christ were talking about — freedom of the spirit. I stopped telling people what was right and wrong for them. Instead I would tell them what different people in the church, and outside, were saying about a particular problem, and encourage them to make the decision. Birth control was the issue which was the catalyst in the church. It brought to the forefront the whole question of individual conscience, especially when it was opposed to the teaching authority of the church. In the time that I grew up conscience was never mentioned. I found the change very liberating.

Gradually, I was changing my attitude to God. I got the idea, I can't remember where it came from, that God loves us, no matter what. Nothing that we do can stop God from loving us. It's a very liberating idea. The new Rite of Reconciliation in the church had an effect on me too and it encompassed the idea of an all forgiving God. This was very important in changing my idea of God, and it became an important advance in my spirituality.

I was also developing a healthy disrespect for the authority of the church. I felt that the church was binding people more than I thought God wished to bind them, especially in the areas of marriage and sexuality. The church wasn't forgiving, and God was. The church was more interested in external observance than in genuine justice.

I left Bondi Beach parish at the beginning of 1980, when I was thirty-eight, and after four months at Cronulla and two months at Surry Hills I went to Maroubra. I was administrator of the parish, which in effect meant I was in charge and could make the rules. There was a full time religious sister there and she gave me my first contact working in partnership with a woman. It put me in touch with female spirituality. We also had a full time youth worker, and a couple of other priests living in the parish, one working in the Catholic Education Office and one in adult education. It was a place where different ideas were constantly being discussed.

One of the things I introduced into the parish was the general absolution of sins — it wasn't being done in Sydney then. This meant that people didn't have to confess individually — they could come in a community. The idea of marriage and divorce was something else that I thought the church was being unjust about, and I was able to marry people in the church who, legally, shouldn't have been married there. Or I would encourage them to be married somewhere else and I would go along, to a Uniting Church perhaps, and be part of the service. I encouraged freedom of conscience and the belief that people could differ from but still be part of the church.

The most important thing that happened for me in those years was my own spiritual development. It was fairly traumatic and went hand in hand with my idea of God. What I came to believe, and what I still believe, is that God is always present in people. I don't accept the traditional Christian belief that after the great sin of Adam and Eve, the gates of heaven were shut, and they were opened by Jesus when he died on the cross and rose again. I believe that God has always been present in people everywhere, and our understanding of Him varies. The Bible is a record of a people, and of a special people's understanding of His presence, and we see them getting different glimpses of the reality of God. Some individuals, I think, see God a lot more clearly than others, and some have had marvellous glimpses of His tenderness. God isn't a God who lays down laws — he's a God who calls people into a relationship. Christ is the ultimate revelation of what God is like, and he redeemed us not by dying on the cross but by becoming like ourselves, by becoming flesh and calling us to that intimate union with Him. He was saying, hey, this is what I'm like, this is what I'm inviting you to — I'm inviting you to be a lover in an intimate relationship.

Now that was great, but it started to pose problems in my own life. On a human level, I hadn't been able to give myself to anyone in that way. I'd had relationships with lots of people, but I'd always kept the mask on. I wasn't really going to reveal myself to anyone. Two things happened at different levels in my life. There was the spiritual idea of God forming, and my relationship with Annette, who's now my wife, developing. She was someone that I'd known for a long time and we'd formed a relationship. I gave her an awful time. I wasn't going to let myself love anybody, or let anybody in. I'd been preaching marvellous things for years about the importance of love, talking about God's love and how we respond in love, and how people love and forgive one another. Yet in my own life, I wasn't prepared to take the risk of love.

Leaving the priesthood and marrying was a step into the unknown. I was in my early forties, and there was a lot of security in the priesthood — a roof over your head and three meals a day for the rest of your life. It was also something I could do well, and enjoy. So there was a lot of soul searching. I realised I had to decide what I was going to do with the rest of my life. Was I going to stay in the priesthood, and still not come to terms with having an intimate relationship, exposing myself to the risk that, when they know what I'm really like they may not love me back? I thought, if I was ever going to make anything out of life, and understand what God's calling was, and even get some idea of what God and love were all about, I'd take the risk and do that. When I actually made the decision it was fairly quick. It was also a very big step in my spiritual growth. I don't want you to get the idea that I married Annette for spiritual reasons — that's not it at all. The two just went hand in hand.

The congregation at Maroubra was marvellously supportive although a bit surprised. The Bishop condemned me and said I was being unfaithful to God, giving up on my commitment and not caring about the people. I was hurt and angered by his attitude.

I left with absolutely no idea of what I was going to do except marry Annette. She was great. She had a job that paid reasonably well and believed we could live on one wage until something turned up. After we were married a friend of Annette's asked me if I could do a funeral service for her uncle. He hadn't been to church for sixty years and she couldn't think of any priest who would do it. So I started doing funeral services for people who didn't have a minister. After twelve months a firm of funeral directors approached me and asked me if I'd work for them doing funeral services and follow up counselling. This is the work I do now and I've settled down to being a husband and stepfather to Martin, who's now eighteen. Our lives together are marvellous.

Being able to enter into an intimacy with Annette, letting each other know what we're like, preparing to love and be loved, has given me another insight into God's intimacy with us. My growth in spirituality will be because my knowledge of God will grow. Most of my prayer time now is reflection, sometimes on a particular subject, or just trying to get in touch with the God within me. I still regard myself as a Catholic, but I have difficulties with the church. It's a reaction to hurt in one sense as I feel that the church rejected me and, even deeper than that, because officially it doesn't recognise what I've done. Theoretically, I should have applied for permission, not to leave, but to get married. The Pope at the present time isn't giving that unless you go through a whole rigmarole of a process which could take a couple of years. I just don't believe they've got the right to do that, in justice and charity...I wasn't going to subject myself to that. I also find myself being affronted by a church which is clerical and masculine and anti-feminine in its practices. I've never missed the priesthood, which has surprised me, seeing that I didn't leave out of dissatisfaction with the work. Perhaps the work I'm doing now is part of the reason, as I've always enjoyed preaching and trying to say things that mean something to people.

Thea Rainbow

'One of the images that's most helpful for me is
that I am a little new seed that has dropped into
being. What I need to do is compost it, so that
it will root and grow, but there is no way I can
know what the flower is going to be.'

After many years as a minister in the Congregational
and the Uniting Churches, Thea Rainbow, born in 1931,
left what she came to see as an excessively hierarchical
and patriarchal institution in pursuit of a more women
oriented spirituality. In her life since then, periods of
contemplative solitude have been interposed with times
of intense activity, during which Thea has taught and
facilitated courses, workshops and groups for women
seeking to discover their own expression of the spirit. Thea
has researched ancient symbols of the Goddess as female,
a project which culminated in the production of a series
of posters depicting these images. Although profoundly
feminist in her spiritual sensibilities, Thea has come to feel
that traditions and belief structures of any sort are less
important for her than growing from the now of her being
in directions she cannot envisage.

Thea Rainbow was raised in rural Queensland as
a member of the Congregational Church. During her
teenage years, the feeling that she had something special to

do in her life grew within her. She trained as a teacher, and taught deaf children. Her story begins with her decision to become a minister.

—————————— ✳✳✳ ——————————

At the end of my third year teaching, I decided to offer myself for theological training. In those days I had no role models of women participating in the church as leaders or teachers, and I felt that my urgency to serve would be expressed as a missionary. India seemed the most needy country in the world. When I went to the interview, the committee reminded me that, within the Congregational tradition, women as well as men could be ministers. There had been no women trained for ministry in Queensland, and I didn't know of any in Australia at that time.

I was in theological college for six years. I did an arts degree, the theological training and almost completed my Bachelor of Divinity. Near the end of my training, I wondered where God wanted me to go. The church acted under a call system. Local churches, where people made decisions as a community, would call or invite people to be their ministers. I began to feel that my place was in Australia rather than overseas. I could use my gifts here as much as I could in another country, so I said that I was ready to be called by the church. I was ordained in 1959, the first woman ordained in Queensland. I became minister of two churches that were connected.

I was in that church for six years. It was a wonderful experience. I was a very good pastor, in the pastoral care sense. I enjoyed what the world calls 'ordinary' people. I found wisdom and responsiveness in them. I tramped miles, those first few years. I didn't have a car, and I was determined to visit everyone connected with the church. I remember calling on a woman who had four children at the Sunday School. She said I was the first person to call without wanting something since her children had been at Sunday School. She asked me some profound questions about the Bible, which she had never felt she could ask anyone before. Because she'd had this steady stream of children, she'd never been able to go to church. Later, she and her husband became members of the church, and she became a deacon. That sort of response gave me a lot of energy.

After six years I was ready for another place. I moved to a double position. I was director of Christian Education for the Congregationalists in Queensland, and I was also responsible for a small church on the north side of Brisbane. I had not married. I had a feminist view about being independent and flexible and, although I was involved in a deep relationship, it was secondary to my feeling that I needed to be free. I once put on a census form that I had no private life, just simply one integrated life. The Congregational Church states that the one thing required for a covenant of people is that they believe in Jesus Christ. It was Christ centred, but freely gave people the opportunity to work out what that relationship meant. I saw Jesus as a role model for openness and availability, and for a cosmic view of reality and the significance of the person within that reality.

I felt happy. I also felt questioning. I always sensed that there was a movement in my life, and that I needed to be stretched further. At that time, we changed the structure of the Congregational Church in Queensland, and it seemed good for me to finish at the Department of Christian Education. I did that without severing my ties with the Brisbane church. In 1970 I was called to a church in Perth where I spent seven years with an open, spontaneous, self-sufficient, group of people. That was a particularly special time in my life. It was the first time I had moved out of Queensland, and I found it creative and a tremendous challenge. We worked through all sorts of ways of expressing our relationship to ourselves, to the universe and to one another. One of the ways in which the Congregational Church functioned was for people to make a covenant with one another, and, through Christ, with God; to join together and to live as a church. When I was called to a church in Perth, we decided that we would look at the covenant, and restate it in words that were suitable for the day. We spent months over it, and the new covenant was like a marriage vow. I can't repeat all the words now, but it started: 'In joyful response to God's word and Christ's word, we come together, deeply sensitive to the needs of these times.' We used to repeat it at church meetings, communion services or at times when we welcomed children or adults through baptism. We also considered whether we actually needed the church community, or whether it was just holding onto the past and we could scatter to different congregations. I learned more there about being a community than I did in any other group I've known. It was a group of young adults, from different backgrounds and understandings connected in caring and resolving seriously and joyously what it meant to be together.

After some months overseas on long service leave I decided to leave Perth. I accepted a call to the city church in Adelaide. It was in an inner city area and it was a very creative church, particularly in the area of worship.

What I discovered there was the patriarchal nature of the church. There was great excitement at my being there, because I was their first woman minister. Alongside that excitement, there was a fairly clear expectation of what would and would not be acceptable. I had never had that before — I had always felt free to be who I was. I felt cramped and confined, isolated and uncreative. I was being constantly assessed rather than related to. I was aware of the power of men in the church, and, for the first time, of what it meant always to be seen as a woman. At the first parish meeting I went to, there was a great furore about a sexist joke in the parish newsletter. It seemed significant afterwards to me that at my very first meeting with these people there was an emphasis on sexism. We had difficulties with words in hymns. I can remember being with another two staff members one morning when words had been changed to make them non-sexist. One of the men who had a great musical interest was really upset, and adamant that we shouldn't change copyrighted hymns or songs. I had a very deep experience at that time. I felt that I was surrounded by women of all time and all places, and that I was there on their behalf.

It was a union of Congregationalists and Methodists, a conservative community, with a hierarchy which I hadn't experienced before. It was partly due to the history of that church, and also to the union, and to the particular people who were there — people who were very conscious of power and how it could be used. There were communities within the congregation which were quite different from one another. Some focussed on a traditional expression of their faith, some on experiential and spontaneous responses within the worship setting, and some were very catholic. There was a great emphasis on worship as being central to the life of the church. I'd always enjoyed that too, but I found the division between the communities painful, and something I hadn't anticipated.

In 1977, when I went to South Australia, I became President of the South Australian Council of Churches — it was the Congregationalist's turn to fill that role. I did a lot of work on the position of women in the church, and followed that up by going to Japan as a consultant to an Asian Christian Women's Conference. Not long afterwards, I went to Hong Kong as an Australian representative to a small group of women examining what women in this age were all about. Another woman and I from the Asian conference organised the one and only theological consultation of women throughout Australia in Adelaide, and I chaired it. I was being pushed by circumstances and by my openness to my journey to look at what being a woman was about in a way I hadn't anticipated. Some of the people with whom I worked saw that as outside my job.

Towards the end of my second year, I felt traumatised by this ambiguity within me, this loss of creativity, this sense of aloneness, and the sense that something had worn out for me. I had worked tremendously hard, and made the church the centre of my life, but somehow it wasn't working for me anymore. I knew that I had to move out. I resigned first as a minister, and then from the church. In my final letter of resignation, I said that religious experience was too fluid, mobile and ever changing to be systematised. My religious experience was valid in itself, and I didn't need to compare it to that of Jesus. Being a woman in this period of history was demanding new thought and understanding of me, and I needed to be free to continue my journey.

In 1979, somebody asked me to follow up what I'd done in Japan. I thought it was difficult to transfer a conference experience to another space, and suggested instead that we study a book together. A group of us studied *God the Father* by Mary Daly[1]. It was like a whirlwind. There were seventeen of us, and when we finished we did it again with another group of people. That gave me a lot of energy. The following year thirty-five of us met every Monday night and looked at all of Mary Daly's books. We did workshops on anger and on our different needs. That was my feminist training, that concentrated work. Mary Daly gave me a connection with someone who was strongly Christian, and yet could see other possibilities. She validated my experience by giving words to my anger and despair. A tremendous amount of energy and power was generated by her books. Some of that was directed, by those still part of the church, into a series of contemporary worship services. We did one on the fact that evil is 'live' spelled backwards. We did some skits on how evil was presented in the Bible, and we had Bible readings about the Hebrew people's cruelty to women — taking over tribes and killing women and keeping virgins. The second one was on God. There was a pyramid of people with God at the top and women right on the bottom. Then all the women walked out, and the pyramid collapsed. We reclaimed Eve's role and gave out apples at the end of one service. We had to deal with the anger of people who didn't want those questions raised, or thought we were being blasphemous.

I thought that I would have a year off, and rest. I would find myself, and work out where my journey was taking me. Three things happened. I reclaimed my relationship with nature, which I'd never allowed myself time for — I did a lot of gardening and walking. I had allowed myself to be deprived of the spiritual wisdom of non-Christian traditions, so I did a course in Buddhism, and one on ways of being religious. At the College of Advanced Education, I found courses in religious studies and a group with whom I could work.

I spent a great deal of time in quietness. I was sharing a house with a woman who did a lot of meditation, so my worship was channelled in that direction. I thought that by the end of the year I would have some clue as to what to do. After so many years, I was tired, and didn't want to make a decision about doing anything — I wanted to continue the journey. So I gave myself permission to have six years of study under my own auspices, recreating my life and balancing the six years I'd spent in theological college. Those six years would be a springboard for the next twenty, because I was in the ministry for twenty years.

During the first of those six years I did an orgy of study at the CAE — religious and women's studies combined. The second year, I decided I had been over peopled, and I needed a contemplative year. So I lived by the sea in a little cottage. I was there for fifteen months. I connected with people one day a week, and I lived the rest of the time with the sun and the sand and the water. While I was there I followed through a project from the previous year's study on the deities symbolised as female. I did the equivalent of a Phd thesis for a one term unit at the CAE. I produced slides and a script on female images of God, and how they had been hidden within our culture. When I finished, I invited groups of women to look at the slides, and found that they were put directly in touch with their own being. The other important thing about that year was the creative work I did with meditation. I did walking meditation, and worked out rituals facing North, South, East and West. I walked through the rainbow in all directions, and I planted a native garden, and felt the earth move instead of the sun. I changed my name at that time. My Christian name had been Dorothy, and I changed it to Thea, a theological statement in itself, although I felt the name chose me. Dorothy meant gift of God, and I didn't want to be a gift of anyone or anything. Thea meant God in me, a female or Goddess. Rainbow was a statement about my significance in the universe, symbolised by an aspect of nature. A rainbow, with all its different strands, has many symbolic possibilities. One of my tasks this lifetime is to harmonise those strands, those colours. I had a wonderful companion in a cat, and if I get nostalgic for anything, it's for that period.

I went back to the city because I wanted to connect with people again. I worked part time for six months as an activities therapist in a nursing home, to pay the rent. I put some money aside, and I decided to use that to go to the United States. In that year by the sea, I had been by myself, but the women who were my companions were the writers of the books I read. I wanted to connect with them in person. I had met Mary Daly in Sydney, but I didn't meet her in America because she wasn't in Boston when I was there. I stayed with Carol Christus in San Francisco, and in Oregon with the women who had been responsible for creating *Womenspirit* magazine. I did a ritual course with Star Hawke, and I met Z. Budapest[2]. I became part of a women's quest movement based in San Francisco. It was a group of women looking for a spiritual path more affirmative of women's experiences, and articulated by them. That was a very rich period. It gave me my world setting, and sent me back to Australia feeling ready to move. I didn't have a church community anymore, but I became aware that I could create my own community, if I knew what I wanted.

Back in Adelaide, two of us initiated a course on women in religion as part of the Women's Study course of the CAE. We also organised a ritual in February which we called the Feast of the Flame. It's part of the seasonal rituals that have been round for thousand of years. As a result of that, we formed a small group that worked out women's rituals and celebrated once a month. Later we started a magazine, *The Rippling Web*, which was for women interested in their spiritual journeys, and in naming them for themselves. Five of us formed a group which was special for us all. It had no agenda, but we were intensely occupied for three hours once a fortnight, discussing where we were, and pushing each other to say what we felt. In that year I did my first private course on 'Goddesses and Ancient Images of Women'. These have continued ever since.

When I moved out of the church, I focussed on my inner journey as a woman, and I expected the women's community to be what the church community had been. What I discovered along the way was that I was all alone. There were no structures out there, nothing at all. I shed copious tears about being on my own. I'm just beginning to rejoice in that now, but I've kept the women's community around me by being a resource person, and by organising and teaching. My journey has been thoroughly connected with the journeys of other women, and I'm just moving out of that now, letting it go to get my own spiritual being together. I've become less head centred and more trusting of myself. I've moved from the time I felt firm in the community of the church to a time when I feel totally affirmed within my own being. I can stand alone and I can connect with other people without expectations or dependence on them. I can name the universe in female terms without having to explain it. The cosmic force at the centre of the universe is expressed through woman form, and we are all expressions of that. I don't feel the need for a system, as I used to. I feel that my community makes and unmakes itself, and flows on. Last year, at a meditation day, I was asked how I would name my spiritual journey now. I found myself saying that it's about being present to the now of my being, and giving expression to that, rather than having a set of beliefs.

I wanted to work in the system again for a while, to decide whether I would spend some of the rest of my life there. I got the first job I applied for, at a CAE in an Equal Opportunity Project in External Studies. It was about looking at the participation of women, and what the studies were all about. It was hard, I was criticised, but I didn't compromise. I was able to live out of my centre in a way I would have doubted I could before. No matter how strong I'd been, I'd always been conscious of wanting to please, to have others connected to me. So I was very pleased about that year, which actually went on to be eighteen months. During that time, we continued our groups, and that's when I started using the name 'Womandala,' from the word 'mandala.'

When I had finished that project, I decided to have the last six months free. I'd earned enough money to look after myself for that time. Then I was going to throw it all up in the air in 1987, and I'm still throwing it up in the air. One of the things that came down was that a friend who had been involved in the first Goddess course decided that she'd like some money she had saved to be used for a women's project. She wondered whether we could provide images of the Goddess in a form readily accessible to women. When I had been in the States, I had done a book crawl looking for images that could be used in our courses, and I had found very few. We decided to make posters of the ancient Goddess images, and checked art and museum spaces throughout the world to see what was available. We ended up not getting all that we asked for, and therefore it was a fairly ad hoc selection, but we feel pleased with it. That has led us into new contacts — for instance we've sold them at the show in Adelaide — and we've had deep conversations with people ranging from those who are repelled by them to those who are positive.

The word God has been thoroughly masculinised in our culture. We need to feminise it and to do that we need to say Goddess. That word earths it more for me, and gives it an immanence. The Goddess is within me, and I love her fiercely. My woman body is a context in which the cosmos is being worked out. 'Goddess' also implies an interconnection of all life. We are not here to have domination over the earth, with God at the top and the earth at the bottom. We are here to connect with the earth who is our sister, another form of energy, and to be alert to our response to the seasons. That's part of a coven or a Goddess tradition. Another aspect of the difference between 'God' and 'Goddess' is that 'Goddess' integrates darkness more than 'God' does. Darkness is about the deepest mystery and struggle, through which we move on our journey. It's a shift away from duality to a sense that life is one. One of the tools I have come to treasure most over the last couple of years is Tarot, the Mother of Peace and Daughters of the Moon decks. They are round — it's like saying that we can experience life anywhere on the circle, and treasure darkness as much as light. I've talked about the moon waxing light and waxing dark, rather than waning, which has a certain connotation. So it's full light and full dark moon, to give fullness to the dark as well as the light.

I find mindfulness meditation very helpful, though I also use visualisation and other techniques. Just to sit and breathe in and breathe out empties the mind and stills me. I find it useful to have a rhythm of quietness and activity which is connected to the meditation practice. One of the ways I've named myself in recent years is a social solitary. I'll have times when I long to be a recluse and then I have times of beehive activity. Sometimes that rhythm will be a on a daily basis, other times it might be six months quietness and six months business. I have also found it good to have worked into my life some form of connectedness with energies other than human — gardening, or beaching. This gives me clarity, and takes away stress by giving me a sense of belonging to more than myself.

I've felt less and less need for men. I find it very difficult to read a book by a man. The first part of my life was so full of men's words, teachings, stories and authority that I need to balance that in the next half of my life. I don't have any sense of loss. I'm not angry now, that's the way it was — I'm quite contained and satisfied. I have men friends, and I can converse and argue with men, but I don't go out looking for them. If they are part of my world, I'll deal with them, and I've no desire to put them down or annihilate them, but I'm clear that I'm not here to belong to them, or build them up, or to do their journeying for them.

One of the images that's helpful for me is that I am a new little seed that has dropped into being. What I need to do is to compost it, so that it will root and grow, but there is no way I can know what the flower is going to be. I would encourage each person, female and male to push their boundaries to the ultimate, but I do not encourage myself to speak on behalf of anyone else. Sometimes I think, how dare I assume anything about anybody — I only know what happens within myself, and I find that difficult enough. I've moved away from believing. I don't want to say what I believe in — it's not a belief system, it's more like poetry. Part of the change for me has been moving away from an overwhelming sense of purpose to just letting it happen. My sense of vocation, being called and being different, has gone, and with it my sense of my own importance. In the third cycle of my life, I want to work more on personal relationships. I had a very deep relationship with a woman in the second cycle, but at the time I was more committed to group activities and the community. Now I want to be more mindful of relating to another person.

---

1   Mary Daly: leading feminist writer and scholar.

2   All these women write about contemporary feminist spirituality.

Stephen Bewlay

'If you go to church, there should be supernatural things going on, otherwise there is no
evidence that God is at work there. Jesus said that
there'd be signs that would accompany believers
in Him. In His name, we'll kick out demons,
speak in new languages, and be able to pick up
live snakes.'

Stephen Bewlay was born in 1959, and works as a scientist.
He is a member of the Assembly of God, a Christian
fundamentalist group. Converted to a Christianity he
rejected in his teens by his acceptance of creation science,
Stephen is highly committed to a small Assembly of God
congregation in Springwood, in the Blue Mountains close
to Sydney. His account of the beliefs of this group, their
mode of worship and the faith in God that guides them
gives a vivid picture of what is one of the most rapidly
growing faiths in Australia today.

The Assembly of God is one of the largest Pentecostal
groups in Australia. In common with other Pentecostal
groups, it is committed to an evangelical (literal)
understanding of the Bible. Thus such classic Christian
doctrines as virgin birth and the second coming are widely
believed. A personal commitment to Christ, expressed
in a water baptism, is held necessary for a person to

be considered a member of the church, and a child of God. Pentecostals value highly what are considered to be manifestations of God in their lives and church services; healing (illness is seen to be a result of humanity's fallen state); speaking in tongues; prophecy and miracle working.

Mum and Dad and my sister were all Christians in a traditional church with a missionary outlook. They wanted to get out and be useful to people in other countries. I didn't want anything to do with it. It seemed unscientific and impractical, boring and limiting. My parents were strict in their Old Testament observance of the scriptures. We wouldn't buy or sell anything, or go anywhere, on a Sunday. I was made to go to church until I was thirteen. Then, at thirteen, I used to make sure that whenever it was time to get ready for church, I'd be nowhere in sight. After a while, Mum and Dad had realised there was no point forcing me. I did a degree in Applied Physics at the Institute of Technology followed by a higher degree at the University of New South Wales. That's where God got me in a corner, and got my attention.

I had never doubted there was a God, a being much bigger than us. I had never done anything about it until one day at uni I went to a lunchtime lecture on total creation versus evolution. The fine print explained that the lecture would be given by a biologist who was also a Christian. I assumed then that God had made everything by the process of evolution, because it's what I had been taught. I thought I'd go along for a laugh and to put the lecturer straight on a few points.

The lecturer was a softly spoken guy who discussed interesting scientific evidence and observations. He looked carefully into what we could conclude from this. It was absolutely staggering to me — it virtually cut my world view out from under me. He showed that many of the fossil facts didn't fit well with the idea of evolution. In fact, they contradicted evolution, and fitted perfectly with Bible history. I didn't become a Christian on the spot — I was fairly sceptical. But it made me think, and from then on whenever I had to look up a technical reference for my thesis, I'd look at a few of the scientific journals that he'd quoted. He was right, he hadn't misquoted or distorted anything. All the facts fitted together exactly the way he had suggested. So I realised how much chemical, biological and archeological evidence there is that God created everything in six days. It made the Bible look like a fantastic minefield of scientific information, an eyewitness record of early times. Until then I'd thought Genesis was a myth. It had never occurred to me that it could be taken literally.

So that was where God got my attention. Over the months, I gradually began to believe that what I'd understood before was totally wrong. Most teachers and lecturers believe in evolution. They teach it because it was taught to them without ever checking. Mum told me about a summer school run by the Creation Science Foundation. It was informative and interesting. I bought a few books and magazines to check into it further. I checked up the Bible references, making sure nothing had been misquoted — always the sceptic, systematic, just as I'd been trained to be in science. Creationist lecturers are some of the best scientific researchers around. They are careful and meticulous about using scientific method and avoiding hidden assumptions. Other scientists are biased right from the beginning, whereas the creationists come into things with an open mind. They are portrayed as dogmatic and people say that they believe in the Bible, and twist their science around to fit it. For me, that's blatantly untrue. I was the other way around. I knew a few facts, and then I started looking at how they fitted the Bible. I didn't do it from the starting point of believing the Bible.

My folks and my sister went to a charismatic church at

Penrith. It wasn't a boring, traditional church. The people were aware and energetic and good things happened there. Cripples would hobble in on their crutches and walk out not needing them. People who had been blind for a few years would walk out able to read fine print. God was working supernaturally, showing that He loved people and cared about them. When I wasn't a Christian, I heard about these things, but they didn't particularly click. I had no desire to go there. But after realising that God had made everything in six days, I realised He had done me a beauty. He'd fooled me on my own ground. I always had thought that all the evidence fitted evolution, and He showed me that the Bible which my parents lived and swore by had been right all along. He proved to me that you can see without seeing. That really shook me up. You have to be very careful. If God can be there the whole time, and you don't even know it, that's living dangerously. If you ignore Him, it's risky, because He's big, and He made everything, and He owns it. So I apologised to God for ignoring Him. That's where I became a Christian and took Jesus as my boss.

I was water baptised a year after I became a Christian, at the Christian Fellowship Centre at Penrith. I stayed there for about a year and a half. The way they ran things was excellent. As well as the usual Sunday church services, they had teaching sessions, where you could do elective subjects. I did everything they offered over that period — prayer, basic Bible principles, Old Testament history, the Bible and counselling and a topic on the Bible and science. Scientists have convinced ninety per cent of the population into believing that the universe is a billion years old, whereas I know it's only six or seven thousand years old.

If you go to a church, there should be supernatural things going on, otherwise there is no evidence that God's at work there. Jesus said there'd be signs that would accompany believers in Him. In His name, we'll kick out demons, speak in new languages, and be able to pick up live snakes. If we drink any deadly things, they won't harm us, and we can lay hands on sick people and they'll recover. God has given me the ability to speak in tongues. It's one of the signs, so you've got to come to grips with it. You can use tongues any time you sense it's needed. It's a way of being in touch continually with God.

After I'd been going to Penrith Christian Fellowship for a year and a half, Assembly of God started up in Springwood. The place was glistening with potential for the future, and there were lots of people interested in doing something useful for God. So I thought I'd get into it and help it become something useful and decent. Over a period of a few months in 1981–2, I pulled out of going to Penrith, and started going to Springwood. I've been there ever since. It was different from Penrith in that we had to depend on ourselves a lot more. We were just a bunch of fairy ordinary local people, that God had thrown together for purposes of His own. He was going to mould us, and teach us, and fit us together, but in ways that we didn't know at the time. So it taught us a lot more patience and trust in God.

We had small signs. There was a little guy, the son of a friend of mine in church, who had a bad crop of warts on his hands. He had tried all the standard old wives' remedies, with no success. If one disappeared, another would pop up. I prayed for him, and all his warts except one disappeared over a fortnight. Although he got some more two years later but it was a sign to me that, if I cooperated with God, He would use me for exciting things.

We decided it would be more convenient if we had our own building instead of having to move stuff in and out of the primary school hall where we first met. A big church hall came up for sale, but it was a pretty crippling price. The church believed God wanted useful work done in Springwood so it got a bank loan and bought the building.

Repaying the mortgage has been a constant hassle. We have had to work at it, and everyone has had to make sacrifices. But, every time people made up their minds to give, God would go out of His way to show His favour, and they'd know they'd done the right thing. God never failed to look after us. After five years, we have only $10 000 left to go on a $55 000 building. God has brought talent to the place.

Being a fairly small church, we want to be useful wherever God wants. God convinced us once that we should go out and visit people, door to door like the Jehovah's Witnesses, to tell them how the universe works, and that there is a Heaven and a Hell. We've done it a few times and there are three women who are now Christians as a result. I don't know where they'd be now if they weren't with Jesus, because they were flirting around with a lot of bad habits. A couple of them were divorced, and were gadding about with heaps of other guys. It's really interesting when you see God gradually working on people's lives, and you see the changes.

Usually our services start off with singing, serving God in music. Then announcements of whatever is coming up — a curry night, Bible studies, prayer meetings, special guest speakers and musicians — then a sermon. We take up a collection, which we use to pay off the church building and give the pastor a part time salary. He's trained in hotel management, and works in a restaurant in Sydney two days a week. Having to hold down a job like the rest of us keeps him in touch with the rest of the world. I can think of at least one time when the pastor threw the timetable out the window and didn't worry about his sermon. We sang and worshipped God for about two and a half hours. Checking around later, we found that there were people who had wandered in absolutely down in the pits. We kept on singing and they realised they had better not keep dwelling on their problems. They could let God work them out, not try to solve them all on their own. So there is always some practical reason why God does things. You have to be careful, because He knows more than we do, and He's wiser than we are, so it may not always look practical or logical at the time.

We also get prophetic words back. God will actually speak through someone. They don't fall on the floor in a trance, speaking in strange voices. They suddenly feel they want to say something, and they speak in a relatively normal voice. What they say will turn out to be useful and significant to somebody there. God can use anybody. If you are a child of God cooperating with Him, and He chooses to give you a message to bless someone, it makes sense.

I like being with the people at the church, growing and being made ready for Heaven. It's like any club in that you like being with people that have the same interests. Another exciting thing about it is that the people are from such different backgrounds. There are housewives bringing up their families, business people, government and private industry workers, self employed people and retired folks and kids. God treats each at his own level, and yet you are all part of the same body. It's quite amazing, supernatural. It doesn't matter where you came from, Jesus got you, and you're going forward together. God's been working on all the people there. We've all had our personalities mellowed and learned to love and appreciate each other. When you are first Christian, you don't realise how many bad habits you are carrying. You tend to be running around trying to do God a favour, trying to do this and that for Him. It takes a while for Him to slow you down. You try to be a missionary, or try to run other people's lives for them. You forget that one of the things God built into us is free will. No one has a licence to run over the top of somebody else's free will.

The issue that God's working me through now is getting my relationship with women right. I'm convinced that God wants me single, at least for the time being — maybe for five or ten years or all my earthly life, I don't know. I spend too much time thinking about girls, or admiring them going down the road. This came to a head a couple of weeks ago. I could tell that if I didn't do something about it I could go the same way as Pastor Jimmy Swaggart[1]. He wasn't particularly bad, just ordinary, the same as me. It bugs me that you can be called a Christian, and be committed wholly to God, but a lot of your habits are too big for you. The devil usually knows exactly what your weakness is. Jimmy Swaggart is an excellent example. He had a problem with lusting after women which got out of hand. If you're not being honest with yourself, and something is more of a problem than you admit, you'll have problems until you get honest. If people expect Christianity to give them instant answers, they're going to be very disappointed.

It's important to start the day with getting on side with God. I've got it easy, because usually on the week days I'm travelling down to work on the train. I've got an hour and twenty minutes of quiet time to read. As soon as I'm on the train, I'm straight into the Bible, getting some more insights into the way the universe works, and basic principles on what the Christian life is supposed to be. God will sometimes plan my reading. Sometimes I feel, for example, that I need to know more about someone like Elijah. So I'll read the historical books of First and Second Kings, all about him. What's amazing is that you read the insights that you need for that particular day. God honours your desire to learn more of His ways, and He'll teach you exactly what you need. The Scripture Union puts out daily Bible study notes. I've gone through them heaps of times and they're absolutely spot on. You might have been finding that some person is rubbing you up the wrong way, and you are having trouble loving them. In fact, you hate their guts. Your reading for the morning is all about the fruits of the Holy Spirit — joy, peace, kindness. You get zonked right between the eyes, and you start contrasting

your behaviour with the way that God wants you to be.
Then you know what you have to work on that day.

I guarantee a lot of the people think I'm a docile
individual, totally unenergetic and thick, who never does
anything exciting. They see me on the train, and probably
think I'm asleep. In fact, I hardly ever sleep on trains.
Before I was a Christian, I was always busy on tutorial
problems, or writing out an essay, or studying. It's only
lately that God has taught me the value of slowing down,
shutting up and doing nothing. Sometimes I pray on the
train.

Prayer is communication with God, and it's got to be
two ways. If you just go to God with your shopping list,
I want this, I want that, bless this person and look after
that one — it'll be pretty boring for God. As you get to
know Him better, it becomes a lot more casual. It's like
two friends conversing. Usually we are the weaker person
in the relationship, because He's the one with the power
to give and we need so much. There is a lot of asking for
favours, although sometimes you'll sense that you've got
the authority to command something. Jesus says, if you
have faith in Him, you can even command a mountain to
be removed into the sea and it will happen. When you're
doing God's work, and you know He wants something
done, you can give the command and it will happen.

I like to go to church for all the activities. There is
a Sunday morning service, but it's more like a Sunday
school for the children. I prefer the afternoon service. I
help out with the music — I play drums. I go to Bible
study on a Wednesday night, and we usually get together
for prayer on Friday nights. That's three formal things I
go to regularly. Maybe one week out of ten, I'll skip a
beat, if I have to work back but that's the usual pattern.
Other people are different. Single parents have to look
after their kids, so it's harder for them to get out to the
night meetings. Occasionally we pool in with a couple of

the other churches to have a weekend camp.

The only reason I'm in my current job is that God got it for me. In my previous job, the guy I worked for was brilliant, but poor on dealing with people. He'd communicate by grunting and he left me too much on my own without adequate information. I started asking God if He wanted me to stay. I asked if I should love my enemy, or should I look for another job. I applied for a few jobs and ended up getting one at Plesseys. Working there was like a breath of fresh air. The boss was sensible, the other workers were good, and there's good morale in the place. I'm there because God put me there. He expects me to do a good job of it and while I'm there I meet other people. They are people He's created too, so my job is to love them. I've done that. He's taught me heaps. I get more practice at loving people, and also finding out more nasty things about myself. You don't realise how much you tend to slacken off if there isn't someone cracking the whip.

I don't talk about my beliefs all the time at work. If you are one of God's servants, people will see it eventually. What is on the inside gets expressed on the outside. We get so preoccupied with the physical universe. The apostle Paul told us that the things we see are just temporary. The most important things in the universe are things we can't see. People live as if everything is going to roll on much the same as it always has, whereas I know there is going to be a final day. God will wind up the whole show. There will be a big accounting and justice will be dealt out. That has to change the way you work. Some of the other people at work are casual, joking all the time. It bugs me. I wish I could tell them we have to be careful — we can joke too much. There's Heaven and Hell to deal with — life's not a continual joke.

Politics is unreal to me, because it doesn't touch on the key issues of life. It's like a mock battle with one bunch of people's opinions stacked against another. The main conflict going on in the universe is quite different. It's God's people versus the destruction that the devil has done in people's lives. How many people do you think there are in the room right now? I'd say there is God, and there is you and me. I know the devil is running around, but I'm not so egotistical as to think that he'd bother putting in an appearance just for my sake. So probably he's not around, but I bet some of his henchmen are, and some guardian angels too. The Bible tells us that this universe is in a cosmic battle between God and the devil. There was a big coup in Heaven. The devil tried to become the top dog, which was pretty silly. He was good and powerful, and had lots of amazing talents, but he was totally outclassed by God. He shouldn't have attempted to exalt himself as he did. Now he's a real dog-in-the-manger sour grapes type trying to get back at God. He's very annoyed with God's little jewel, God's favourite toy, Earth, with all his creations running around, so he is trying to create havoc.

In everybody's life, there must be times when God tries to get their attention. God said it's a narrow way that leads to eternal life, and there are few that find it. But He didn't say that none find it, and He didn't say He's going out of the way to hide Himself .What God wants with the universe, and what its purpose is, can be discovered from the facts around you. You don't need a university education, because that would make God incredibly elitist. You have only to go out and look at a flower to recognise His design and complexity. You can pull it apart, and look at the component parts, and they are complex in themselves. If you look at it under a microscope you will see all its complicated sub-structures. It cries out there is a Creator.

In fairness to God, I have to stress that finding Christianity is not something I've done by myself. It was God who got my attention, and showed me stuff I hadn't known before. He revolutionised my life. My life has two periods — before I knew about Jesus, and after I'd become a follower. I've been born twice, that's for sure. I call myself a born again Christian with the utmost reluctance, because of the way they have been devalued in the press. But, yes, I'm born again, because when I met Jesus it was so radical that it was like being born all over again. I'm starting from scratch, and it's all being done differently. Going His way, I'm only eight and a quarter years down the track in Christianity. That puts me half way through second grade. I'm looking forward to what it'll be like cooperating with God when I get to about sixth grade and graduate into high school.

Sometimes I'm happier as a Christian, but sometimes I cop the flack. When people misunderstand me, when the devil makes me a target and I struggle or have doubts or get depressed, I'm not happy. If you want to be happy, Christianity is not going to help you. Often the people of God will go through hard times. He'll refine us with fire. We'll be happier in the long run, because we'll have a long run. God made us eternal beings, but we've got a choice about where to spend eternity. God's given me a chance to find the path of eternal life, and I'm sure He must be doing the same for other people.

1 Pastor Jimmy Swaggart: American television evangelist whose relationships with women led to considerable controversy in 1988.

Petrea King

'I knew that I'd never given myself an ounce of
permission just to be. I knew that every spiritual
technique that I'd ever employed was to make
myself different from who I was.'

Born in 1950, Petrea King is a natural therapist who
specialises in working with patients with life-threatening
illnesses. From childhood, her inner experiences gave
her a sense that there was more to spirituality than
was presented to her in the church. She spent many
years involved in two structured spiritual traditions, the
School of Philosophy in Sydney and the Self-Realization
Fellowship, the teachings of which are based on those of
the Indian sage, Yogananda. Although these movements
gave her much, she eventually came to realise that her
spirituality had not altered her basic lack of self-acceptance;
in fact it had given her techniques she could use to
avoid looking at the parts of her psyche she condemned.
A diagnosis of leukemia forced Petrea to reevaluate her
beliefs radically. She discovered that to live in the present,
guided by her feelings, with a deeply non-judgmental
attitude to herself was a mode of spirituality more
appropriate for her than one based on highly disciplined
practices aimed at turning her into what she felt was an
abstract idealised image.

Petrea describes her philosophy of healing in her recently published book, *Quest for Life*, Equinox Press, Sydney, 1988.

———————————— ✶ ✶ ✶ ————————————

I was raised in an Anglican family. Everyone attended church and the family were all in the church choir. I found it difficult that often beautiful things were said in the service but said no mechanically. When I was eight years old I had an experience where I was running around the side of the house, and I was suddenly rooted to the spot. Everything dissolved into a grey mist, and I could see through the earth, and through the house behind me, and through the dog and the cars. It was as if there was something brilliant in everything — physical creation was so insubstantial and nebulous. Yet there was no one I could talk to about that, because the world dealt in solid matter — what you could see, feel, taste and touch. So it was locked away inside me for many years. I didn't understand it and I had no framework for it. I remember asking the minister at the church questions of great significance to me, and feeling that his answers were lies. That destroyed a lot of my faith in the church.

I found it extremely difficult to cope with the idea of being a teenager, I did not have any of the physical equipment — I was very underdeveloped for my age. I grew nine inches in one year. The bones and muscles in my legs became disarranged — they had difficulty in growing the right way. So I left school when I was twelve, and spent three years in hospital, many months flat on my back in traction, and all kinds of reconstructive surgery to my legs.

During that time, I had some wonderful experiences of leaving my body when it was in great pain, and looking at it from the ceiling, and from the trees outside. I was scared of these experiences at first, but then I thought they were wonderful fun. When you have been in bed for nine months, it's a boon to be able to get out. A little old lady came to my bedside one day. Though I'd never seen her before, she knew all about the pain I used to get. She said that the next time the pain came, I'd find a place inside me that was just watching. If I took a deep breath, and went to that place, I wouldn't feel any pain. When I did that, it was the first time I went to the ceiling. I think she was an angel, and she'd given me a gift that was to be used in times of pain. I always felt a bit guilty going out into the trees or up into the ceiling or around other parts of the hospital when I wasn't in pain, because it felt like that was a misuse of my gift. I was having a great number of pain killers. Some of those were mind altering. I had a second taste of that experience I had had in earlier childhood. In lots of ways, it was very comforting, because here was something that was familiar to me. Yet it was still inexplicable, and there was still no one I could talk to about it. I was very lonely because there were so many things that were important to me, but there was no one I could share them with. For a long time, they thought I'd never walk again. I had churches praying for me. It was a weird experience, being connected to religion, and yet feeling that I was having experiences that were spiritual, but couldn't be explained by my religion.

It took about three years of calipers and crutches and plasters and operations to get me well again. It was pretty heavy duty, but it was a great way of getting out of being a teenager — I was immediately precipitated into a world of adults, and I felt quite at home with them. When I had recovered, I went into nursing but my body wasn't strong enough for it. I went to New Zealand as a roustabout in shearing sheds and became a boundary rider in Western Queensland. Then I went to Europe, and became involved with psychedelic drugs, mostly LSD. I did a tremendous amount of those drugs in a short time. Again, that was a very similar experience to the one in my childhood. Every part of me ached to understand something. Yet I wasn't even sure what it was that I was trying to understand. Then I went back to nursing, because I found tremendous satisfaction in caring for people in a hands on way.

I'd learned to meditate by that time, and meditation was certainly a part of my life from then on. It was time out for me, and I enjoyed it very much. I had one of those personalities which is very typical of a lot of people who develop cancer, which I did later. I set extremely high standards for myself, and beat myself up unmercifully when I didn't reach them. I felt as if everybody else got a manual for life when they got here, and I didn't get my copy. I felt worse than lost. I felt that everybody else knew something that I didn't.

In my mid-twenties I married and had my two children. The marriage was rocky right from the beginning. I tried all the time to be a nice person, the perfect wife who anticipated his every need. We were both involved in the School of Philosophy[1] for many years. The teachings were based on the ideas of Gurdjieff and Ouspensky[2]. There were some wonderfully valuable aspects to it, but it was a very Victorian atmosphere. Victorian in that the women looked after the men, wore long dresses, and were meant to be at home baking bread, tending children and keeping the house clean. I did that with great diligence for many years. We were up at four thirty every morning meditating, and did calligraphy and Sanskrit and all kinds of other good things. I gained tremendously from that time. I could sit for hours and meditate. I could keep a house absolutely spic and span, children fed and clean, gardens tended and fresh bread on the table. The discipline was valuable, but it was the only aspect that was nurtured.

I found after a while that it was stifling. There wasn't a lot of love involved at all. In fact, if you mentioned the word 'love', you were told that you didn't know anything about what it was. I left the group shortly after my husband did.

I felt a necessity to get in touch with my heart. That was terribly difficult, because hearts were never featured in our house. The people in the School of Philosophy didn't seem to manifest much joy, and I think the closest thing to love is joy. Becoming enlightened seemed awfully hard work. When I left, I still didn't know what I was going to do. There was a part of me that just wanted acceptance of myself as I am now, instead of the person that I have to become when I'm enlightened, or when I'm spiritual. Yet I was my own hardest task master.

Not long after I left the School of Philosophy, my brother took his life. He was a brother whom I was extremely close to. I was born eighteen months after him, and, as it turned out, I was diagnosed as dying eighteen months after his death. In many ways, he usurped my childhood, because he had many difficulties right from the minute he got here, and I was a very placid baby. So I didn't get a great deal of attention and cuddles when I was little. I worshipped him. I was always extremely proud to be Brendan's sister. I was Brendan's sister, I must be okay. When he died, he set the rest of us free, because he had completely dominated the family.

My mother and I began to get much closer. She and I enjoyed meditating together. We heard about the Self-Realization Fellowship, a spiritual community based on the teachings of Yogananda[3]. There was a centre in America with an annual conference. We decided to go to America to the conference and to visit the community. When I was there, I had a strong feeling that I should return and do the yoga and meditation teacher training course. Five weeks later, we had sold our home in Sydney, taken the kids out of school, and moved to America. We lived in a little single roomed yurt in the wilderness surrounded by deer and squirrels and with no gas, electricity or running water. I did a three month full time yoga and meditation teacher training course. My husband and I separated a month after we got there. He returned to Australia, so that left me with the two children in America, living in a spiritual community. In some ways, I felt very happy. A three month full time course devoted only to your own spiritual development is very nurturing and nourishing. At the same time, there was a lot of sadness connected with the breakup of the marriage, and the stress on the children who were upset and disturbed at being in a foreign country in unfamiliar circumstances.

At the end of that course, the swami who had founded the community asked me if I would like to be his housekeeper cum secretary. He was born in Rumania, educated in England and Switzerland, and had come to America when he was nineteen. He immediately became a disciple of Yogananda. I told him that I didn't want to work for him — I was fed up with spiritual hierarchies and I didn't want to put him on a pedestal. He said that was why he wanted me: he wanted someone who would say no, and argue with and challenge him. I worked closely with Swami for six weeks, until I returned to Australia. It was a rich time. He was extraordinary. The first day I went to work with him, he told me an Indian saint was coming to dinner probably with about half a dozen people. We were millions of miles from anywhere, in the mountains of California. So I made some banana bread and some cookies, and found out where the tea cups and the milk were kept. An hour later, he came back and told me it could be ten, but certainly not more than fifteen. An hour later he said it might be twenty, but not more than twenty-five. This went on all day until we got to fifty. In the end we had seventy-five people for tea. God knows how, but every person got a cup of tea and a piece of banana bread and a cookie. We were in a huge geodesic dome, and the kitchen was on a raised platform. I was looking down at Swami and the Indian saint in his white turban, white beard and white clothes. I thought, this is really what the job is all about. It's not about being housekeeper, it's about responding joyfully to whatever happens. It was a great lesson. From then until I left him a long time later, every day he did something that just turned my world upside down. Every concept, every belief, every thought I had ever had about what was spiritual and what wasn't, he completely disrupted.

In that time, I was diagnosed as having leukemia, and was given a very short time to live. It was the end of September, and I was told I wouldn't see Christmas. I would have been thirty-two. I went back to Australia within two weeks. There was a part of me that was aware that I had created the whole situation. That sounds ridiculous to most people's ears, but I knew that I hated myself. I knew that I'd never given myself an ounce of permission just to be. I knew that every spiritual discipline that I'd ever employed was to make myself different from who I was.

At first, I didn't believe the diagnosis. As I got weaker over the following weeks, I realised that I had pushed death over into a corner. Every now and then, I would catch sight of it, and it was this great monster. I had been practising spiritual disciplines for many years, and I was quite adept at changing my focus of concentration. If the thought of death came up, or panic, or fear, or terror, I had a whole range of activities that I could indulge in to flood my consciousness with another thought or another feeling. I saw myself doing that, and I realised that I had lived all my life on the edge of a black hole. This black hole was all the parts of myself that I didn't accept — the panics, the terrors, the feelings of rejection, of isolation, of abandonment.

I decided that, rather than seeing death in a corner, and filling it with something else, I would jump into the black hole. I thought, if I have spent my entire life avoiding the black hole, be damned if I am going to die in five weeks without having seen what's there. What happened was, up came despair. Instead of switching my attention to something else, I breathed into being in despair, and allowed the whole ghastly mess to come up and assail me. There were moments of being absolutely consumed by despair but there were moments of being able to observe. It was like when I was a child, and could go up on the ceiling, and observe this body in pain. In the same way, I could observe how it was to be a being in despair. In ten days, I went through loneliness, isolation, rejection, panic, terror and anger. Instead of fighting off all those feelings, I allowed them to be there. In the end, it felt that a flower that had been in bud was finally given some space to open and breathe. When I looked at the sunshine on the leaves, there was a lightness about it that I hadn't experienced before.

My first feeling was that if I allowed myself to have any of these emotions I would shatter into a million pieces. I felt that I was asking myself to leave the structure I had created to survive in the world, and to let go of all control. It felt like stepping off a cliff with a blindfold on. It was terrifying to let go and trust. But, after a little while, it became so much fun to feel. The willingness to have the pain of being human has meant more tears, but more joy and more depth of experience and connectedness with and vulnerability to others — the best thing ever. Now, as a therapist, I see that I can only be valuable with a client to the extent that I am willing to be with my own pain. If there are parts of my own pain that I can't address, then I can only share their pain to a certain extent.

I went back to America. I still had leukemia, but I was so lit up with this new adventure of finding out what I felt, instead of what I thought about things, that whether I lived or died became of secondary importance. It was extraordinary and wonderful to feel. There was no treatment for the kind of leukemia I had but I felt that these internal changes and meditation were what I was most interested in. It took about a year until I felt confident that I knew about leukemia for me. I knew about my self-destruction and I knew about my self-hatred. I'm not saying that it's because I hated myself that I got leukemia. That's much too simplistic — it's far more involved than that.

The next year was spent mostly in Italy. Swami was over there teaching. I went into a Franciscan monastery outside Assisi, where St Francis himself used to go to retreat. I'm not quite sure how all that happened. We went to visit one day, and loved it. The superior of the monastery, who didn't speak English — I didn't speak Italian — asked me if I would like to stay, and I said yes. I moved into a simple little room, and spent eighteen hours a day in a cave in the mountain where St Francis used to meditate and pray. It wasn't all meditation. Sometimes I was banging my head against the wall, looking inside at all of my shortcomings and still beating up on myself for having them, and then forgiving myself for beating myself up. It was a long process. It got to the stage where I could go into the cave and know that for eighteen hours I would experience peace and bliss and joy. Weird as it might sound, it became boring. I felt that I could only experience peace and bliss and joy in a cave in Italy, away from my children, away from my family, away from everybody. I wanted to have this quality in my relationships with people. So I decided that, even if I was going to go out of remission and die in a month, I would sooner go back and share that in relationships than have it just to myself.

It sounds strange but being well again, or at least being in remission, was worse than dying. When you are dying, you have such an intense experience every day of being alive. You look with awareness at everything that happens. So I came back and wondered what I was going to do. Swami had kicked me out of the nest. He said he had taught me everything and it was time for me to go and use it in my own life.

He was quite right — my work is very different. I

had done naturopathy a long time ago, after nursing, before the yoga and meditation teacher training course. When I was nursing, it was obvious that we were mostly mopping up after catastrophes. We weren't actually healing people. I thought natural therapies might hold something. They did to some extent, but the people I saw who made progress through natural therapies did so because they made fundamental changes within themselves. They became more philosophically oriented, more interested in taking responsibility for their own health, and took an active part in their treatment.

I decided to go into naturopathic practice. I did it reluctantly, but I had to pay the rent. Two weeks after I started the practice, the first person with cancer walked in. She had been told that she wouldn't see Christmas. The day after, the first person with AIDS walked in. He had been told he wouldn't see Christmas either. I'd never worked with anyone with AIDS and I knew very little about it at the time. I shared with him my experience that Christmas isn't always something to mark your life by. They are wrong sometimes, and they certainly were in my case. He is very much alive now, four and a bit years down the track. I felt that these people were my brothers, and I knew what they were going through. When you are diagnosed with a life threatening disease it's a very isolating experience. The only other thing I can vaguely relate it to is giving birth. When you are in labour, even though you are surrounded by well meaning people who would do anything to relieve you of your pain, it's your experience. Even though they might be floating in and out of your awareness, the experience itself is so incredibly intense that you feel very separate.

When I started practising, part of me believed that because I got well, everyone could get well. Very quickly I began to see that there was a lot more to treating people with life threatening diseases than meditation

and changing their ways of thinking and diet. I'm still
in the process of healing, and, when I teach someone
how magnificent and unique and wonderful they are, it
reminds me that I'm okay too. It's not that I'm healed,
therefore I can show you how to heal yourself, but that in
sharing our experiences we both get healed. That might
be healing into life, or healing into death. Bodies being
well is not a necessary criterion for healing. People often
come to me saying that the doctor has told them they
are going to die and they don't want to die. So we
start off with the physical therapies. But my primary goal
is how we can establish peace. For me now, healing is
people experiencing self-acceptance, peace, love and joy
in everyday life. The only failure, if there is one, is seeing
people living or dying in fear and isolation. That is sad, and
yet some people need to experience that as well.

My only religion is love. Christ and I became good mates
when I was sick. I went through a period of praying with
every ounce of my being not to wake up in the morning. I
hated being dependent on my parents — my mother had
to dry me after my shower — and I loathed the physical
exhaustion and weakness. I thought it would be much
better not to be there, but every morning I'd wake up. I
took to visualising Christ sitting on the end of my bed. I
figured there must have been lots of times when He wanted
to split. But He didn't, He stuck it out. I would visualise
Him, and reflect on His qualities, and see them radiating
out from Him as light. I would breathe in that light, and
I'd see it going through my body right down into my feet.
In five minutes I'd be feeling those qualities, instead of
despair, or depression. It wasn't just Christ, it was Mary
and St Francis and Yogananda and Sai Baba[4] and angels
and every good guy I'd ever heard about that I'd have in
my room. I still do that. There are lots of times when I'm
with a client and I don't know what to say. I might visualise
that I'm sitting inside the body of Christ or in the body of an

angel, and I let them do the talking. It helps me to realise that I don't need to fix the situation. I just need to be there. If I can be there, in a space of love and compassion with this person, they are going to find their own solutions. It's not that I have to trot out a nice neat package. Very often there aren't any nice neat answers at all. They are tragic and painful experiences, and the best way to help someone is just to be there, and allow your openness to encompass and share in their pain.

I don't know what God is. I'm sure God's only a label that we pin on love. What it comes down to for me now is that I'm not attached to any religion, though I've drawn deeply and richly from many. When I was in Italy, I went to Mass twice a day. Every day I cleaned cathedrals. In the cathedral in Sorento there was a black crucifix that was actually brass. I decided one day that I would clean it. It took me a couple of months, starting at the top and working for hours every day. It was a mind blowing experience to clean the thorns on His head, and the blood on the hands and the nails, and to share in the passion of Christ. So many religions, including the Eastern religions and Sanskrit and everything we did in the School of Philosophy have been enormously valuable for me.

What gives me support now is the people I work with. They are profoundly courageous and willing to be human. The love that we share together is deep. That's what nourishes me. It's the light that shines out of other people. I'm sure that is God. I sometimes feel lonely. I get to hug lots of people, and to a great extent I feel nurtured and cared for in that. But there are times when I wish I had more support. Yet I know that I have created a lifestyle in which I have very little time. If I were to have a one to one relationship I'd have to shift my schedule to make space for it. It would have to wait until I saw that it was a priority because there was somebody there. All the men in my life are either gay, married, or have cancer.

When I look around the room and see fifty people, and I realise that in five years a lot of them will probably be dead, that can be fairly overwhelming. I love my people. We go away for weekends together, we go on picnics, we go out for dinner and we visit each other's homes. When a person dies, it's a slow process with both of us working through the separation of the relationship. They leave a body, and, in a way, I feel their presence as much as when they were alive. Often when I am with a child with cancer, I'll think of Charlie, who was the first child I ever worked with and from whom I learned such a lot. Feeling his presence again enables me to be more with this child. The people I have worked with are still very real to me, and the relationship is still intact, even though I can't hug them anymore. So I don't get down very much. I get overtired, but that just means having a walk along the beach and a sleep.

I know I have created a lifestyle that makes it difficult for me to have a relationship. Yet I know I am committed to having that relationship. I feel that now I am ready for it. Before, I wasn't. I was scared to be that vulnerable with someone else. And that's another great gift all these people have given to me. They have helped me to learn that it's all right to be vulnerable and open with my feelings, and that our relationship can remain intact in the midst of anger or frustration or fear or panic.

I used to have spiritual disciplines that I adhered to because I felt they were necessary. Now, it feels that my heart belongs to being. It's a relief not to feel that I have to have a guru or a church or a ritual or a dogma. I like meditation, when I get the chance. Most of the time I meditate in the middle of the night for a couple of hours. The phone doesn't ring, nobody needs me, and I have the wonderful stillness of the night. That's my time, and it's very sacred to me. I don't do it every night — just when the angels wake me up. I don't get time to meditate during the day. I teach it to a lot of people, which means

I get to slot in and out of it. I have used just about every meditation technique there is, from Kriya yoga to mantras and breath work. My method now is just being. If anything, it's tied into breathing, as a way of getting to that state, but I don't practise a technique. I find meditation now is second nature, not something that I practise, or set aside time for. When I'm with people, I'm with people, and I'm not thinking about what we are going to have for dinner that night. There used to be a time when there were different parts of my life. I was a mother, I was a therapist, I was a lover. Now I'm exactly the same person, whether I'm being mother or therapist, facilitator or lover. It doesn't make any difference, and that's a relief. I don't have time to switch roles for one thing, but I don't have the inclination or desire to.

The concept of having to get somewhere in order to be spiritual has dissolved entirely. Partly because I don't have time to think about it anymore, and also because goals are only beliefs and concepts. While I'm believing that I'll be good enough later on, I'm missing out on being here now. I went through stages of believing in reincarnation but, frankly, when you are dying, all of that stuff goes right out of the window. This is the only moment you have. If reincarnation exists, terrific. I'm sure if I live life to the fullest now, with openness and the courage to be, then reincarnation will take good care of itself.

---

1 School of Philosophy: a group which both gives basic instruction in philosophy and teaches more advanced students techniques of spiritual development.

2 Gurdjieff was an Armenian-born philosopher and teacher who came to prominence in the inter-war period. His teachings combined Eastern and Western thought into a system still taught today by Gurdjieff groups around the world. Ouspensky was one of Gurdjieff's chief disciples, and wrote several books expounding his theories.

3 Yogananda: Indian sage and teacher.

4 Sai Baba: Indian sage and healer.

Philip Maxwell

'My concept of spiritual development had been limited to the mystic, the ascetic, the hermit in the cave. Recognising that I could continue to grow spiritually, and become a family man, and that that was precisely the direction I had to go, was a breakthrough.'

Philip Maxwell was born in 1951. Disillusioned with the emptiness of a life based purely on materialistic values, Philip left his highly-paid executive job in pursuit of emotional and spiritual growth. Bio-energetics, Vipassana meditation and the eclectic teachings and techniques of the Self-Transformation Centre have all influenced his journey deeply. 'Opening his heart' is now central to his spirituality, and he finds opportunity for this in his work as an osteopath and in his marriage. Philip describes many aspects of the human potential movement's philosophy, including its fundamental principle that beliefs create reality. He also gives an interesting account of different ways of centreing, and of contacting the wisdom within.

Philip Maxwell was born in England and raised as a Roman Catholic. His childhood faith faded in adolescence, and at university he found in politics 'the grand ideal ... (that) filled the niche that spirituality might have'. Not wanting to be 'trapped in a box', he left his sheltered

English life. His story begins in Sydney, where he settled after two years travelling in Asia and working in the Australian outback.

✳ ✳ ✳

It was an interesting time back then. I met a character who had a major impact on me, although we were only in contact for a couple of months. He introduced me to Gurdjieff[1]. The idea of remembering is very big in Gurdjieff's teachings. He says that we are all machines, that our natural resting state is machine-like consciousness. The first main goal of development is to awake from that state by 'remembering'. Herculean efforts have to be put into this task of remaining alert, in the present, completely aware of what's going on, and not simply reacting, responding as a machine would to outside stimuli. On and off, over the next three or four years, this concept of trying to tap into and live from who I really was, became my touchstone. What I really liked about those teachings was the sense of personal power and responsibility. You didn't need teachers, priests or the ministry. There was just you, and you worked on yourself from a book, and were responsible for your own results.

After a few months, I realised that Sydney was for me. Rather than going back into labouring and that kind of work, I began working as a warehouse manager. I had very little experience of either warehouses or management but, basically, I worked hard and tried to do my job well. At first I was going by the seat of my pants, firefighting. I got to the point where most of the fires were out, and then quite suddenly my boss was called back to head office and I was thrust into the job of administration manager. Once again I was running around, frantically coping. Initially, the new position took most of my time and energy, but after about a year I was doing a good job and the novelty was wearing off.

During that time, I was keeping a journal. I'd write down what was going on, how I was feeling, insights and particular passages from a book that had inspired me. A lot of the time, though, I was into raging. I had become an apprentice yuppie — I was into image, appearance, parties. But my dissatisfaction was growing. More and more, I begrudged the energy I put into the job. I started to become lazy, to do less — it was increasingly clear that there was something missing.

After about three years, I was radically dissatisfied with my life. I had zero job satisfaction, and most of my friendships were superficial. I had no other creative outlets. My concept of relationships was limited to two adults tolerating each other's presence, only I found even that really difficult. I was absolutely incapable of expressing my feelings, even if I had been aware of them. In my relationships, the frustrations, pain and hurt I felt would build up and increasingly became a barrier between me and the other person. Sooner or later, it would reach the point where I would withdraw — my way of coping has always been to withdraw from difficult and painful situations. I had one fairly long relationship which lasted more from the tolerance of the other person than from any contribution I made. When that ended, there began a series of casual relationships that were increasingly brief and dissatisfying. My memories of that period are a blur. I was drinking a lot. Every night, three or four of us from work would go and have a few drinks. The weekends would be an alcoholic haze.

One day I was in a meeting at work, talking about forward planning, and I just found myself quitting. I said, I won't be part of your forward plans. On the face of it, it was a crazy thing to do — I didn't have another job to go to.

But even though I was immediately offered an increase in salary and better conditions, I realised I had done the right thing. Looking back, I think I was extremely fortunate to get out before I was heavily committed to the system, locked into mortgage payments and superannuation, and all the sorts of things that might have made it more difficult for me to change direction.

In the period that followed I did all kinds of strange jobs — presenting motivation programs to middle managers, selling gimmicks to newsagents, working as a builder, a shopfitter, moving furniture. When all else failed, I drove taxicabs. Above all, I read. I read vast amounts of materials — everything from Alan Watts to Steiner to Alistair Crowley. I was looking for a new direction but I couldn't seem to make anything happen: the ideas weren't enough. I felt a tremendous inertia. It was a hard time, as I fluctuated from tremendous excitement about the potential for new growth, and yet despaired of my ability to make it happen.

Yet I was beginning to discover more about myself. My identity had formerly resided entirely in my intellect. I started to discover more about my body, about sensation, about my *feelings*. Spending less time in my head, breaking away from the rational and the logical, I actually had more and more insights. I was beginning to trust my intuition, and to recognise that my previous concept of who I was was limited, that there were other ways of being which were equally, if not more, valid than those I had considered to be right.

Around this time, I heard about a general interest course in massage at the NSW College of Natural Therapies, and went down there to do it. I so liked what was going on that I enrolled in osteopathy at the College. I thought, I'll give it a go, but I'll only give it a year, then I'll redecide. On that basis, I actually ended up completing the course.

One night, at home, I had this quite clear message that spiritual growth should not be my main goal for the moment. It was more important that I learn about emotions, otherwise my imbalance at the emotional level would spill over and mar any work I did in other directions. Soon after this message, a friend suggested that it would be good if I came to the meditation course she had enrolled in. I'd never meditated in my life, but in a spirit of complete trust, I went along. It was a ten day Intensive. We did little except sleep, eat and meditate, all in total silence. I found it extremely scary at first. I'd gone along expecting to learn how to be serene, and I had nothing but pain and turmoil — all kinds of powerful emotional stuff. I didn't understand what was happening. I'd been told that I was releasing samskaras[2] and I was just to observe these, which I did dutifully, but a whole new door had opened. Coming out of that meditation Intensive, I went as high as I'd ever been. I felt filled with ease and grace and a sense of myself that I'd never experienced before. I thought, I want more of this.

Another friend was beginning a course in bio-energetics[3] (which I'd never heard of) with a well respected trainer from England. Once again, in a spirit of trust, I signed up. This was a six month course — a weekend every month and follow up sessions in between. Originally I went in thinking that this would be valuable information that I could use in my professional career as an osteopath. And of course the real reason I went was that I had a huge amount to learn about what was going on inside me. The first few sessions were spent in total confusion and absolute terror. Bio-energetics recognises that unresolved tensions can be released through peristalsis in the gut. So I'd spend entire weekends lying down, gurgling and churning, watching everything that was going on and trying desperately to process it without speaking out or working myself. The saving grace was that we paired up in co-counselling sessions between the major workshops. Working with one other person, I was able for the first time to get in touch with some of the more powerful feelings that had, totally unbeknownst to me, been running me all my life. Delightfully, the first major charge of emotional energy I felt was joy and love. It was incredibly powerful and intensely moving. After that, a lot of anger came out, and later I tapped into some of the other feelings, sadness and loss included.

About that time, I felt it important that I go back to England and my family. I began looking closely at how my stay in Australia had stretched from what was originally an extended working holiday to about seven or eight years. I recognised that a big component of my staying here had been the need to break away from the expectations of family, of friends and the institutions that I was a part of in England. Now that I had recognised that being here had a function, suddenly it was OK to go back and talk to my parents about it. So I went back to England for three months in the college holidays, and went a long way towards re-establishing a relationship with my parents. I also went to Findhorn[4] and really loved what they were doing there.

When I came back to Australia, a lot happened in quite a short space of time. I'd begun to understand that relationships weren't just a mutual tolerance thing, and I'd gone out eager to relate, and got a bit hurt. Now I met Sue, who was to become my wife. Instant attraction. There was a real sense of, yes this is right. It was delightful — for the first time I was truly in love. Another major thing that happened was the basic course I did at the Self-Transformation Centre[5]. The Centre taught simple but powerful psycho-therapeutic techniques coupled with Eastern meditation tools in a way that wasn't off puttingly religious but which was spiritual, in the sense of giving a purpose to your life.

My second course there was about creating your life. The idea is that our beliefs about the world will to a greater or lesser extent actually come about. This is not to say that we can create yachts and swimming pools and fancy cars.

At the simplest level, someone whose head is filled with aggressive thoughts will often find themselves attracting aggression back. Someone whose basic mode is loving will find lots of love and acceptance around them. Often the influences are coming from the deep unconscious — we may have stored away within us beliefs that have a radical effect on our entire lives. If we can find the point where these beliefs are operating, and work at this level, we then become able to create our lives as they happen. I'd never realised that this applied to everything in our lives, not just the big events but the small ones too. Nothing happens by accident. There's a whole new world involved once that shift is made.

I then signed up for the six month Being of Service (BOS) course the Transformation Centre was running. Sue managed to get on the course as well. A lot of major shifts came out of that period. Probably the biggest one was the decision for Sue and I to get married. I'd always thought that marriage was too big a responsibility for me, and the idea of kids, well that was responsibility times ten — I was terrified of it. Now, I started to recognise the role that a relationship could play in a spiritual sense. I'd seen quite clearly how easily I'd got bogged down in my own rationalising and inertia. Outside stimulus was what had helped me — firstly the meditation course, then the bio-energetics group and finally all the work I did with Self-Transformation. The role of a teacher is to mirror for you areas that you are totally unaware of, and another human being who is intimately part of your life can do precisely that — give you the feedback, the mirror of what you're really doing. Sue and I work very well for each other in that area.

For the last seven or eight years, I'd conceived of my spiritual growth as the most important thing. But my concept of spirituality had been limited to the mystic, the ascetic, the hermit in the cave. I had never aligned spirituality with family life. Recognising that I could in fact continue to grow spiritually and become a family man, and that that was precisely the direction I had to go, was a breakthrough. I'm by nature a very solitary person, I like to hold myself back, and to withdraw if threatened. The challenge this time round is to do just the opposite — to be there, much more present, sharing, giving, opening my heart. This is far more easily achieved in a family than in a monastery. So my spiritual growth lies in the direction of family life, especially with children; the challenge of unconditional giving and being there. Giving of myself applies also to my job. As an osteopath, I have a lot of contact with people, many opportunities to share some of what I've learnt.

The next major development for me was doing a second Vipassana[5] course. I started to have experiences of energy moving around my body and, having read about chakras and energy centres, it was delightful to actually feel them. I began to understand some of the experiences I'd been having in the meditation through the BOS period, when I'd have major shaking and shuddering. I could put them into a framework of energy moving in my body, particularly in my spine, and hitting into all kinds of tensions. I started to understand the very immediate correlation between issues and tensions in my life, and tension in my body. It's like an early warning system. I can sense what's going on in my body, and relate it to events in my life — it's been a tremendous boost to what I do as an osteopath.

All these experiences have been taking me towards awareness. Life itself is the teacher, we simply need to be aware of what is going on beneath the surface of things. Every single event that happens to us has a lesson somewhere within it. Ideally, this awareness takes you to the point where you are able to cooperate with the process. Rather than being a victim of the circumstances of your life, you become part of the creation of the whole process. I think of the process of life as a spiral. We often go in a circle, but if we are taking the chances and opportunities presented to us, we will actually move through three dimensions and go deeper into who we are. If the challenge is too great, or if we are unaware that there is even a challenge, we tend to remain at the same level, and go back like a stuck record, playing the same kinds of things again and again. If you can break out of that mould, yes, you might come back around to the same area, but on a much deeper and more intense level. I feel this is happening now with my early problems with inertia. Now that I'm away from all the encouragement and support of the various groups and therapies that I did, the challenge of motivation is there once more, but at a new and deeper level. The stimulus now comes from other sources. Sue provides very clear and direct insights. Often we function quite dispassionately at this level, at a level of channelling. At other times we get caught up in games like everybody else.

One of the most powerful spiritual experiences that I've had was a long conversation with what I suppose would be called a guide. As I was going to sleep, I was suddenly in the presence of this person. It was a reassuring and informative session. My main direction right from the very start has been to seek the answers within. The guide said that we all know the answers to all of the questions within ourselves. I'm not at the stage where I can read those answers right off, but what I have developed is a sense of the rightness of things. That's my touchstone, and increasingly I'm getting more clarity in inner dialogue. I was told that there is always someone there — that support system is there with us for our entire lives. It's simply a question of tuning in. If we were only to take the trouble, we could tune into that level at any time.

The process of personal growth and spiritual develop-ment is a bit like carving. It's a slow paring away of the unwanted parts to reveal the perfection locked within. The perfection is often disguised; for instance, the endless love that we are all capable of is often blocked by old patterns of pain and hurt. The actual process feels a bit like peeling off old rusty bits of armour. There is a sense of feeling very vulnerable, perhaps a little awkward, but also suddenly very free and liberated and a hell of a lot lighter. That sense of liberation and lightness is a signal for me of the completion of a particular cycle, another successful expansion of my being. It's like identifying less with the small ego-centred self and more with the bigger self, and through that, with the universe. There's an analogy that I really like where the individual is seen as a wave, and the actual stuff of the wave, the sea itself, is the universe, the cosmos. We have for a moment an individual identity, and then it's reabsorbed into the unity. There's another lesson in that for me. With my desire to grow personally and spiritually, I am aware that the goal is not to move completely out of being a wave. It's not that I wish to live in a realm so far removed from corporeal reality that I might as well not be in a body. It seems to me that we are incarnated on the planet to do things that we can only do in bodies. I conceive of my role as being to use the various techniques of understanding that I have found to identify more and more with the higher self, a higher sense of purpose.

To use the analogy of a spiral again, I'm on an outward going part of the cycle at the moment, not learning or looking inward but sharing what I know. There will be a further period when I'll be learning again, but the last eighteen months have been the laying of a foundation for this outward stage. I've put a lot of energy into setting up a new practice as an osteopath. Sue and I have moved out of Sydney to Newcastle, and we're both establishing social contacts, getting the feel of a new place and making some choices about lifestyle. I'm quite content to limit myself to a fairly humble role of just introducing some of the ideas I've learned about. I don't see myself as some intense therapist doing wonderful work with individuals. I'd far rather be doing basic construction work with lots of people, so I see myself moving on to doing work with groups in the near future. The whole issue of materialism has very much diminished in importance. Beyond a certain level of comfort, chasing possessions is an amazingly distracting process. There's nothing particularly spiritual about living your life in a continual paper chase, getting so far into debt that the only thing you can do to prevent yourself from falling flat on your face is to run flat out. I enjoy comfort, but I live simply, and I want to avoid major debts.

The main focus in my current spiritual practice is opening my heart, and sharing as widely, and with as many people, as possible. Staying aware is very important, staying on the surfboard riding with balance and poise so that the energy of the wave can move me. There is a succession of waves — if you miss one, it's not the end of the world. I've learned that each wave has the potential to move you more towards the direction you are seeking. Sue and her feedback is a major assistance in staying aware. I meditate regularly. My basic meditation is the Vipassana technique of awareness of my body in the mornings; if I do an evening meditation it's nearly always more calming, with a breath or mantra technique, and then a conversation with the inner voice. Often the dialogue will be quite a silent one — there'll be an unspoken question, and then up to ten minutes of waiting, depending on how clear I am. I'm getting to the point now where I recognise a distinction between the kind of thoughts that run willy nilly thought my head and the short sharp clean bursts of communication from some other part of me. My thoughts tend to follow a sequence, word after word, like a conversation in my head. The more profound levels of my being seem to communicate in total, an entire thought in an instant.

My life at the moment is hectic, and I spend quite a lot of my time off centre, out of touch with my inner core. I've found several techniques that can help me through this. I sometimes use a pendulum — simple yes/no answers. More often, I'll use a technique of book opening. I have books that are full of inspiring and significant messages. I'll just open the book at a page, jab my finger in, and find unerring appropriateness in the passage selected. Then there are the Runes, a system based on an old Nordic way of divination. It's a series of stones, each with an old Nordic letter with a different meaning on them. You pull one out of a bag, and then read off the appropriate message. That I find quite useful, sometimes, if I'm stuck with a major confusion and I'm not getting any clear answers. Another delightful system that I use more frequently is something that comes from Findhorn — the Angel Cards. This is a series of fifty odd cards, each with a quality written on them. It might be love, or joy, or abundance, or awareness, or any one of a number of qualities. You pick one, and that can give you an aspect to focus on in a particularly confusing or murky period. None of these systems will give you a 'you must do this' answer. Basically, we have free will, and it's important that we exercise it. It's important that we take responsibility for our decisions — we can't just abdicate it all and let them up there do the deciding. But we can be assisted and supported — we *can* have our confusions illuminated, and the issues at stake clarified.

---

1 Gurdjieff was an Armenian born philosopher and teacher, who came to prominence in the inter-war period. His psychological and spiritual teachings combined Eastern and Western thought into a system which is still taught today by Gurdjieff groups around the world.

2   samskaras: Sanskrit term for impressions of past lives, said to be stored in the subtle nervous system and released during meditation. Personality in this life is held to be shaped in part by samskaras from past lives.

3   bio-energetics: a school of psychotherapy developed, inter alia, by Alexander Lowen, in turn influenced deeply by Wilhelm Reich. It works with the body to release emotional trauma stored therein.

4   Findhorn: a community in Scotland, U.K., where New Age philosophies of attunement to the spirit and community are practised and taught.

5   Vipassana: literally (in Pali) insight, intuitive knowledge. A Buddhist meditation technique for developing right mindfulness.

Jan Goodman

'We had been called to live together. I had moved
in with people that I hardly knew. Suddenly our
lives and our futures were bound up together.'

Jan Goodman's is the story of a profound attempt to
live out a new vision of Christianity. Born in 1949, Jan
in her mid-twenties joined a small Christian community
in a working-class suburb of Adelaide. There, income
sharing, common prayer and shared housing have been
for ten years the framework for a life oriented to service
in the neighbourhood: first in building up a sense of
community amongst church-goers and then in providing
training facilities for the unemployed. Jan is an Anglican.
She would like to see less emphasis on hierarchy and
on preserving tradition in the church, and more lay
involvement, receptivity to women's experiences, and
openness to the movement of the spirit.

Jan Goodman was raised in Sydney, by parents to whom
hospitality and caring were important expressions of their
Presbyterian faith. She was very involved with church
activities as a teenager. Her story begins when she was a
student at Sydney University.

At university, I did science with a major in zoology

176

and botany. I became involved in the Evangelical Union (EU). This was a Bible based Christian group which was there both to support Christians at university and to further Christian truths. It was an evangelical group, which acknowledged the Bible to be the authoritative word of God, and authoritative in people's lives. I had a dual response to EU: I really appreciated being with a Christian group, but I was a bit cynical about what they were doing, and the intensity with which it was all done. So I determined that it wasn't going to be my whole world — I was there to experience university life. I joined the rowing club which put me in touch with a completely different strata of university. So I moved between the rowing club and inter-varsity, and EU and my Christian friends.

Zoology and botany were wonderful. I remember sitting in lectures, marvelling at the wonder of creation and the mystery of life. I can still recall all of the lecture on pollination and its mechanisms, and the grandeur of some of those amazing creations. So science enhanced my awe for God, and my excitement at the power and beauty of creation. But there was a lack of integration between the Christianity that was expressed by the group that I wanted to align myself with, and my own experience of faith and life. In some ways, I felt more at home with the rowing crew than I did with the Christian group. My sense of wonder at life, and at the mystery of creation, and the grandeur of God did not sit easily with the intense and narrow EU attitudes. The question of predestination came up, and I knew that I couldn't accept that God had ordained some people not to be saved. The church at that stage wasn't meeting my needs as a Christian or my needs as a person. It just didn't seem wholesome or life-giving. I had a hunger not just for talking about a truth, but for experiencing it with others — a meeting of people, an enjoyment of life and a sharing of that experience. This is what I was finding in a totally different way in the rowing club and at the pub. Yet I still wanted to to be with Christians, so I was living a double life.

Both these worlds must have been important to me, because I kept both going in my first teaching position in the country. I lived with people who weren't Christians, and all my social life was with people who wouldn't have called themselves Christians — in fact, many of their practices would have been considered abhorrent to the church. Yet they were my friends, with whom I lived and shared and grew. At the same time, I would leave a party and go to church, and come back again. I was aware of the inconsistency and wondered why I kept doing it, and yet I knew that there was something in me that had to.

I was in Mt Gambier for three years, and then I went to Pt Augusta. There, I shared a house with two Christian girls. The culture shock was enormous — I felt as if I was in a straitjacket. They were just very nice Christian people, but their lives were so narrow. Yet, with the people in Pt Augusta, I was probably pushed to think about my faith more than I ever was in Mt Gambier — to think about church, and what church was meant to do and be, and to reflect on my past experiences with it. That was good, because it forced me to discover a sense of who I was, and from that centre then to interact with the different parts of the environment.

At that stage, early in the seventies, the concept of community in the church was starting to emerge. Christian community within the church was one of the 'in' things — a sense of different people having different gifts to contribute. When they were contributed in the right way, they made a whole. There was a sense of the corporate rather than the individual, a sense of 'Kingdom of God' theology rather than a more Calvinistic doctrinaire 'do what you should, get it right' attitude. Kingdom of God theology is a much broader sense of God being present in the world, and in the church and in our lives. That sense of God being present was very important to me. By then, praying was not just praying that God would do X, but that I would know what I was meant to be doing, that I would know what the movement of life was, what the movement of God was. So rather than the individual becoming the centre of the world, I was almost becoming part of God's world, or a world where God permeated reality. The patterns of life were drawn into God, and it was finding the pattern that God gave that was important.

I left teaching at the end of that year. I had always thought of teaching as first stage to something else. Actually the move was very much done in response to prayer, a prayer in terms of 'show me the way', and reading a scripture that spoke about what was happening in my life. I returned to Adelaide, and started to work for an interdenominational Christian organisation which provided consultancy and support for Christian groups in the country. I did a lot of travelling, visiting school groups, training people, talking to principals and teachers, parents and kids. In the first year I was involved in Girls Brigade, a uniformed organisation that was far too ordered and disciplined for where I was going at that stage. I'd done a fair bit of training within the movement, but I was beginning to question its value. I recall thinking that what we really need to be doing is helping people to understand themselves, and getting them to talk about what they are doing. We need to create an environment in which people can develop what is inside them. The sense of vision, and knowing where a person or a group is going is far more important than ten little hints on how to lead a Bible study group.

That coincided with my sense of the importance of personal growth and development and journey. So life is not just doing what needs to be done, but is pursuing your call, your journey, your vocation. That understanding came partly from the realisation that forcing material into people in training was pretty useless, partly from an experience at Pt Augusta with the Charismatic movement and its sense of the presence of God, as well as going around the countryside and seeing that everybody had a different understanding about everything. You could have groups that were functioning very effectively with totally different theology. I was coming to see that what determined wholeness and goodness and truth was something other than merely the code of ethics or the theology behind it.

At that stage too, the absence of a Protestant Christian presence in the inner city was an eye opener to me. Ferretting it out, finding people in ones and twos, and bringing them together to share their experiences awakened within me an understanding of the degree to which the traditional Protestant and probably Catholic Church is middle-class in values and perspective. Its values are materialism, security, profit and respectability which insulate people from real life, and in particular from people who are struggling with not enough money and not enough personal or spiritual resources. Those people find life very much more difficult than those who may not have many personal or spiritual resources, but have material resources that can take up the slack. My experience of God, Christianity and life didn't seem to me to be contained in middle-class values. If it was, then it wasn't what I was looking for. So the quest for urban ministry, an understanding of God that transcended middle-class culture was an important part of my journey. Relating cross culturally somehow reflected a much deeper perception of life and of God. The more you get in touch with life and people, the more in touch with God you are. If you go the other way, the more you are in touch with God, the more you are in touch with the reality of life.

I stayed with the church organisation for three years. Halfway through that time, I became part of a small Christian community in Elizabeth. I had been flatting in

Adelaide with one of the girls from Pt Augusta. She and I moved in with a couple, and we moved into a new house. Some people living in another house close by made up the rest of the community. The group had been together for six months. Our aim was to put together everything that we had so that we could be committed to work for renewal of the church and the neighbourhood. I'm not sure that I knew what I was doing when I joined the community. I had a sense of church needing to be corporate, from my understanding of God and of people. I found a group of people whose experience and understanding of church were similar to mine. So moving in together didn't feel like a radical thing to be doing, but the next step. Pooling our incomes was more radical, because I had come from a background where money was important — you looked after it and it was your security.

We had incredible expectations of each other and of ourselves. I don't think I had the expectation that there would be no relationship conflicts, because that's part of life. We were living and working so closely together, that it demanded pastoral resources which most people don't have. We were experiencing each other as adults in ways that were atypical to society. A husband and wife are experienced at handling the relationship patterns between them, as are two friends living together, but when a group of adults are committed to sharing their incomes and their lives it is different. There are few patterns for adults living committed lives in a non-related way. We hadn't chosen to live with each other. We had been called to live together. I had moved in with people that I hardly knew. Suddenly our lives and our futures were bound up together. We didn't have a lot of spare money because we were trying to live simply, so you couldn't just get out of it, because there was nowhere to go. You could go and see your friends, but they didn't understand because they were still living conventional lives.

We had a sense of having been called to be corporate. Being Christian wasn't giving individual assent to a set of beliefs but it was a call to relationship, and a call to relationship with God. We couldn't be in relationship with Christ and with God, and not give expression to that in our day to day lives. The expression we felt called to give was the expression of community. We wanted to work towards wholeness in the world, and particularly in this neighbourhood. 'Think globally, act locally' was the key to what we were doing.

At the beginning there were ten of us. We lived in two houses and a flat. The flat and the house were next to each other, and the other house was about five minutes drive away — about thirty minutes walk. It was more of a challenge to have a good life giving house than it was to have a good life giving community. When people are living in other houses, it's much easier to be nice and a friendly than when they are living in the same house. We had a meal together on Tuesday nights, and met every morning for prayer. From the end of 1976 we pooled our incomes. The community now consists of six adults and three children. One guy has just left, because he was about to get married and felt the need to establish the relationship apart from the group. Six months ago another family joined the group. We have had some people from overseas living with us for a while, and they are just about to move on. So there is a fairly stable nucleus of a family and two single people, and others who come and go. There are others in the neighbourhood who are very close to us, who know what is going on intimately, but are not committed in the same way. We are very closely involved with the local Anglican Church, so our worship and our life is inter-related.

When I first joined the community, I was still working for the church organisation. From 1978 I worked for the local Anglican church. We formed a ministry team with a sense of the corporate. I was responsible for developing a pastoral structure within the parish, a sense of infrastructure. I encouraged people to meet together weekly, and to reflect on and discuss their perceptions of God. I encouraged them to be open with each other, and to help each other out in times of need. If children were at home, some mothers cooked evening meals together, rather than all doing it separately. I encouraged people to look after each other's kids, to talk to each other and to be aware of the person next door. On the one hand, it was pretty ordinary stuff, and yet, on the other, it was looking at the fabric of our lives from the perspective of God being present. There was a sense of seeing 'the Kingdom'. You look at something and you can see all the negatives or you can look at it and perceive another reality. How can we be in touch with that reality, and respond to it so that we find our lives in God in each other?

I was working mainly with church people, and their friends, so I didn't challenge the local neighbourhood outright. We were in touch with the neighbourhood. We had the lease from Australia Post to run the local post office, and we had a secondhand clothes shop in there as well. We were involved in running kids' holiday programmes, and we had a horse and cart and used to give people rides around local tourist spots. In retrospect, I think it was very successful. People formed very deep relationships across generations. I think we were tapping into life at a deeper level because of our diversity. When people came among us, they received something different in the quality of relationship. It was a local attempt to experience a depth of spirituality that was both individual and corporate. Sunday worship grew out of that, so that going to church wasn't just the formal liturgy, but the culmination of a week of individual reflection and corporate understanding.

I did that for nine years, until the end of 1987. Then I moved to Hilltop Community Services. It's a ministry of the parish, a non-profit company incorporated by guarantee. The members of the company are members of the parish, so that, while it is an independent structure, it has that people linkage. We started off as a community development agency which ran the post office, the holiday centre and the horse and cart, and set up the retail shop. Our activities more recently have been focussed on employment creation and training for unemployed people. I see this as a parish response to unemployment. I'm responsible for Hilltop Community Services, and liaison with the parish, and other business ventures in recycling, plus the development of new projects and the organisation of the office. We have two centres where we train people to work in the information industry, in word processing, office skills and computer applications. We run twelve week courses which are free for people who come to us through the Commonwealth Employment Service. We have many people working for us who aren't Christians. We also do life skills and job search skills and work experience. We are thinking of moving into the hospitality industry.

There have been sacrifices made in order to live in the community. I've been following a journey, responding to a call, and it's happened, not without me thinking about it, but without there being a sense of choice. Potentially, as a single person, I could have been earning reasonable money and been in a very different financial position. It's most unlikely that I will ever own a home, given the choices I have made, and the fact that the community tends to work on a needs basis rather than a market salary basis. That has meant that we have been able to build up our current projects.

I don't have a sense of having given up my independence. When we moved in together, we didn't give up our independence, we grew to be interdependent. We chose to find our lives amidst others. We are not committed for life. We need to be free to move. Yet I know that the people that I share most deeply with form my life. They give perspective

— I can't imagine not being in relationship with them. So long as I remain single, I will remain celibate. I haven't chosen not to marry, but I can't imagine that I will. Marriage is not a major issue for me. If I fell in love, then I would need to consider it, but it's not an issue in my life. I've made the choice to follow my own journey.

Years ago, before I came to the community, I went looking for a church. For two or three months I visited different churches on Sunday mornings. I was about to give up when I came to Sunday morning service at the Anglican Church in this parish. I felt that God was present — there was a strong sense of awe and yet intimacy. The minister had a lot to do with it, and the community — it was only embryonic at that stage, but people in the church were open and aware of the spirit and felt free to respond. There wasn't a sense of restriction. So I didn't make a choice to be Anglican — it was a finding of a people. My experience has often been that the church, the place where the tradition is and should be guarded, is the place that somehow loses it. The church has actually alienated me from my spiritual journey, because it is so keen to preserve the truth that it holds on to it in a way that is not free, not open to what the spirit might be doing, and what people might be needing to do. Tradition gives so much, and yet if tradition is not linked with the present reality, there is no creative tension between it and the experience of God. That experience of God is never wholly present. You can't contain it, because once you do it is not what you are looking for. I think we sometimes glimpse some of it, and that was what I perceived at that first service.

I call myself Anglican, in that I've made a commitment to these people, and this tradition, and this tradition is Anglican. Yet in so many ways, I distance myself from the Anglican Church, because of the sense of power vested in the bishop and the clergy rather than in the people. Sometimes I think that institutional power doesn't coincide with the power of the spirit, nor does it affirm the journey of an individual or a congregation. It's probably a fear thing — we are afraid that these people are going to go off the rails, so we keep them on a tight rein. Yet that's the very thing that, by trying to contain life, loses it. The other thing about the Anglican Church is that it tends to withdraw from the world to retain truth, and then to impose that truth on the world. Yet, more and more I think that truth and Christ is found within the world, and its broken people. Christ exists in giving, and hanging on to something and insisting that this is the way, seems to be at odds with the relational aspect of God. In some ways, I feel more in touch spiritually with people of other faiths who are committed to life in the same way that I am, than I do with Christians who are committed to maintaining the status quo and aren't aware of the call of the people, of justice and life.

There are many times when I am out of touch with that centre of quietness and peace within. The times when I probably most need to be aware of God are the times that I'm least aware. I can't say that when things go wrong I stop and say a quick prayer and everything is all right. I just don't function like that. For me, it's a matter of taking time out, and thinking back over the day, and becoming aware of what the points of irritation were, and reflecting on that in the light of God's presence. That might be doing very little. I don't find myself praying much. I find myself needing to take time to be still, and to wander down to the beach, and to reflect on the scriptures. Sometimes it's just living the day out, and waiting to get some space, or trying to take some space in the middle of the day. Some things last much longer than that. Sometimes there has been an issue for a couple of years, and there seems to be no answer to it. Rather than continue to confront it, I need to let it be and find another way around.

We meet every morning between 7.15 and 7.30 for

prayer and scripture reading. There is time for prayer for what we are doing in the day. That's terrific, I really appreciate it. I tend to take the next hour just to be quiet. That's not a highly active prayer time, but it's a time for centreing, for being quiet. My understanding of prayer is making space and being attentive rather than being particularly active.

I've been involved in Woman Church, the group out of which the magazine arose. In 1980, I spent some time in America in a group where someone described God as mother, and how they found themselves relating to God very differently from when they thought of God as father. I thought that was a lot of nonsense until I actually experienced it. I don't object to calling God father, but a lot of the time I like to call God mother. It seems more nurturing. I feel more in touch and intimate with God as mother. God as father has a lot of those old connotations of God up there, looking at what you are doing wrong, rather than of a God who is with you and cares for you.

Woman Church is pretty important to me. There's not much opportunity in the church for the expression of feminist ideas, so it's good to be with other women, and with men too, who want to relate to God as feminine. Woman Church is a collective of women who want to find ways of encouraging each other, and of being in touch with God. It's not just relating to God as feminine, as mother, as woman — it explores patterns which are non-patriarchal and non-hierarchical. We use music that is written by women with patterns to it that are different from those found in music written by men. Much of our liturgy is inclusive and participatory, rather than given and dominating. Much of the church has despised women's experience, or ignored it. Yet women's experience is very important, because it is in that, too, that God is found — the sense of intuition rather than head knowledge and 'thus said the Lord'.

In the community, I feel free to be who I am, and for women's experience to be received and acknowledged. We have always shared jobs and there has not been a strong delineation according to sex. Our church is very accepting of women, but it is still tarred with the brush of centuries of patriarchy and of both men and women being threatened by changing roles and expectations. You have to move slowly. I've grown up in a world dominated by men, and I'm used to functioning in that milieu. So, when I'm tired it's easy for me to slip back into not listening to myself, not taking seriously the things I think or feel, or have hunches about. I know that there is a dull monotony about what I am doing then, but I don't do anything about it, until I take seriously my own life and experience. And it's experience not just in terms of what I can do, but experience in the thinking, feeling, being wholeness of my person. It's that whole sense of being attentive that brings me in touch with God.

Bruce Nicholas

'A lot of people say, how can you be a butcher and be a spiritual person? . . . you're cutting up poor little animals.'

Born in 1941, Bruce Nicholas left school at thirteen and has been a butcher all his life. A nervous breakdown set off his spiritual search, and, untaught and unguided, he has explored many branches of New Age thought, inspired by mystical visions in the streets of Sydney and his own deepening understanding of himself and the universe. Rejecting any concept of himself as one with a special mission, Bruce feels that his role is to love, and help others overcome the fears that block them from experiencing life as bliss. His contact with people in his butchery gives him some opportunity for this, as does his unpaid work as a minister in the Spiritualist Church and organiser of a Planetary Healing Group (a small and innovative New Age structure).

The Spiritualist movement developed in the USA in the mid-nineteenth century, and was introduced to Australia around the same time. There are sixty formally organised Spiritualist Churches in Australia today, with a membership of over five thousand. Although many of its beliefs are similar to those of Christianity, the Spiritualists believe that the soul is everlasting and that communication with the dead is held to be possible, via mediums, and is considered a valuable source of guidance for living individuals. The experiences of mediums are seen as the fundamental validation of the truths of Spiritualist philosophy.

As a child I never had any spiritual experiences or unusual happenings. I left school when I was thirteen; I wish now that I had continued my education because it would be a help to me nowadays. I've always been a butcher. I married in my early twenties and had four children. I had my own business and I used to throw everything into it. I'd be off to work at four in the morning, home at nine at night, and thoroughly enjoying every minute of the pressure and the rush. I neglected my family. A man took a shine to my wife and though nothing ever happened I got very suspicious and it became an obsession with me. One day, I found a note written to her by this guy, saying how much he liked her. Something snapped inside me, and I fell to the floor. I felt as if I was being electrocuted, but not with electricity coming in — with the electricity going out, bursting out of me in all directions. It was like pins and needles from the tip of my head to the tip of my toes ... the weirdest feeling.

I went through quite a bad period, it was basically a breakdown. The doctor put me on tranquillisers. I'd never been involved in meditation, but I found the tablets calmed me down so much that I'd go into a dream world. I'd sit, shut my mind off and go somewhere different. It was a real dream world, because the people in it weren't people I knew — it was like sitting down watching television. What it actually was, I would say now, was all my fears passing before my eyes, as if I was releasing them.

I became very interested in the psychic. I wanted to have my cards read. I knew there was a message for me, but I didn't know who to ask for it. I went from one to the other and occasionally I'd strike one that could tell me something that was going to happen. One day I met a woman who suggested that I should read *Handbook to Higher Consciousness* by Ken Keyes and told me I could buy it at the Adyar[1] or the New Awareness bookstore. I got it at the Adyar bookstore and the woman in the shop invited me to attend their regular Monday night meditation group. I read the book from front to back, and did not understand one thing in it. Driving to the meditation on the first night, I was frightened. I'd never been involved in meditation before, and I had visions of all sorts of weird and wonderful things that might happen. But the people were just ordinary like myself; there was nobody who looked like a guru or anything special. We were led verbally into a planetary healing meditation. I had a vision of those big grotesque things that Chinese have besides their temples — there were two dragon figures standing beside me, one on each side. I was terrified. When I talked to people afterwards, they explained that they were probably doorkeepers. In spirituality there are 'doorkeepers' to protect you from incoming evil entities.

I kept going to the meditation group. We sat with our feet on the floor, and our backs straight in ordinary chairs. In the centre of the room was a little log of wood with a candle on it, and a flower. The energies from the other people in the group would become one, and everyone became very still and deep and quiet inside. After going three times I had an experience on my way to work one morning. Everything looked as if it was brand new. I had the strangest sensation that I was seeing everything for the first time. The sunlight seemed ten times brighter and there seemed to be a light radiating from me for ten or twelve metres. Everything shone and sparkled and glistened and was lovely and peaceful. I had an incredible feeling of inner peace. I never knew what peace was until then.

One night after meditation I drove a woman home who was going to start courses on unconditional love. We talked about unconditional love, and how to attain that state. We pulled up in front of her unit and when I looked at her she was no longer the person I thought she was. It was a different person sitting beside me, a man. It frightened me a little at first but then I got my calm back and started talking again. Next minute I had visions like great big teardrops, like the Ying and Yang symbols. One was blue, and one was indigo, and in the heavier part of the teardrop was a tiny little silver star. I went into a state of total bliss. Tears rolled from my eyes. I was so happy and peaceful that I could have stayed in that state forever. I still see the blue that was in that teardrop when I'm driving around at night. If I go to a spiritual person's home, or somewhere where there is a lot of love, I can see this blue light — it might be around a pot plant or a stereo. It's not an aura, it's an electric blue that shimmers for a while and then goes away. One day I was talking to a woman in a health food store and I saw two great shafts of blue light come from her throat. On either side of the blue lights were silvery sparkles — it was the most magnificent sight. She told me that she'd done a favour at an old people's home nearby, and they had said that they would pray for her. She was touched by it, and as she spoke I saw the light coming from her. She was feeling the joy and beauty and love that these people were giving her. I've seen other things like that. One day a woman asked me for help as her son was on drugs. I gave her some advice, and on the way home I felt good about what I'd done. Out of the blue, through the roof of my car and straight into me, came a brilliant white flash of light. It was just like a streak of lightning, but dead straight, not jagged. When I'm in a state of feeling happy and blissful, these things happen. I'm sure other people can experience them, if they only allow themselves to be in that state of bliss.

When I first started meditating, I became a real meditation nut, all I wanted to do was meditate. Once

I went into a paddock beside a churchyard and started meditating there. That's when I got one of the biggest shocks of all. A voice spoke to me, and asked what is the meaning of God. That took me away from all the cards, and I started searching for what God is really all about. I had a mad craze to read about spiritual things. I read books about everything, from auras to the teachings of different spiritual leaders, even ones that I wasn't interested in. I realised I had a lot of study to do, and that I had to start thinking and getting deep down into what life and spirituality were all about.

I used to study in the morning tea break, and in half my lunch hour — the other half I would meditate. Then I would race home and read books till three o'clock every morning. I would be up at five o'clock the next morning for work. I never felt tired. The only time I feel tired is when I do nothing. I've just done a massage course, I've looked very seriously at chakras and auras, and I've gone through 'A Course in Miracles,' which takes twelve months to complete. I've studied a little bit about Buddhism, Hinduism, Sai Baba and spiritual healing. I was very involved with crystals until I came to the realisation that all these things are only little tools. The crystal doesn't have any power at all, it's you that has the power. They are beautiful, and I love them dearly, but they are only a stepping stone, a tool that has to be used for concentration. I went to some of the seminars at the Theosophical Society. Most of them didn't hold any interest for me, except one on listening to your inner self. From then on, I've always listened. Now, I have a very broad view of everything happening around me. I can see the whole picture. It's as if you're sitting in a circle, and everything around you is a stage. It's all being acted, and you can see the acting, see the game that's going on. You can see the people that are coming up, and different people learning, and other people that are stuck in a little spot. I decided that

I would never get stuck on one particular thing. If you do that, get stuck on rebirthing or past lives or whatever, you are not going to grow. You have to look at it, take what is there for you, and then leave it and move on to the next thing. Otherwise, you don't grow in a spiritual sense, which means learning to have unconditional love — to love everybody and everything, and see the whole picture of life, not just one thing.

During my search for readings, I went to the Spiritualist Church. I used to attend every Sunday, hoping for the magic word that would change everything. When you first start getting all these wonderful feelings, this sense of peace, you feel as if you have been given a special mission. That's just a stage that you go through, and then you settle down to realise that what it's all about is living and learning to help and love other people. I can help people conquer their own fear. Their own fear is the greatest enemy they have got. Of course, they think their husband or their kids are the problem, but it's all of their own making. Everything that happens around you is your own responsibility, your creation.

A medium brought me to that realisation. She spoke at the church one day, and apologised for teaching the wrong thing for many years. She's eighty-four, and she had come to realise what she had been searching for all her life was the Christ within. The silly part about it is that you look on the outside for it, when it's there inside, and all you have to do is recognise it. Then you realise where you are. You are in a total state of bliss, you are peaceful, and you have the power to change everything around you to that state. It is only your own fear, disbelief and rejection of these thoughts that stop you being there.

What held me at the Spiritualist Church was the beautiful brotherhood with the people there. Everybody tried to help one another, there was no backbiting, no do's and dont's. Everybody was interested in what was going on, and if someone came up with an idea, our little group said, let's try it and see what happens. I don't agree with some of the ideas of the Church. I don't believe in any evil forces or devils.

I went along every Sunday for five years, and then they asked me to become a minister of the Church. I felt nervous, and then I thought, why not, maybe I can help somebody. It takes two years to become a minister. In the two years training period, you look after the church, and you study its philosophy, the Science of Spiritualism which we believe is a science, not a philosophy. After two years, you become a full minister, and, when you're registered with Corporate Affairs, you can carry out weddings and funerals. I do all the church work at the moment, from the prayers and the address right through. After the church service is finished, we have the 'demonstration'. You read flowers, or someone puts a ring in the bag and you read the ring for them. Most people bring a flower, and you read from it. You do it out front so everyone can hear. I do readings, but not as fortune telling ... I do a spiritual reading where I can feel things that they should know, or experiences that they may have, from objects that they have had in their hands. I don't do past lives, and I won't do fortune telling. I try to give spiritual guidance, and help people to take away their own fears.

With the Spiritualist Church, the main thing is the science of proving life after death. That wasn't attractive to me. It was not why I became involved, and still isn't. I don't care if there is life after death or not, because I intend living this life with affection. If there is life after death, it will be beautiful, if there is not, I've missed nothing. My concern is this life, here and now, and to take away fear in people, to help them realise that the only fear there is is fear itself. There is nothing that can hurt them. If they stop and listen to themselves, they will find out that the reason that everything is happening is that it's all part of a master plan, all to do with cause and effect and karma. Quite often, if you look at it properly, things smooth out again. When you are learning something in the spiritual world, it's like a carpet. The harder you push a carpet, the harder it is to move. It buckles up under your foot and you can't move at all. But if you let your foot slide across the top, your foot just glides across and life is so easy. This is what we do in our life. We push too hard, and everything goes wrong.

We are given a lot of lessons on counselling in the ministerial training. We are taught to speak from our hearts. When you speak from your heart, it doesn't matter whether you are educated or uneducated, you are speaking the truth. What most people want, when they seek counselling, is to be loved. There is a lack of love somewhere, and all most people want to do is tell you. All you have to do is listen and you are counselling, because they are pouring out their hearts. You wouldn't be asked to be a minister unless you had the ability to give people a reading, to be able to speak from your heart, and to love people and let them be loved back. I was ordained this year, at a service which was very similar to being ordained in any other church. None of my family would come, because they have been brought up Catholics, and they were taught Catholics aren't allowed to go into another church. They don't know all the experiences I've been through — they're not interested.

Being a minister is a voluntary job, and it hasn't changed my life in any way. Nobody calls me 'reverend', and I don't sign anything 'reverend'. I just know in my heart that I have been ordained in the Church, and I'll do the best I can. It's a lifelong commitment to our principles and to our Church, but I can pull out anytime. You do not have to be excommunicated from the Church if you want to back out of it, because there is no 'church' as such. We believe that whenever there are more than two, there is a church. We often hold our church services at Lakemba's Masonic

Hall. There is a very small charge, and what we collect from a free will offering is almost always enough to cover the charge. We don't want a great big church, because we can hold a service in our home, or in a park, or in a paddock. Sometimes there are fifty people at service. We are all very close, it's like a family. We have a seminar at Yarramundi once a year. All our little churches go and spend a weekend listening to different speakers — people like Chris Cole, a psychic healer, and Jackie Warren, an astrologer. They give us lectures on their beliefs, and if something is nice we will take it. If it's not nice, we will let it go.

I hold a planetary healing group in a school at Lakemba on Wednesday nights. We run the group absolutely free of charge. People hear of it by word of mouth. Last week we had two Indians, two Czechs, two Muslims, four Australians and one Greek. Sometimes the numbers might go down to twelve, sometimes they build up, but it's always a cross section of nationalities. Originally, our meditation was similar to the Findhorn group's technique. They used to bring the Christ light down to the centre of the group, and then send it to the Archibald fountain. They would fill the fountain with light, and then they would slowly flood Sydney with this light, which is unconditional love. Then they would see it going into all the dark lanes and filling the hearts of derelicts and all those who needed it. They would send great shafts to Ayres rock, and link up with other groups doing similar things in Australia, and then flood the whole of Australia, and the planet, with light. In our meditation, we first pass the light through our bodies. When we do that, we are cleansing them. You feel an energy force going through you, as you tap into the life force itself. Then we send the light to the centre of the earth, the heart of mother earth, and then we see it expanding inside the earth. Then it seeps through the earth, and goes to all its inhabitants, whether they are animate or inanimate objects. Everything, to our way of thinking, is alive, because it's all part of the life force, and if one molecule was taken out of the whole system, the whole system would cease to exist. This is our way of sending love to the world.

I meditate whenever I can, because I love it, it's the greatest form of relaxation. I don't use a particular technique. Meditation is being still, and making yourself still inside. I don't know how long I meditate for — it doesn't have any significance. About ten minutes is sufficient to create through meditation, to learn to project. That's what meditation is to me — it's projection. Usually when we pray, we are asking for something — for forgiveness, for someone to get well. I believe that God is all loving, and we have everything we ask for. When we want something to happen, we must project it, and make it happen. We actually create what we are praying for. One of the greatest things I experience through meditation is the ability to project my feelings. If somebody is in trouble, I project my love to them. I don't care who it is, or whether I like or dislike them, I'll send them my love. If they pick up a fraction of it, and it makes a little bit of happiness in their life, I've achieved something. I don't read much anymore. I spend most of my time either in meditation, or in deep thought or projection. Sometimes when I meditate, I will feel my etheric body get up and leave my body. It will go to a certain place — it might be to somebody in trouble. I can feel my body go, and actually cover the person and give their soul comfort. I honestly don't know what's happening. I tried to work it out, but I thought, it's not for me to know. It's something higher than I understand.

A lot of people ask how I can be a butcher and a spiritual person when I am cutting up poor little animals. I started butchering before I was involved in spirituality, and it's only another form of feeding the masses. The people who need help are the people who come to the shop. I feel quite confident that I have been put there for a reason. I have been given a job where I will always have personal contact with people. I could have ended up in an office, and looked at a desk all day, and never spoken to a soul. That wouldn't be where I'm supposed to be. Sometimes I don't have to say anything to a person. There is a force far greater than our material being with which we contact one another.

I would like to stay in the Church and give more to people. I'm convinced that my goal in life is to help people to turn away fear. If they've got a problem, be it a spiritual or a household one, I will help if I can. I'm not an educated person, so most of my work will be with people of like mind, less educated people. I can communicate with them because I have a very simple philosophy, and I don't go into the academic side of things. I can explain eternal life: Imagine yourself as a cloud. You fall to the ground as a raindrop. You wonder what you have come down for. You see a seed beside you, and it reaches out to you. You go through adolescence and maturity, and then a flower comes from within you. You blossom and you feel the bees and life going by. All of a sudden you start to wither, and you realise you are getting old, that you are going to die. The petals fall off your flower, and the seeds fall onto the ground. You look at the seed and realise that is your offspring. You wither away, and the sun dries up your withered leaves. As you are dying you realise what you are. You are the moisture in the plant, and you are taken up to the cloud to start all over again.

---

1 Adyar bookstores are run by the Theosophical Society, and stock spiritual literature from all the great world traditions.

2 *The Course in Miracles* is a spiritual text, first published in 1976, which draws on contemporary psychology, Eastern teachings and Christianity.

Elizabeth Cain

'At some point I came to know that my energy
was not moving in the same way as the group
was choosing to go. There was a level at which
I wasn't psychically strong enough to stay on
there. And I wasn't meant to, because the leaving
of a formed religious life has been the birth into
a new and deeper sense of spirituality.'

Elizabeth Cain was born in 1933. A Dominican nun for
over twenty-five years, she derobed in search of time for
contemplation, unavailable to her in an Order oriented
to service and in turmoil after Vatican II. She has studied
Jung extensively, and undergone Jungian analysis. Her
journey has taken her to the Blue Mountains outside
Sydney, where she lives a simple life concerned less with
establishing financial security than with having space for
contemplation, the basis of her spirituality. Her work is
spiritually innovative. As a lay person, she gives spiritual
direction, and runs courses on a variety of spiritual
subjects, including Australian spirituality and the links
between depth psychology and spirituality. Her search has
been undertaken within the Christian tradition, but she
is planning a trip to India to explore the connections
between Hindu and Christian mysticism.

Elizabeth Cain was raised in a strongly Catholic family

in rural South Australia. Her story begins with her, at the age of sixteen, attending a Catholic boarding school and thinking of becoming a nun.

——————————————— ✳ ✳ ✳ ———————————————

Becoming a nun meant leaving home and being prepared to spend your life in some form of service. In the Catholic Church, at that time, religious life was a natural way in which to follow the desire for service. Somehow, I had an obscure sense of wanting a contemplative direction in life, an obscure longing to have a directness of attention towards God, and to express that. It's not easily articulated — it's a sense of a direct expression of your life towards the centre. In retrospect, I have thought that maybe it would have been better if I had gone to an absolute contemplative order. But I didn't. I went to the Dominicans, a teaching order. The nuns at my school were dedicated and quite influential in the religious dimension of life. I had a lot of admiration for some of them, so that would have been one major factor influencing my decision to become a nun.

My parents mildly discouraged me, suggesting that I took a bit more time to make such a radical choice. Yet the values of religious life were those I'd heard all my life. They thought it was a bit too soon, and they didn't want to lose me. It wasn't a heated discussion. I lived in a generation where open communication between parents and children happened much more rarely than it does now. Also, I am a fairly reserved person, and I can be difficult to talk to about things that matter. In the end, I can remember my father saying that my happiness was the major thing.

I have asked myself whether going into the convent was an escape from life. It could have been partly that. I didn't think adequately about relationships or children. I was too young, I didn't know enough of life to consider properly any of those things. The lack of that knowledge has to be made up later. There was no counselling beforehand.

It was very haphazard and informal. I had a teacher for whom I had strong respect and love, and I talked to her sometimes. She never tried to influence me. She would listen — maybe not discourage. In general, the nuns were, in my experience, though not in everyone's, fairly careful not to apply pressure.

I was nineteen when I joined in 1954. I was a postulant for nine months during that time. I was taught about the Church, and got used to community life. After that I became a novice which was a time to focus on spiritual life. At the end of that period I took my first vows, and, at the end of three years, final vows.

We would rise at 5.30 am, and pray together, then meditate for half an hour. The focus of the meditation would be Christ. We would take a passage from the scriptures, and think about it in relation to our own lives. After that was the Eucharist and Mass. By then it was breakfast time. Next, we'd have some form of class. We were taught scripture, and about our new life in the community. We had recreation in the afternoon, and we'd play tennis, or sew, or go for walks in the beautiful Adelaide hills. At night, from nine o'clock, was the great silence. So it was a mixture of work, prayer, silence and community — people searching out their vocation.

There were difficult times. I found it hard to get up in the morning. In fact, when I left religious life, it took a long time for my body to get back into its own rhythm. I was teaching under supervision, and the school experiences were hard. I hadn't enough training to know what was good for the children, and I used to get anxious about them. The ups and downs of friendship with the other sisters could be trying. But, on the whole, I look back on that period as a happy time in my life.

I remember myself as being quite fervent and energised in my spiritual life. I valued times of prayer. But as time was coming up for profession, I had severe doubts about my vocation. The future was unknown, and I doubted whether I was meant for the life, whether I knew myself well enough to make a decision. Being in a convent then meant that you were in a fish net. It was closed and one-sided, and didn't allow other life experiences. It's changed radically now, but at that time it was very separatist, with a lot of emphasis on silence and prayer. The doubts went on for some time — that's not unusual, apparently. Then, I came to the decision to take my vows.

Taking the vows didn't change my life in a radical way. I continued to do the same sort of things. I became a teacher, and taught at all levels. But life became extremely hurried and busy. I remember being constantly tired, and not getting enough relaxation. It was a totally work oriented existence. People were looked on as work energy, for what they could contribute to the institution. So it became for me a survival exercise. It was done for spiritual motives, and had a lot of happiness and creativity. But my pattern was one of quiet exhaustion.

This period went on for twenty years, and I was fundamentally happy. I enjoyed the teaching, I loved the children, and I had good friends among the sisters. I had progressively more responsibility in the community. I studied literature, Greek and Roman Classics, music and history. The study was done in between everything else, after a whole day's teaching. There was a lot of pressure. That's how I remember life — as extremely pressured. But that wasn't unusual for the religious life. I was developing spiritually, within the rather confined limits of the institution. The orientation was certainly spiritual. But, as I look back, unknowingly I existed there just to supply energy for the institution.

I had been teaching, and tremendously committed, for twenty-two years. The custom was that at the end of a long period of service, you were given the opportunity to replenish yourself. I wanted to study spirituality, and I had read about a place in Berkeley, USA where lectures were being given on St John of the Cross and other Christian mystics. That really attracted me. I went to Berkeley in 1979, to an ecumenical centre, part of which was a Jesuit school of theology attached to the University of California. There I discovered that Jung was taken extremely seriously, and considered highly relevant. Initially that surprised me, and then I saw it as a wonderful opportunity to find out why that was so. I had been interested in Jung for a long time. When I first read him, it was like an enlightenment of the psychological aspects of my faith, and I had read a great deal.

It was a very rich time. My study became a search for the interface between depth psychology and spirituality. I gained from it a basic psychological insight, and the philosophy behind that. I did a lot of work with my dreams, and came to understand more the relationship between the conscious and the unconscious, and the relationship of all that to the Scriptures. I did some spiritual direction, exploring with a person their inner world, and seeing how it was affecting their life. Towards the end of my time in Berkeley, I searched out whether it was right for me to move towards doing more of that kind of work. My director encouraged me, and the Order, before I left, had said I might like to work with adults when I returned. By the time I came back, I knew it was a good time for me to move towards education with adults.

When I returned, it was suggested that I would go onto a school staff. Always before in my life, if a suggestion were made, I would agree because that was the way to be obedient. But when the suggestion was made this time, I knew I had some rich things to offer people. So I asked if I would be able to use the insights I had been given. That experience was like the transition between two different modes of being. It was a major change for me to say, 'I have something to give, and I would like the opportunity to give it'. In a general way, there was an openness to Jung in the Order, but I can remember my Provincial asking what Jung had got to do with the faith. I tried to answer, but because not many people had read Jung at that stage, it was hard. Nevertheless, permission to teach, and do spiritual direction was given. There was a good deal of wisdom in the leadership at that time.

Progressively I began to be asked to give workshops on aspects of Jung's thought. That just built up. It wasn't customary for a nun to give workshops, but that was a time when great changes were happening in the Catholic Church. As time went on, I realised it would be good to undergo a Jungian analysis myself. I thought that one day I might become an analyst, and one prerequisite for that was to have had two hundred therapy sessions. So I got permission from the Order to work with John Jansen, the Jungian analyst, in Sydney. There was no Jungian analyst in Adelaide in 1981.

The analysis went on for several years, and affected me deeply. It was a great joy to work with John Jansen. I saw him twice a week. It was a purification of my psychic existence, a wonderful journey. I could perceptibly feel a freeing up within, the uncrumpling of something that had been a bit crumpled up, an opening out of my being to who I am, in an essential way, beyond roles. The analysis enabled me to release anger and resentment, and to realise that I had been governed by a lot of fear. I became able to get more in touch with what was really happening inside me. I learned to work with my dreams. Whereas before I had had a gift for helping others to work symbolically with their dreams, I hadn't had such a gift for working with my own. So it enabled me to touch into my symbolic life at a much deeper level. I had been trying to explore the connection between Jungian analysis and the spiritual direction process. What I found was that, for me, the two were equivalent. My search was clearly directed in the

Jungian way.

Meanwhile, the changes set in motion by Vatican II had been working their way through the church. It was a time of renewal, an opening out of what had been an extremely constricted form. Religious life before Vatican II had been set in an exceedingly solid mode, and I had lived in that unaware, preconscious stage. The forms had come from medieval times or earlier, and nothing had radically changed since. Overlaying that, we had the Irish tradition of a narrow expression of faith. So we had inherited an anachronism.

People started to question, and everything was challenged. Modes of worship, modes of prayer — the old ones were not nourishing — the meaning of community. What Vatican II meant, eventually, was that people had to get in touch with their own religious experience, rather than depending on nourishment from outside. That meant a movement from the collective to individual responsibility.

Within the group identity crisis, individuals were also having their own crises. I was caught between two modes — the older, more established mode and the newer, more personalised independent view of creative expression, and taking responsibility for your own life. The group I was in experienced this tension between the two modes as extremely painful. I was right in the middle. Some people can contain the coexistence of differences like that, but it was highly destructive for me. It tore me apart, and I almost had to make a decision between the two. I also tended to internalise some of the pain people were going through, and that made the whole period worse.

I struggled for a number of years, and then I decided to leave the Order. It wasn't a matter of a loss of faith, or a sense of a different calling. My basic orientation was very much the same. It was a matter of admitting that the Order was no longer nourishing my spirit. Too much of me was being spent on the formal. A whole value system collapsed in front of me. My whole person had been suffering deprivation. What had nourished me in the past no longer did — not the Mass nor the Eucharist because that is the foundation of the faith. Maybe it was that the group had become so fragmented, and it was so hard to find the centre. At some point I came to know that my energy was not moving in the same way as the group. There was a level at which I wasn't psychically strong enough to stay. And I wasn't meant to, because leaving formal religious life has been the birth into a new and deeper sense of spirituality.

At one level, you can also look at the fact that I had the energy for a contemplative mode way back, and that group didn't value it. Nor did it pretend that it did. It was a teaching order, which had a base in contemplation. So I could truthfully say that I was slow to pick up that this wasn't the right place to nourish my essential spiritual direction. It would have been possible to have changed to a more contemplative order. But religious life in contemplative groups has such an overlay from centuries of tradition and custom — the unquestioning expectation that things will happen in a certain way. It's like an encrustation that can obscure the essence. For me, it would have meant retaking something that was no longer necessary. I didn't seriously consider it.

The analysis may have been a catalyst in helping me to see that I should leave the Order. I wasn't exhorted to stay. The Order was going through its own journey at the time, so there was an openness to, and respect for, the individual. I have a great fondness for that group, and still consider it in some ways as my root. But it was the right decision to go.

I was forty-nine when I left, and it was a major step. I had a sense that I could survive economically, because I had been in Sydney for a year, living on what I could make myself, and paying for my therapy. The invitations for workshops built up, so I was doing a lot of work. I also had an excellent 'break' in being taken on in an unusual manner at the Aquinas Academy[1], where I still work.

I moved to a community in Darlinghurst run by a Dominican brother, an open community for people who had nowhere else to go. That was wonderful, because I had people around me who were supports at a very tenuous time in my life. However, gradually I came to know that I wanted a lifestyle where I could give more time to the meditative aspects. I found that giving workshops, and living in an open house, I was getting too exhausted. I also knew that it wasn't right for me at that time to be part of a community. I needed some solitary time to locate and articulate where my own journey was going.

I moved to the Blue Mountains. I had driven through them once, and been overcome by their beauty. That move was a real simplification. I wasn't setting out to get enough work to build up security. It was a big step, and I remember early in the piece getting very anxious about having enough to survive on, and the fact of being a single woman, no longer young. I used to get quite distressed and anxious if I was short of money. But, working with the unconscious, with prayer and with therapy, I now have come to know that I have to trust in Providence.

I have come to know that a basic orientation of discipleship and a prayerful life is what I want most. By discipleship, I mean that, as a Catholic or Christian, the nature of the journey is following Christ. So it's articulating that, and making that a primary value in my life. In the Dominican Order, there used to be a phrase: 'To contemplate and give to others the fruits of contemplation.' I always could locate myself in that. Being an inner kind of person, I've always needed to root myself in a contemplative, still mode of being, and to let the action of my life come out of that. So it's not moving away from action, but it is a way of life where the action comes out of the right base. I find now that, when I do have time for prayer and meditation, the work I do happens in an amazing way, quite differently from the way it is when I don't have that time. There is a deep connection between my external work and my inner life.

In my work, I am exploring my own journey, and doing it with others, which I find really creative. Most Fridays I take off somewhere to give a weekend workshop. The workshops are on a variety of topics. The Meyer-Briggs typology[2]; one called 'The Inner Journey,' which is a Jungian exploration of the journey in dreams; one on Jung and the Christian mystics; one on the Progroff Journal[3] and other forms of journal keeping; one on Christian meditation, and another one I've developed with the help of colleagues: 'Towards an Australian Spirituality'. The workshops are becoming more and more of a mix of Catholics and non-Catholics, just because their nature is so broad. At one 'Journal Process', I had eight young Buddhists. So there's a broadening out, which I love. It's very valuable.

Sometimes people come up to the Mountains for a retreat, or for interviews or spiritual direction. Other than that, I lead a fairly simple existence. When I'm in the Mountains, I meditate regularly. How much depends on the movement of the day. At least a couple of hours. When I have retreats I might do four hours a day. The times I don't meditate so much are when I'm away, and I get very tired giving workshops. Nevertheless, I'm home enough to have a consistent pattern.

I have regular spiritual direction from a Carmelite monk. It involves looking at what is happening in my prayer life, and discerning what is happening in my relationship with God. It's splendid direction, and I find it extremely valuable to locate some of my own experience in the understanding of Teresa of Avila, or John of the Cross, as well as in relation to the Jungian side. I see John Jansen occasionally, and talk about my dreams and my experiences. That's been very important — he has remarkable insight. I have done some rebirthing[4] over the last four years. I have found it valuable, and I often suggest to others that they have a session, or do a retreat that's a combination of rebirthing and spiritual direction. For me, it led to a freeing up of certain blocked energies. But I try too hard, as I did in the convent, and the trying too hard can almost stop the process. It's not a mode in which I can relax sufficiently to get the full benefits.

I have found my right mode, which is a simple and still form of presence, maybe with a mantra, or with the awareness of the person of Jesus. It's not an explosive mode — the energies are being touched and stirred, but not at the kind of level that dramatises. That suits my psyche much better. I also do a fair bit of journal keeping to support my prayer life.

My main teacher is Jesus Christ. But there are others who've mediated in a very powerful way. I don't know that I'd give them the name of 'guru'. As a person, I'm slow to give anyone that name. In the end, a person is responsible for whatever the journey is. Maybe I have a fear of handing over the authority of my journey to someone else. I would look to a spiritual director as a wisdom figure, but I would see them more as helping me to discern the movement guiding my life, than as giving me directions, or telling me how I ought to do it. If I can touch into the spirit of Jesus Christ, and live that out in my life, that is enough.

My spirituality does imply enlightened political commitment, and I think when I am convinced about something, I will commit myself. However, I tend to be a little slow regarding the political dimensions of the spiritual journey. I have a question and a hesitation about political movements that are obviously not coming out of a deep centre. They're coming out of a level in the person or the group that is not looking at ultimate values. If I did commit myself to political action, peace certainly would be one cause, and values that have reverence for the environment. Anything that would be a genuine full discipleship, in the sense of the values that are held, and lived by, the political group. Often my sense is that the values are articulated, but not lived. That holds a dilemma for me. Being truthful, and having eternal values is no problem. At the same time, I have a critical mind about the words that are expressed, and the reality that's lived. Sometimes I don't cope well with the vast difference between the two.

In the Australian context, we've inherited the Western tradition of power politics. There is another way that we hardly know of, a way practised by people closer to the unconscious in their way of life. You find it in tribal groups, and in communities where people are on a genuine journey themselves. The search that is likely to happen in these groups is likely to be creative for the world. I know a number of Christian communities like that. There is a powerful energy for the transformation of the universe in that kind of group.

My primary value is that direct, contemplative aspect of life. If I met someone who would walk with me, I would be open to walking with them in a conscious way. Certainly I would think that at some point I would become a member of perhaps a Christian community that has a contemplative orientation, a mixed community — male and female — and I may meet a particular person that can be on that journey with me. I don't put an ultimate value on celibacy. Sometimes I miss the intimacy of a close physical relationship. Any choice has a cost, and there's a big cost in a solitary choice. But I have very close friendships, and I find a lot of nourishment in them. So my essential needs are being attended to.

I tend not to put too many names on God, because I think that whatever God is goes beyond anything I can conceive. However, being transformed in love is the essence of my understanding of God. I believe that God is love, and my life is oriented to that love. There are two kinds of suffering: the kind you bring on yourself; and the kind that you're called to, which is redemptive. I tended to bring quite a lot of the first sort on myself, through unawareness, getting sick, anxiety, tension. I would question how redemptive that has been.

But, when one reaches a certain level of presence to God, there's an insight that suffering can be a precious means of deepening that awareness. There is a lot of pain involved in needing to separate from a group to respond to a genuine call in your life. That is suffering, but it's not one that is self-inflicted. It can be redemptive, and I probably have done some of that sort too. The suffering of experiences like World War II remains a mystery for me, and I am content to leave it at that. The Christian crucifix expresses some of that mystery — the unanswerableness of a being in anguish in the face of His God.

Some years ago, I was asked to give a workshop on Australian spirituality. My immediate response was to go to it through the symbols. Symbols are spiritual in the sense that they hold meaning. The essence of the spiritual quest is the search for meaning — the institution is not intrinsic to it. Jung's understanding is that there is an energy in the psyche of all human beings, whether they have a Christian background or not, that is God-directed. With Australian spirituality, that is the level of the person that is being touched into. Helping people to contact that level is not like being a missionary, or preaching. It is educating in the true sense of the word — to bring life out of a person.

My aim in the workshops is to help people to locate their journey and symbols within the Australian context. We discuss what a symbol is, and help people to discover their own. Their symbol might be a little Irish house, or it might be the cane fires that burn in Queensland. The land is a very powerful symbol for people, the bush, camping, the desert. The desert is an extraordinary symbol in that it holds so much meaning — emptiness, absence, no edges. Symbolically, in any tradition, it's the place where a naked encounter with God is unavoidable. Australia has so many symbols, it's unbelievable. In any group of Australians, there would be such an amazing variety of backgrounds that to articulate an Australian spirituality is incredibly complex.

These workshops have proved to be very exciting, and affirm the fact that many Australians are on a powerful spiritual journey. Les Murray says something like: 'It's bad form to talk religion in Australia, but Australians will talk spirituality for hours on end.' I travel a lot, and it's amazing how often, in the oddest of situations, easily and naturally, that search for meaning is happening.

It's out of that search that whatever is the religious dimension in the Australian context, expressed institutionally, will come. When people are on that search for meaning, they come to know that they need time for retreat, time for silence, time for meditation. Institutions come out of a number of people in a certain environment sharing a history. The type of structures that emerge will depend on the particular people, and the form that most attunes them to the spiritual. So it won't be, for example, the Ignatian practices[5] that provided a structure in the Christian tradition that will come, but it will be some form that will express the Australian psyche, in relation to its own environment.

---

1 Aquinas Academy: founded in Sydney in 1945 by a Marist priest to teach adult classes on the basis of Thomist philosophy, the Aquinas Academy today runs courses on a wide variety of spiritual subjects for Catholics and non-Catholics.

2 Meyer-Briggs typology: a personality typology which is an elaboration of the basic Jungian classifications (extrovert/introvert; feeling/sensation; thinking/intuition).

3   Progroff: an American writer who has written extensively about the uses of journal-keeping to develop self-awareness.

4   rebirthing: a psychotherapeutic/spiritual process developed originally by Polish-born and American resident psychiatrist, Stanislav Grof, aimed at releasing unconscious material and facilitating transpersonal experiences.

5   Ignatious of Loyola: medieval Spanish Catholic, whose spiritual exercises form the basic of many contemporary Catholic retreats and practices.

Annie Stockford

'You take it so seriously at the time. This is what I'm into — I'm a married woman forever, I'm a nun forever, I'm a lesbian feminist forever. Only my spirit is forever — all the other identities and clothing keep changing.'

Annie Stockford was born in 1950, and has been involved in the Indian movement Ananda Marga for over fifteen years. Her journey has been, in some ways, a struggle to reconcile the different elements of her nature. Her desire for transcendence has at times clashed with her desire to be part of the world, and the need for relationship and intense political commitment which that entails. Her strong feminism has led to conflict with the male dominated hierarchy of Ananda Marga. In a journey that has had many dramatic highlights: her training as an acharya (an ordained woman in the Ananda Marga tradition) in India, and her imprisonment by Vietnamese soldiers in Kampuchea stand out. Annie tells her story with the insight and tolerance of one who has come to integrate all the different parts of her being, and is now 'daring to be ordinary'.

Annie explains the philosophy and development of Ananda Marga early in the interview.

I'm not conscious of having had spiritual experiences when I was a child, except that when I felt unhappy or couldn't cope at school, I used to imagine myself flying up into the sky. As a teenager, I wasn't attracted to church or any of those institutional structures, but I was conscious of looking. In a way, it was spiritual, but I didn't call it that. At about fifteen, I started to feel restless, that I didn't fit in, that what I'd been told about the purpose of life didn't make sense.

In my late teens, I dropped out of university. I got a bus, painted it and drove around New Zealand. I was into drugs, LSD, trying to find truth and enlightenment through hallucinogens. It's funny now, but at the time it was a serious business. Physically, it probably wasn't good, but what it did was to open my mind to the possibility of other realities. Later, when I got into meditation, I thought it was going to be like that, and of course it wasn't. Chemicals have a certain effect on the mind which isn't at all related to meditation. But drugs and Indian mysticism were part of the lifestyle of the time, quite different from the frustration and boredom that I associated with conventionality.

When I was twenty-one, a friend of mine got involved with Ananda Marga. I didn't know exactly what Ananda Marga was. All I knew was that there was an Indian monk and teacher, and it involved meditation, yoga and chanting — a devotional approach to spirituality. I was attracted to the feeling of the movement — the concept of a universal spirituality rather than one linked to churches, God internally rather than something external. As it turned out, there were structures and limited concepts of God, but the initial impact and inspiration was more the Eastern mystical concept of God as pervasive, a being in yourself.

Almost overnight, I stopped taking all drugs and alcohol. I gave up coffee and tea. I lived in an Ananda Marga house and gave away all my possessions. I got into quite a strict yogi practice — yoga, meditation, fasting, silence, devotional singing, retreats, reading the philosophy. I was ready for it, I wanted it. It was also fairly typical of me, then, at the age of twenty-one, to do things by extremes and look for total answers.

Ananda Marga and Prout Universal were both started by B. R. Sarkhar[1]. In an Ananda Marga context, as a spiritual teacher, we know him affectionately as Baba. The function of Ananda Marga is to teach the spiritual practices and philosophy of Baba, and to do service. The function of Prout Universal is to promote the teachings of Progressive Utilisation Theory, and in that context Baba is universally known as B. R. Sarhkar. Ananda Marga means path of bliss. The motto is self-realisation and service to humanity. The philosophy is that the purpose of human life is to know our spiritual goal, our inner divinity. Baba talks a lot about neo-humanism, which is a philosophy of welfare for all creation, not just human beings. The idea is that we have physical, psychic, and spiritual needs, and they all need to be fulfilled. That's where Proutism takes over — it has a more political orientation. In a social and political sense, Baba propounds a theory of change, of a just society where people's needs are met on a material level. It's a socialist approach, with a spiritual basis, a real mixture. Most people who are Margies also feel for Prout, but some people who work for Prout are not Margies — they just like its philosophy. To Westerners, service often connotes paternalism and charity. It's not about that. Service in a spiritual sense is about giving without any attachment to results, and seeing everything as an expression of the divine. For me, Baba's approach has been a fulfilling combination of pure and ancient spiritual ideals, and a modern, realistic approach to the injustice and exploitation of society.

At the time I got into Ananda Marga, Baba was in gaol. Shock, horror that this so-called spiritual being was in gaol. We had such a pacifist and hippie idea of spirituality. Everyone had long hair and beards, and sat in the Himalayas. Baba didn't fit any of this image, except that he was Indian. At that time, although I cared about things, I had no political analysis at all. But, looking back, I could almost say I had a political consciousness, because the fact that Baba was in gaol made it more attractive to me. I'm hesitant to say why he was in gaol, because I wasn't in India and I don't think I ever understood its internal politics, but I think he was accused of being behind the murder of ex-members. It was basically political. Ananda Marga was not liked by the Indian government. Baba was seen as a strong force — if he were removed, the movement might collapse.

After six months, I started travelling. I went to the States and did the 'Local Full Timer' training. It's like a trial as to whether you want to be a nun for the rest of your life — a middle step. Then I went to Jamaica for six months as a Local Full Time Worker. That involved teaching yoga and organising group meditation. It was a challenge for me, and I went through a lot. It was the first time I'd been out of a Western country, and I was young, and not very confident. It was a highly politicising time. I'd lived a sheltered life in New Zealand. I had a social conscience, but no real political awareness. I was in San Francisco at the time Patti Hearst was kidnapped by the Symbionese Liberation Army, and, when I was in Jamaica, I was exposed to third world poverty and racism. I started feeling strongly about class, colonialism and race.

I went back to New Zealand and married the man who had introduced me to Ananda Marga. Our lives were geared to the Ananda Marga way. We had jobs just to pay the rent. There was no question of looking for a career or job fulfilment. We taught courses in Ananda Marga philosophy. We went to an old people's home every weekend and took them for outings. We had a stall at the flea market where we sold clothes cheaply, and we used that money for relief funds.

In 1977 I moved to Sydney. My involvement in Ananda Marga had changed from being a focus on personal spiritual development to having a lot of social awareness. Looking back, I think that would have happened to me anyway, as part of getting older. Because Ananda Marga does have a social philosophy, the two were quite compatible, and that was encouraged. We had a strong concept of a spiritually based revolution — radical, quick, dramatic change. It was partly our youth If we hadn't been in Ananda Marga, we might just as well have been in another left wing revolutionary group. We saw life in a particular way — we had the answer, and everyone should see it. We were committed to breaking down corrupt power structures, to cooperatives and women's liberation, to reform within prisons.

At first our activities focussed around Baba's imprisonment, agitating for his release. Then there was the sale of *Dharma*, a socially orientated Ananda Marga magazine. Then the three Margie men were arrested in '78, so that brought us into direct contact with prison activists.

With a couple of other women I got much more involved with the women's movement and this began the big clash. Until that time, everything had fitted like a glove. Then, when I began seeing and feeling issues around women's suppression and patriarchy, I began to feel that it didn't. I began to see that every structure and group reflects the macrocosm. Unfortunately, there's a tendency when you're young and get involved in groups to see yourself as different, as having all the answers. It's embarrassing now, but that's how it was. Then there was the shock of discovering that within Ananda Marga, we also had these struggles, this inequality and suppression of women.

I felt this suppression not in the concepts of spirituality, but in the practice, how we lived it out. There was a hierarchical male dominated power structure and a particular way of working which I associated with the patriarchal mentality. Not only was there that traditional hierarchy, but there was also the spiritual hierarchy of single life being better than marriage That's not common in our culture, but within spiritual groups it is. Baba states clearly that that is not the philosophy of Ananda Marga, but still that dynamic was there. It's an old tradition in India. I've gone through many phases about hierarchical power structures. First of all I accepted them, then I rejected them. Now I can see that, as with everything, there is a place for them, though it was imbalanced.

What I wanted was for Ananda Marga, our family, to acknowledge that there were the same faults in it as in society. Women didn't hold positions of power in the organisation, and the women's way of seeing things wasn't given its rightful place. For example, the hub of the Ananda Marga organisation in Australia and New Zealand was a big collective house. Lots of energy, lots of things going on — I loved it. But, I was practically the only woman involved in it, because any woman who had children, or who couldn't be an honorary man as I was, just didn't have a place there. I wanted more women working there, and child care, to allow that to happen. That brought up issues of skills. We were doing a lot of public relations — interviews, demonstrations, publications — stuff that a lot of women in Ananda Marga didn't have experience in. My desire was to see affirmative action, so that women could get those skills.

In the beginning, I was very optimistic and idealistic. I thought that, if we explained things clearly, all my family would of course be happy to change. It was quite a shock to realise that that wasn't how things were going to be. There were some people who did respond, but there was a real polarisation. Some felt the focus on women's struggle was divisive, undermining the unity of the human family. Others believed there was no real unity when there was suppression. People I had been close to became almost like enemies, because they did not agree with the analysis of patriarchy, the relinquishing of male power, and allowing women's ways of doing and thinking to become stronger. So, within Ananda Marga, we were suspect because we were involved with the women's movement. Within the women's movement, we were regarded with suspicion, being Margies and therefore associated with a patriarchal structure and a male guru. We didn't fit in anywhere! Spiritually, it was good, because it reminded us that you don't fit in anywhere — you fit in with the universe. But it was quite difficult for those of us who were attached to having a safe identity.

Over a period of years, we got involved with anti-pornography action, the women's peace movement, women's music, women's publications. We went to women's marches, and got involved with self-defence. Instead of working as a women's editor on *Dharma*, I started *Sister*, which tried to blend feminism with a more overt spirituality. We're only talking about twenty or thirty women, but our effect was disproportionate to our numbers, because we had such strong ideals and a lot of energy. Within Ananda Marga, there was so much commitment to working for what you believed in. That provided a lot of vitality, direction, and positivity.

My primary loyalty was still Ananda Marga, and I was still doing all the practices. I was always conscious of my spiritual development. I defined it as self-transcendence — being immersed in the inner self that is beyond body, mind, and emotion. The practices were giving me a lot of energy: one to four hours meditation a day, a vegetarian diet, no cigarettes or alcohol. This is very conducive to feeling positive about life and not repressing feelings with drugs. I was living in a women's house, and having a strong spiritual connection with the group of women there. Women often make strong connections anyway.

When you get a feeling of spiritual connection, that's very powerful, and then when as well you start affirming your womanhood, and linking with the woman spirit, that's even more powerful. It's such a strong bond.

When I was married, I didn't know how to be in a relationship. I had a deep yearning for a spiritual life, and a real fear of human life. I needed companionship and human intimacy, but I didn't accept this need in myself. I was always trying to turn it into something nobler. After a few years of marriage, it was obvious that I had to come to terms with this dilemma, because the man I was married to wanted to have children. I was living more like a revolutionary nun than a married woman. I felt there was only one choice for me, and that was to pursue what I was only half heartedly doing, and become an acharya. He also felt that — it was his suggestion, actually. So we separated.

'Nun' is not an adequate word for 'acharya'. The feeling behind the Eastern concept of sannyasin, or renunciate, is a little different from that behind Christian nuns. There's a lot that overlaps, and, as time goes on, I can see more and more similarities. Once I couldn't, because I was reacting against the Christian way, and embracing, a little bit blindly, the Eastern way. Acharyas, within Ananda Marga, are renunciates and full time teachers. They lead a much stricter life than members do. There are many special practices, you don't have relationships, and you are sent to work in a particular area. You try to surrender your personal needs for security and control over your own life. It's pretty much the tradition of people who give their lives to their spiritual paths.

I lived in a women's house for a while, preparing to go to India for the training. At the same time, I was getting much more involved with feminism and the women's movement. I also became involved in a relationship with a woman, which wasn't normal in Ananda Marga at that time. But I'd already made the decision to go, so I thought I'd stick to it.

I had a problem integrating my head and my heart in those days. I'd make a decision and stick to it, no matter what, and not allow any feelings to get in the way. That can seem to be a strength, but it is not really. If there are other things happening inside, they eventually make themselves felt.

At the end of the training, I was posted to Calcutta, and then to the Manilla sector, which covers the Phillipines, Malaysia, Thailand, Vietnam, Kampuchea, Burma and Singapore. Baba was encouraging workers to go to countries where we hadn't been before, to build up communities of people who were meditating and giving service, based on the concept of a universal family, transcending barriers of race and politics. What I was supposed to be doing wasn't clear. The practices and the discipline were defined, but the work wasn't directed. I still had a need to express myself politically and socially, and not just play the role of the meditation teacher. I was in Bangkok, and I got involved in teaching English in refugee camps, more as an individual than as an Ananda Marga representative. I wasn't being much of a spiritual teacher — I was being an activist and a social worker.

I went to Laos briefly, to build up a meditating group and prepare the way for regular contact. I had great ideals, and lots of spirit, but not many practical ideals. I had no money and Laos is extremely poverty stricken. I had a real problem accepting money from others, so I didn't stay long. I went back to Thailand. I was faced with the problem of colonisation, of moving in to another country and trying to impose ideas. That's something I've come more and more to detest. On another level, I felt more and more inspired by the concept of a universal spirituality, yoga and meditation. Those practices are good for anybody, anywhere, anytime. Whatever the personal concept of God, they can strengthen and enhance it.

I was in the Phillipines for a while when it was proposed that someone go to Kampuchea. As a result of my work in refugee camps in Thailand, I had developed a strong interest in what was happening there. This was two years after Pol Pot had been driven out by the Vietnamese. I wasn't afraid of doing it, I was more than happy to. I walked, via a landbridge[3], across the border into Kampuchea from one of the refugee camps. I faced so much in that process. So much pain, so much moral dilemma, feelings of incredible powerlessness about all those thousands and thousands of people stuck in a particular area without passports, controlled by the Khmer bandits, controlled by the Thais, controlled by the army. And here was I, so privileged, able to move here, there and everywhere.

I had to go through a subterfuge to stay in the camp. Some Khmer people took me in and helped me get ready. I set off in the middle of the night carrying a plastic bag with pens and pencils in it for kids. The forest was ringing with cries of, 'Barang', which meant foreigner. 'Barang' 'Barang'. For miles I could hear it. People asked me where I was going, and, when I said, Pnom Penh, they laughed. I didn't get very far at all when I was arrested by Vietnamese soldiers, and taken into detention.

I spent two months in a political detention centre in Pnom Penh. They thought I was a spy. If I wasn't a spy, why the hell did I walk over the border. They interrogated me several times a day. There was no threat of physical torture. On the contrary, they were keen to show me how human they were, compared to those rotten Khmer Rouge. It was mentally draining. I'd get summonsed to a room upstairs regularly. They'd give me a piece of paper and ask me to write my autobiography. Then they'd demand that I write more, write what I was thinking. It was very invasive. Then they'd ask me questions. Then the next day they'd ask me more and try to trick me. I didn't want them to know I was involved in Ananda Marga, because there was a lot of hostility there. So I told them that I went to Kampuchea to have a look. In the end, they thought I must be a smuggler as no one would face all the danger, the bandits and the war, unless they had a mission. I did have a mission. I wanted to see if anyone wanted to meditate. But I wasn't going to tell them that.

I used to meditate sitting up in a chair, with my eyes open, and do my self-defence practice in the bathroom. The soldiers used to patrol all the time, and look through the window, so I had absolutely no privacy except in the toilet. My overall feeling was that in Kampuchea there were people who wanted a spiritual way of life that was non-dogmatic, more to do with the inner being than with the trappings and safety of a religion. I actually did teach a little bit of meditation and yoga and self-defence. The Kampuchean women were very stroppy, and really wanted to learn karate, and people did want to know about meditation, because they have such a strong Buddhist tradition. But it was limited. I was kept in one house, a political detention centre, so I taught the neighbours and caretakers I had contact with.

It was a peak experience; I went through the process of thinking I'd never leave. I felt so isolated from the rest of the world, and I thought I'd never speak English again. But after a while I felt almost ecstatic. I was freed from my normal attachments and ways of seeing things. I felt a strong connection with my spiritual being, and with Baba. Then I'd get sentimental, and see a plane flying by, and cry, wanting to be on that plane. It was only for a short time, but it was a taste of what people go through when they are imprisoned, and it was good for me to feel that.

The International Red Cross arranged for my release. I had thought that no one knew where I was. That was silly, because I stuck out like a sore thumb. All through Kampuchea, it was known that there was this white woman who'd disappeared. Another acharya in Bangkok told the Australian Embassy that I hadn't come back. But no one told me any of this, least of all the people I was being questioned by.

The last day I was in Pnom Penh, I asked to see the detention centre where about sixteen thousand people had been tortured to death. It was heavy. I had had a tendency to be a little 'head' about revolution. For the cause, you don't let too many feelings get in the way. That was already coming undone through the women's movement, allowing myself to feel. Seeing what had happened in Kampuchea in the name of ideology and revolutionary fervour pushed it a lot further. They have rooms full of photos of the victims. Their pain — all the torture instruments and shackles were still there, and the rules were still on the wall.

Foreign Affairs contacted my parents and they paid my fare home. It was very confronting. I'd done a lot of the old typical stuff about rejecting my family, as part of my rejection of mundane life. When you go off to be an acharya, you don't have any contact with them, but, as soon as I got into any trouble, they were called on to help me. I had to face the fact that a lot of people had to make a lot of effort for me, because I hadn't thought things through properly. My idealism and missionary zeal had caused considerable distress. It's good to have spirit, but you also have to take responsibility for yourself.

I ended up back in Sydney, right in the middle of all the things I hadn't resolved — my attachment to a particular woman, and what that symbolised for me — women's culture and autonomy. The whole thing was absolutely alluring, I wanted it more than anything, but I'd repressed that part of my personality. I used to criticise feminism all the time — so narrow, not universal. Then someone told me that I kept on attacking it so much because it's what I wanted. I realised that was true. I had to attack it to make it less desirable. And I was in conflict about being an acharya. I didn't want to go where I was sent. I wanted control of my own life — I wasn't able to surrender nearly as much as was required. I worked for a couple of months, and then I decided not to be an acharya any more. In one way, I felt that, in myself, nothing had changed. I was changing directions slightly, in terms of roles, but I was still committed to the same ideals. But I really felt the need to develop the feminine part of me. At that time, there was no feminist women's community within Ananda Marga, and I didn't feel the freedom to develop one.

My feminism became much deeper, an acknowledge-ment of God as being She, as much as He. It sounds basic, but that's heresy in a certain context. The fact that the guru was a man did not in any way conflict with my concept that the universal supreme being must have a woman's identity too. As Mary Daly says, when God is male, male is God. That has a powerful effect on women's feelings about their spiritual progress. Indian concepts of God can be androgynous. In Ananda Marga, there's the concept of God as a composite of Shiva and Shakti[4]. The philosophy of Ananda Marga is that women and men have the same spiritual potential. That was never the issue. It was the way it was lived out, the power politics. More and more we came to the conclusion, as many women have in many areas, that once you have an awakening as a woman, you need to be autonomous to some degree. We didn't want to break away from Ananda Marga, but, within the family, we needed to be together, to be free of the pressure to speak, think, and write in a certain way.

I got much more involved in women's issues. This was '83, '84, '85. Very soon, I was working in a women's drug and alcohol service. I started a women's music group and participated in women's spiritual festivals. I had a huge vested interest in trying to make Ananda Marga more progressive, less sexist, more open to change, less hierarchical. A group of us, men and women, tried to introduce new ways of doing things. I felt distraught — so much attachment to it being the perfect vehicle. I got into a lot of strife trying to tackle the powers that be, not being able to accept in myself that some things weren't going to change. I had to find a way of expressing myself that wasn't banging my head against a brick wall, and was more in tune with the culture I lived in.

I tried to go back to being an acharya again. I was thirty-five, and still avoiding the responsibilities of buying a house and making a commitment to a relationship. I was torn. Was I going to face those responsibilities, or was I going to let go of everything and cast my fate to the universe? In the end, I decided that I needed to let go, and focus on the spiritual side. Over a period of a year, I went through a process of gradual withdrawal, letting go of a relationship, trying to let go of political involvement and my country — all the things you identify with in life — to get back in touch with my inner self.

I felt tremendous pain and anger about the misogyny, the rigid hierarchical structure, and the incredible resistance to change I had encountered doing my training in India. So I went to the other acharya training centre in Sweden, which was for Westerners. It blew up very fast. The monk who was in charge had heard of my reputation — trouble making feminist, going to cause a revolution in his training centre. He was an Indian and he didn't understand. I could understand how he felt, but I couldn't stop expressing myself because of that understanding. Change has to happen, and it's often painful and involves struggle. I tried once again to be silent, to accept things. But you have to have a measure of expression of yourself, or you go nuts.

Basically it was impossible. I thought I had worked through all the possible clashes, but the reality and intensity of it was much greater than I had anticipated. What I had to face quickly was that I wasn't going to find the kind of support system I needed to survive. I had thought I could survive, working in the structure, as long as there was a camaraderie amongst the acharya, a women's consciousness. The women who were in training did have love for other women, but there was a long process, which I'd already been through, for them to experience. It was an issue of age as well. Most of them were in their early twenties, and I was a lot older.

I would have had to let go of everything I needed in life to become an acharya, except the most subtle spiritual things — the ideal, the sharing. I would have had to give up or totally suppress my feelings about being a woman, and the whole issue of women's liberation. I felt as if I was going completely mad, trying to follow one part of myself and throw out the other. Perhaps if I had been more developed spiritually, I could have surrendered that much. But I have needs as a human being, to have intimacy and rational intellectual exchange, and openess to new ideas. And I don't want to be controlled by male monks.

So I left the training centre, and eventually, after more travels, came back to Australia. I'd come to a turning point. I knew I was going to live in the world now, and I felt peaceful. That meant coming to grips with things — getting work that was fulfilling, having my personal relationships healthy and constructive.

I'm working as a sexual assault counsellor, and learning a lot from that. Previously, all my energy had been directed to Ananda Marga, so any work I did was a little on the side. Now, my work has become something I put a lot of effort into, and find fulfilment in. I'm finding more and more that it's possible to be a whole person in my work. I don't have to stop at a certain point where the spiritual part of me is at home meditating, and this part of me is separate. I'm also studying for a graduate diploma in adult education, and I would like to teach English as a foreign language. I've worked a lot in other countries on the level of ideas, women's groups, change. Next time, I'd like to have something more practical — not try to foment instant revolution. I'm doing the Psychosynthesis training programme[5]. I like it because it acknowledges all the different parts of me, has a good ethical and transpersonal basis, and gives me techniques I can use in the work I'm doing. The other area that is important is what in Ananda Marga we call 'society building' — wanting to live in a constructive way: sharing ideas and skills, and being part of a community. A group of us are looking at starting a community somewhere out of Sydney, linked to the city, and to a housing cooperative that some of us are involved with. We also work together as women by gathering and celebrating our spirituality with one another.

I had put aside all these things before, because I was too busy doing other important things. They were important, but there was a part of me that I wasn't facing. Now, it's like embracing the world more, daring to be ordinary. I have been afraid of that, and addicted to drama and excitement. Now, it's like embracing the void, the emptiness, and allowing myself to be still. I work hard, and there's a lot happening, but inside, it's a different reality, and it feels perfectly all right. As you get older, you get more philosophical. I can look back on the struggle I had within Ananda Marga over women's issues, and think, what a pain in the arse I must have been, waving a banner at this, and a banner at that, and being so insensitive and impatient, and gung-ho. I think that's how it always is with change.

I do exactly the same spiritual practices — yoga, meditation, chanting, reading the philosophy. I live with people who do the same practice, and we meditate together. I only do one hour's meditation per day, because that's all I have time for. I could make time for more, but this time I very much want to do all the other things that I've left for so long. I don't know if that urge for self-transcendence will manifest externally again. I strongly want and need to be involved in community, ongoing consistent relationships, children. At the same time, I don't want to neglect my deep desire for detachment — that, in this life, I will completely know myself, and not get submerged in finite reality.

I still feel quite strong devotion to Baba. He is still my teacher, though we've had no direct contact since I saw him in gaol back in the seventies. The lesson with that is to find it more inside. The true guru is in ourselves, our own inner being. I do feel that I have a personal relationship with Baba, otherwise I don't think I would have kept going through all the things that have happened. As I get more in touch with my inner self, I see Baba now more as a human being who has ups and downs. Sometimes he is well, sometimes not well, sometimes he is cranky and sometimes absolutely ecstatic. An extraordinary human being. I feel a more human relationship with him. Maybe I could have an argument or discussion with him — before, there would have been no way! The fact that he's a male guru — I think if I had been involved with the women's movement before I became a Margie, I would have found it much harder to develop the relationship. But, if you love someone, you love them. You might be pissed off at what's happening to women, and male power and violence, but you might still have affection and love for your son, or your father or brother. There are contradictions there, but that's part of life. And, lately, I've been feeling more open to having some connections with brothers, men who've worked through issues of power. They're happy to be men, but they want to relinquish the power that comes from being men in a male dominated world.

I'm seeing more and more the connections between the external and the internal — what you're going through in your microcosmic self and what's happening around you. In a way, it feels like a play. What it gives me is greater humility. It's all so serious at the time. This is what I'm into — I'm a married woman forever, I'm a nun forever, I'm a lesbian feminist forever. Only my spirit is forever — all the other identities and clothing keep changing. It's been very humbling for me to look back and think how gung-ho I've been about certain identities and political outlooks. But, at the same time, I think you have to be gung-ho about what you're into, or you don't move.

When I first got into Ananda Marga, I thought, I've found it. That feeling of seeing the light, and everything before was junk and stupid. After years of being full on into Ananda Marga, I started thinking, it was a bit silly to think like that. My whole life has been part of my spiritual path, and I don't want to see things in such a linear way. Then, I moved into another phase in that journey of seeing it as all part of a spiritual journey — that time of initiation into Ananda Marga practice was highly significant. So, it's not an either–or thing, which for me is a much less patriarchal way of seeing existence, inclusive rather than exclusive.

I often feel the most incredible sense of gratitude. I feel strongly that I am on a particular path, and that it is the right one for me. It's fulfilling, because I can feel progress. Sometimes it is hideously painful, but I don't mind the suffering, the pain of separation from the inner self. I just feel a sense of joy. Out of the grace of the supreme, I keep moving. There's nothing external I can pin it on. It's a feeling that life is always new and always vital, a feeling that there is a rightness to whatever happens, even when it is painful. Then, especially. I have had a tendency to be addicted to drama. I've been working on that for a year, and so I've been having fewer crises. But I'm very aware that the universe can make anything happen, and occasionally does. I don't control. Of course, I can have a measure of control over my life, and I want that on a human level. But, on another level, I can't. There is a real peace in knowing that, surrendering to a greater truth — the feeling that there is a reason for everything and that everything happens for the best. It makes it possible to do anything.

1 A highly controversial figure in India, B. R. Sarkhar was arrested in 1971, and charged with two hundred offenses. Each of these charges was eventually dismissed, and he was honorably released from jail in 1978.

2 In 1979, in Sydney, three members of Ananda Marga, Paul Alister, Ross Dunn and Tim Anderson, were convicted of conspiracy to murder the then leader of the National Front in Australia, and suspected of bombing the Sydney Hilton Hotel during the Commonwealth Heads of Government Meeting in 1978. The NSW Government granted each a pardon in 1985.

3 landbridge: landbridges were areas between Thailand and Kampuchea which, by the agreement of all combatants in the area, were war-free zones. Supplies passed into Kampuchea through these landbridges.

4 Shiva and Shakti: in Indian thought, male and female aspects of fundamental cosmic energy.

5 Psychosynthesis is a school of psychotherapy developed by Robert Assagioli. It sees the psyche as consisting of an unchanging self, witness to all phenomena, and different sub-personalities. Actualisation and integration of these sub-personalities, and realisation of the Self are seen as the goals of existence: thus, it has a strong transpersonal basis.

Suzanne Vernon

'The real theology is who I am, how I'm living this life, and how I relate to God here every day. Women have an instinctive sixth sense about that, which we have always kept secret, while barely tolerating the mucking about (of institutional theology and philosophy).'

Born in 1950, Suzanne Vernon works as a teacher of handicapped children. Her story is one of a search for healing, a mode of prayer and spiritual direction which the institutional structures of the Catholic Church could not provide for her when she needed them most. Equally, it is a story of her growing awareness of the exclusion of women's language, gifts, patterns and experiences from the church, and of the growth of her feminist spirituality. Suzanne is currently active in the Wollongong branches of MOW (Movement for the Ordination of Women), and WATAC (Women and the Australian Church), two inter-denominational Christian groups which address the position of women in the church, and in movements for making available better quality education to lay Catholic adults.

Suzanne Vernon was raised in a strongly Catholic family. She left her Catholic high school with a strong personal faith, and a deep sense of a knowing and loving God who accepted her totally. She trained as a teacher at Sydney University, and married an ex-seminarian. Her story begins with the birth of her first child.

My first child was born after eight and a half years of marriage. I was blissfully happy with the pregnancy, but at the same time afraid of the future. The second child came a year later, and at that time I felt strongly that I hadn't been a child myself. I was terrified. I realised I needed a mother, not another baby. After the birth of my second child I was on my own (having moved to Wollongong). Before, I had lived a couple of blocks from my parents and, although I used to fight with them, they were always there. I was still part of the family, and could call on them anytime. Now I was realising that I was central to a new life and family. I was angry and depressed, lonely and bitterly unhappy. Although I loved the babies, that was all there was.

I cut myself off from religion when I was pregnant; I felt as if I didn't belong in a church. I felt a revulsion to celibate men being at the altar, while I was grossly pregnant and thinking different thoughts. Thinking about my fertility — I remember being struck by my physical well-being. I had often had had period pains, and bad skin, and had not been a well person. When I was pregnant, I was more fully alive physically than I had ever been. I wanted to celebrate that, and there was no place to do it in church. That seemed wrong. I was very randy, and thought about sex all the time. It didn't fit in at church, so rather than upset myself, I stayed away.

When Marisa was born, I felt abandoned by God. I had done all the birthing preparations, and been reasonably successful with my first child. With her, it was a much greater physical strain. I couldn't do it, and I couldn't meet the expectations I had of myself. I thought I was a failure, and, if that was the case, there was nothing to sustain me anymore. Perhaps all the judgements I'd made about myself had been completely wrong — where I thought I had great inner strength, I didn't. There was an enormous sense of loss. It was the death of the old person I had been — the child that wasn't a child. Then it was extremely difficult being mother of two young children in a house far away from home. The sense of failure kept on compounding itself. I didn't try to pray the way I had before. I felt so abandoned that I couldn't. It was as if the person I talked to had gone. I described it then as post-natal depression. It's only now that I recognise that it was a deep spiritual crisis. The way I described myself then was as a refugee. There was a great deal of news reporting at the time on boat people and refugees from Vietnam. I can remember thinking that I was one of them. I was floundering around on an open sea with nowhere to go. I was waiting for someone to come and rescue me, almost powerless to do anything. At the same time, I was scathingly critical of myself for feeling like that, when I had a home, two beautiful babies, and a husband. I had worked for years and been professionally successful. I had everything to be grateful for, and yet I was a homeless person, a refugee.

I found no help at my local church. We used to go to Mass there, and it was extremely depressing. We went to the glassed-in room at the back for children. There would be teenagers there, wanting to smoke, and being rude if you wanted to listen to the Mass. The sermons made me feel more distant than ever from the church. It seemed to me they were concerned mainly with rules, and with haranguing people for having secular concerns. Yet there was a complete ignorance of the fact that people could appear to be happy in their secular lives but at the same time be in dire need of something spiritual.

We went from church to church to find someone who might be sympathetic. I did find someone, at Albion Park, about half an hour's drive away. We used to go to Mass there to hear his sermons. Sermons were very important to me. They were the only contact I had, apart from attempts to write essays and read at home. I had no relationship with other Catholics in the parish. I didn't have time. Going to Mass was a major performance. The priest would say, if you can't come on time, don't come. I'd be desperate to get there, and I might arrive ten minutes late. It doesn't matter how well you prepare, you can't get two young kids into the car and on time somewhere easily. Then the nightmare of battling the babies all the way through the Mass, so you could sit and not disturb everyone around; the constant feeling of humiliation that you couldn't bring it off, and then going home feeling worse than ever.

I don't know what the turning point was. A young cousin of mine came to live in the house, and I began to make tentative steps out. Something drove me out. I think it was God. There was a vestige in there that said, no, what you are thinking in your deepest depression is wrong. Don't indulge any more. I joined a play group committee. I heard of a course that was being run by the Aquinas Academy[1] at St Mary's College in Wollongong. That was the start of the upward climb — from there I reestablished contact with the church. I enrolled in the Academy courses and, at the same time, began correspondence courses with the Randwick Centre, one on St Paul and one on John. All this brought me back to God.

I began to do a 'Parent Effectiveness Training Course'[2]. My husband found great difficulties with it. He didn't think it was valid to give so much attention to people's feelings. We had a crisis in our marriage, and undertook some counselling. It was a very positive experience — we learned a lot about each other and about ourselves. I realised that I'd been cast in a role from very young, and my inner child needed to be nurtured. I started to see that I couldn't solve all the problems at once and that I was not failing at this dreadful game. The biggest change was recognising that

how I am, and how I think about an issue is important. I
don't have to think it's stupid. It's what I think and what I
do and that's me, and it's good to be me. It may be different
from everybody else, or it may not be, but it's how I am.
That's given me enormous freedom to be different and to
feel in control of my life. I still have the same husband, the
same parents and the same house, but something inside
me has come home. It's as if I've stopped trying to validate
myself by judging my successes and failures against those of
other people, be they parents, priests, teachers or husband.
I accept that I don't have to be afraid of the feminine, the
competitive or the masculine in me. All those things that
can force you into a ridiculous fight with yourself over
something that doesn't need to be questioned, because it's
who you are.

I admired the way the counsellor led my husband and
myself towards a more healthy understanding of ourselves
and our relationship. I felt that those qualities he had
should be available to us in our spiritual life. Why was it
when the church harangued us all the time about secular
interests that we actually had to go outside the church to
find what we were looking for — a deep inner spiritual
strength and self-knowledge. When I've talked about this
to other people, they have agreed, especially women. They
have often gone through years of psychiatric work, and say
they are doing it to find a confessor, a spiritual guide.

I began to look for a spiritual guide. I'd been reading
about developing spirituality, and I found that I wanted
to pray again, not just as emotional fulfilment, but as a
constant pattern in my life. I wanted to make my life
more prayerful by being prayerful. I had learned from
counselling that, although I can be very undisciplined, I
need to be a reasonably regular person. I then tried to
say the Offices regularly. It's a set of prayers that are said
morning, midday and evening. It's a community prayer,
that's the nice thing about it. You can be praying at home,

but you know that all over the world people are reading or saying the same psalm at the same time. But I found it tiring and stressful. I would get very angry if I were interrupted, and I took that as an indicator that it wasn't the right kind of prayer for me.

At that stage, a priest was doing some prayer work with the handicapped children I teach, to enhance their spiritual life. He was leading us in meditations which he directed to the children, but I did them as well. They were mainly imaginative prayer. You would put yourself back into scriptural times, or be in your own special room and look for Jesus and what he would say to you. I don't think those techniques are deep prayer — they are more analytical, revealing knowledge of yourself. And they were stressful — it was like having a catharsis twice a day. I couldn't do it regularly. Nevertheless, one of my key religious experiences came from the type of meditative prayer I learned from him.

I was at Lake Illawarra, looking at the water. I tried to reenact a prayer he had been leading us in. It was seeing Jesus coming towards me from the lake. I started to do the prayer, and then it came to life. There was a canoeist gliding past, and suddenly I saw Jesus coming towards me on the canoe. He looked a gentle nice sort of bloke, very friendly and empathetic. He pulled up, and I climbed in. I had been thinking, wouldn't it be lovely to go out there and canoe. Without a word, we went out into the lake. Suddenly it appeared that I had opened up, and the lake had come into me — I was full of the lake. I found it such a powerful experience that I can't trivialise it by trying to repeat it again and again.

Then I tried reading scriptures, and responding to them word by word, another method that I had read about. That was good, but it fell short of prayer — it was an intellectual exercise. If there is one thing I do, it is intellectualise. All the time — think, think, think. That's me, that's not prayer.

I began knocking on doors, ringing people up, asking people if they could tell me something about prayer, if they would be my spiritual director. Priests were horrified. I began to think that asking someone to be your spiritual director must be like asking someone to marry you. It must be much more deeply involved than just getting a bit of help in prayer.

Eventually I read an advertisement in the paper for some tapes by Marianne McClelland[3]. Wow, everything happened. This was it. Something different, easy to do — ten minute segments of breathing and relaxation that I could do while dinner was cooking. Once again, there was the use of imagination. I worked with the tapes for a while, and then I realised I needed even more. Marianne came down to Wollongong and led us in prayer there. She taught us other kinds of prayer — walking prayer, and mantra prayer, where you chant a word over and over again. It's very calming. In doing that you are centreing. What I had been searching for was a way of centreing. It took me a long time to work out that there are many different traditions of prayer. Often, a person's personality will determine which is the best type for them. I realised that my discomfort with traditional forms wasn't necessarily an off thing. It was telling me I needed to know more. So I read works by Matthew Fox[4] and Basil Pennington. Gradually I began to understand that real prayer is not me speaking or performing, but me coming home to and being silent to the God within. To pray like that, you have to believe in the God within. I know now what faith is. It's saying that it's worth spending forty minutes sitting with this God.

The priest who had led us in meditation at school and I had begun to be interested in the role of women in the church. We went to a meeting in Sydney to hear Patricia Brennan[5] speak. I began to realise that the trouble I'd been having in getting a spiritual life of my own on the road was that there was a whole part of life that was being denied in the church. Suddenly the lid was lifted on my secret feelings, which I had felt made me part of some sub-culture, almost like witchcraft, which should be driven out. Patricia validated what I had thought all along: that theology was an intellectual philosophical pastime, done merely to amuse people, of very little relationship to the kind of life I live here at home. The underground shared empathy that women have between each other, where we know what it means to relate to somebody, that is often left out of our experience in church. You might go there, and not feel welcome, precisely because you have two little children and you are vulnerable. The way women come together to share and help when they know someone's in need is more Christlike than any ritualised liturgy. When a woman has a baby, her fertility must be celebrated. We don't need a liturgy for cleansing after impurity, which is what we had in the church.

I saw Patricia as a role model, a woman who could speak for those who couldn't and explain that this is how we experience each other. I asked her, at that first meeting, how I could be like her — what training she had done. She explained that her training had been in the school of life. I knew she was on the right track, because when I look at seminary training, in which I'm very interested, I still can't get over the hurdle of institutionalised theology and philosophy. The real theology is who I am, how I'm living this life, and how I relate to God here every day. Women have an instinctive sixth sense about this, which we have always kept secret, while barely tolerating the other mucking about. It's all part of recognising our own inner child, our need to love and relate, and not putting each other down because we are vulnerable.

I also found in the women I met at the first ordination meeting a great model for a ministry — ministry meaning how you serve. Being a Christian is not just a personal experience — there is a sense of community too. That's how we experience Jesus most strongly. Ministry means bringing Jesus to people. That was lost to me when I needed it most. All I can feel is a great responsibility. I have been given something, and I want to share it with others. Ministry is not just being a priest behind an altar.

After meeting Patricia and recognising a sense of direction, it all seemed to come together like a jigsaw falling into place. I had just completed a Master of Arts at Macquarie University in teaching mentally handicapped children. That gave me a great sense of competence. I wanted to apply the skills I used in acquiring that degree to my work, not only at school, but in religion. I felt called to share some perception of God in my life.

I then was motivated to go with Patricia to America. I wanted to do a course on the gospel of John, given by Sandra Schneider, a writer on women and spirituality I very much liked.

It was an incredibly bold step to go to America. I knew it wasn't just a trip overseas — it was a trip away from my old dependent self. At first I thought I would go alone. When I went to the travel agency to book, I was nearly physically ill. I thought, I can't do it. I came home, and felt terrible, because I had paid the large fees at Boston College. I almost bullied Patricia into going with me. She was off to London, so we arranged to go that way. We spent the first week in the States doing interviews in Washington for a radio programme Patricia was making. I had selected the people to interview from newspaper cuttings and books that I had read at home. It was so bold, but I had an incredible belief in the rightness of it, and in my power to do it.

During the time in the States, I was aware of a growing personal spiritual authority. The women we spoke to said that we need to author ourselves. It was as if I'd gone to find a phrase to tell me what I was doing. Teresa Kane said that we need a sense of timeliness. I knew that was right. She also said, we need to respond to that sense of timeliness and that it can come upon us unexpectedly. She had acted without the agreement of her religious group when she spoke to the Pope, and she did that because of her own sense of timeliness and authority. She was the first woman to address the Pope on the needs of women in the church, and ordination, on his first visit to America. It's a long time ago now, so she's almost the matriarch, the pope of women.

All the women I admired had a great personal warmth. They were prepared to put their arms around you, to share, to treat you as if you were a sister. I shared a flat in Boston with three other women, and that was a great experience. I felt a positive surge of life as I realised, yes, even on my own, so far from home, I am real, and God is still with me. Not only that, but I can reach out and experience God in other people too. As well there was the academic input from Sandra Schneider, which was brilliant. It showed me how good scholarship can lead to a greater spirituality, and that theological study doesn't have to be dry. I would love to put together a course on how to better experience the theology of our own lives.

I was away for only three weeks, but not only did we pack a lot into our itinerary, a lot was packed into me in that time. The trip changed many of my ideas. I had had a rather crude idea of women as priests. Now, I'm much happier to say, quite strongly, that we need to accept our own ministries. I agree with women who question the need for ordination in that patriarchal pattern. It is necessary still to fight for that, but it's much more important for us all to acknowledge what we have, and to use it. I learned more about performing liturgies ourselves, recognising that when we come together, that is a basis for liturgy. It's recognising the theology of experience. I remember one of the sisters I was staying with in Boston suggested we had a glass of wine one afternoon. She put four glasses on the table. I realised by the way she put them out that they were special. She had a little bread roll, and then it was a matter of going with her as she led us in a spontaneous liturgy, which actually had started as a pre-dinner drink. She taught me how to see things in our every day actions that are sacred, and to make them even more so. That's what our liturgy needs to be.

I came back less frightened of personal failure. The spirit, the God within, is bigger than me, or any individual. I stopped thinking we always had to import someone from Sydney or America to help us in Wollongong. I was emboldened to run a small scripture course myself, at my local parish. I did a four week session on the Gospel of Mark. It was enormously hard work because I didn't want to prepare it on too superficial a level. Then I realised that there was a lot more work to be done in setting up education programmes here. I'd love to see more diocesan involvement. I'm getting political, in that I'm asking the bishops to do things for us. I'm not the only one. Other people are also asking whether we will get some adult education programmes in Wollongong. When Catholics say they want an education, they want three kinds. They want to know about scripture, they want to know about the laws of the Church, and they want spiritual help. Often people don't know which of those things they want, and often they are interconnected. The Church itself has a certain authority, and it needs to use that. We all contribute financially by going constantly to those meetings on Sunday. Why should we have to duplicate, to use people's private energy? It consumes a lot of time and energy to organise anything outside of job and family. We should have people in the parishes who are trained, and prepared to run lecture courses and provide facilities like books. We do have some counsellors and psychologists at Centre Care, the Catholic counselling service in Wollongong, but there is a great vacuum of spiritual assistance at the parish level. Even within our own community, we have the resources to give spiritual help to each other, but it does need to be organised by a group that already has the structure.

Openness to sharing is the most important quality in spiritual growth. When people are open they can perceive possibilities. It's not the person in authority who has the answers. I have always been awed by those who are competent, and have titles. Studying with Sandra Schneider, and meeting all people overseas, I started to realise that success in religion is the opposite to what we think it is. It's almost powerlessness and failure. If you appear to have all the answers, and you have it right, you are in a bad way. What's most important is openness to possibilities you have not imagined. Things outside my control may happen, and I can't legislate for, or anticipate them. I can only go with them, when they happen. That is openness to God.

What I'm doing now is working with groups like Movement for the Ordination of Women (MOW) and Women and the Australian Church (WATAC), trying to use them as structures to address the needs of women and to put that challenge to the institutional church. We need women's groups, to share our stories and validate each other. We should keep networking with existing groups — radical and conservative. Until I went to the States, I had thought it was a great weakness that there were so many women's groups, all doing different things. I thought, why don't they all get together? Then I talked with an amazing woman in Chicago who works with women who are in gaol, or just out of gaol, or homeless. She explained that we are all in it together, there is only one women's movement, but we all do different jobs, and there is no fear in that. We don't have to conform to a patriarchal idea where there has to be only one kind of theology, one kind of spirituality and one kind of organisation. So, back here at home, the Catholic Women's League, WOTAC and the Uniting Church

are all in the same movement, and we don't defuse each
other.

I can't see how the church can keep denying ordination.
I have just read a book by Schillebeeckx on ministry. He
suggests that changes in the Catholic church will take place
differently from the way I had assumed. I had thought
change would come from above. You lobby, and get people
to change their minds, and then they send the new rule
back down and everything is fixed. Actually, it appears that
the tradition is for the institutional church to ratify already
existing states of affairs. For instance, in the early church,
deacons had been functioning for some time before rules
were made. Therefore, the work I am doing to change the
status of women in the church, is preparing the ground for
a future ratification. It doesn't mean I'm holding my breath,
waiting for acknowledgement. It means that everything I'm
doing now is meaningful, and will eventually seep into
the communal knowledge of the church, and be ratified.
Issues that should be addressed immediately are inclusive
language. Being denied in language is a terrible form
of torture, like brainwashing. We need different kinds of
services. We have only one kind of Mass, and the usual
set of songs. People could be suffering the most shocking
grief or loneliness and it could not be acknowledged in the
liturgy of the day.

I still go to my local church regularly. It gets harder and
harder, and sometimes I can't quite bring it off. However,
I usually do some kind of communal worship weekly.
Sometimes it's a liturgy at a group meeting, but most of
the time it would be to Mass on Sunday with the family.
I try to say the Morning Office every day. It's very brief,
and I use it as an initiation into some quiet time. I run
through a physical relaxation, and then I use a mantra to
stay centred, to be with the God within. It's not stressful
— I don't mind if I'm interrupted, and yet I can have a
very deep religious experience with it. The way I pray now

is almost like the way I prayed as a child. It's different, in that I don't have a discussion with God, as I would with my mother. Now, it's a wordless being. There is no hassle, there is nothing I am trying to compete with or match up to. That experience is so beautiful and simple. I had always thought that you had to be very good and saintly to do that. When you finished, then you got up and everything was in a rosy mist. You never said another bad word and you didn't go crook at the kids. But it doesn't mean that — it's just that you centre for a while. What I hope for my spiritual future is that, gradually, as I become more understanding of myself and others, that prayer time will come to infuse more and more of my life. That's my goal, and I'm not too hassled if it doesn't happen tomorrow. I know that everything else I do in my life contributes somehow to that.

If I've had an especially long session in the morning, and then a bad day later — trouble with the kids, problems at work — I'm not hassled. It's not exactly preventative, but I'm not so self-judging. I'm not heaping scorn on myself. Rather I tell myself that it was a bad day and hope tomorrow is better.

I have been incredibly blessed in my life, but I do have a problem that is starting to become serious. My father has been very ill, and that is hard. Meditation has helped me to accept that I'm not my father's parent. I want to take responsibility for him, and I sit with my God, who lets me know He is my father's God, and I must let be what is. Even if something terrible were to happen to my family, a great challenge to my faith, I feel confident that my knowledge of God would stay with me. It has to do with going with life, an acceptance of what happens.

I see God now primarily as Goddess, as mother. For a long time, I have been searching for mother, so in calling God that I come home to many things. I struggled for a long time trying to picture God and Jesus. I would get stuck on what they were wearing. I don't do that now. We are in a 'cloud of unknowing', as the book says, and I can accept that. It's back to that childhood sense of the person you talk to comfortably and relate with. River of life — the life force — the God within.

---

1 Aquinas Academy: established in Sydney in 1945 by a Marist priest to conduct adult education classes based on Thomist philosophy, the Aquinas Academy today runs courses on a wide variety of spiritual subjects for both Catholics and non-Catholics.

2 Parent Effectiveness Training: a set of ideas and practices aimed at improving relations between parents and children.

3 Marianne McClelland is a Catholic nun who gives courses to help people deepen their spirituality.

4 Matthew Fox is an American priest who has written extensively on 'creation spirituality,' a recent Christian theological understanding which places more emphasis on joy and love than on judgment and guilt, and is sensitive to feminist and ecological values.

5 Patricia Brennan is a Sydney doctor and prominent activist in MOW.

Paul Bourke

'You could say that religion is the opium of the people — it puts everything in place for you and numbs the mind. The reverse is actually true. If you are really practising, you are forced to face issues and deal with them, rather than just saying that it is God's will or some other platitude.'

Bourke's is the story of a gradual movement from a hippie alternative lifestyle, where he pursued a 'hodge-podge' of spiritual teachings, to a serious commitment to Tibetan Buddhism, a commitment which has placed him in such responsible and demanding roles as director of a large spiritual centre and manager of a Buddhist publishing house. The steady yet undramatic nature of his spiritual progress and his emphasis on caring for others as the crux of his spiritual practice give a different perspective on Tibetan Buddhism from accounts which focus on the amazing powers and arcane disciplines of lamas living in remote mountains. Also interesting is his description of the evolution of his relationship with his gurus, and his conscious decision to pursue relationship as a means of spiritual development.

Tibetan Buddhism is one of the Mahayana (literally, great vehicle) schools of Buddhism. Mahayana differs from Hinyana (lesser vehicle) in the number of spiritual techniques it offers seekers, and in its belief that each sentient being *can* and *should* become enlightened. An enlightened being vows never to leave this realm of existence until all beings are freed of suffering. Buddhism was brought to Tibet in the eight century by the great Indian scholar Atisha. The teachings spread and flourished there, and were preserved in their entirety, including the complete tantric teachings, even after the demise of Buddhism in India. After the Chinese takeover of Tibet, many lamas went to India where, in Dharamsala and McLeod Ganj, the exiled Tibetan government is now located. Today Tibetan teachers can be found throughout the Western world. The Foundation for the Preservation of the Mahayana Tradition (FPMT) was set up by a Tibetan lama, Lama Yeshe (one of Paul Bourke's teachers) to preserve the teachings of the Tibetan Buddhist vision, particularly those of the Gelugpa sect. Since Lama Yeshe's death in 1984, the FPMT has been headed by Lama Zopa, Rinpoche.

Paul Bourke was born in 1950 and raised in Sydney in a deeply Catholic family. He drifted away from his childhood faith in his teens and dropped out of Sydney University in the late sixties. His travels took him and his girlfriend to India.

We had planned to go to Kashmir, but there was flooding there and so we decided to go to Nepal for a couple of weeks. We spent a little time in Kathmandu, and then one day we went out to Boudnath[1]. There we met an Australian woman who told us about a course in Buddhism run by two Tibetan lamas. While travelling, I'd continued to read about Hindu philosophy, but I knew nothing about Buddhism. I was particularly taken by the Tibetans in Nepal. They were a warm, wonderful people, with something special about them. This woman had done a month long meditation course with these two particular lamas, and she raved about it. We gradually became friends with her, moved out to that area, and decided to stay for the course in November. In the meantime, she took us up to Kopan[2] to meet the lamas. It was Lama Yeshe who I remember. I had some preconception of what a Tibetan lama would be like, something special. I remember being a little disappointed. He wasn't like that at all — he was quite ordinary. He gave me a guava, and I didn't like guavas at all.

It was the fifth course run, in November '73, and it was intense. I had never done anything like it in my life. We started at five am with a couple of hours of meditation. I'd done a little bit of meditation before with yoga, just breathing, nothing serious. I remember my legs killing me. The lectures were long, and it was very demanding. You fell into bed at nine pm. In the beginning, it was as if everything was falling into place. It was as it Rinpoche[3] was verbalising thoughts that had been floating around in my head in a non-connected way. The main concept was the teaching on Bodhicitta[4], the importance of caring for others, happiness being due to the kindness of others, the interconnectedness of living beings. Rinpoche prefaced each lecture with a long talk on developing Bodhicitta motivation. Then we got into the hells, and spent a long time there. My mind was growing darker, thinking, this is just like Catholicism — it's scare tactics. What a disappointment, here I am with another formal religion. The whole course was going through this cycle of depression — you could almost feel the weight in the tent. Then one night Lama Yeshe came in and gave a lecture. He blew everyone apart. Within minutes, the place was in laughter and the energy was blissful. All I remember was his making fun of us, and how bad we felt. Basically he was patting us on the head and saying, it's all right dear, you are wonderful, you are all Buddhas. That was a turning point in the course, so, by the end I was on an up peak again.

We went from Kopan to a small place some hours by bus from Kathmandu. There was a guest house there, and we took a room. We stayed for a month. I hadn't intended to do this, but it developed into a time of meditation, and going over the notes from the course, and colouring in pictures of deities. During that time, the teachings came back to me strongly. As I look back over my spiritual evolution, that course was a turning point in my life, in the sense of having spiritual experiences rather than just reading about them. It had a profound effect. The actual lectures were happening on one level, but my mind was going through an experience on another level that I only had inklings of at the time. We were in an intense dharma environment — our washing was done for us, our food was cooked — for a month, just focussing the mind. As scattered as the mind was at the time, putting yourself in that intense teaching situation is a purification in itself. It burns up a lot of crap, so that the mind is less deluded, less immersed under the weight of the fantasising and anger that goes through it every day. You are a little detached, observing those energies rather than caught up in them. Even now, years later, when I do a retreat I'm never satisfied with how well I have done it, but I come away with my mind definitely clearer.

I left Nepal and travelled through Asia back to Australia. I got back here at the end of June '74. I didn't know what I was going to do. Some old friends were in Sydney, and they had moved up to the North Coast near Grafton, so I went up there. It was the time when everyone was getting out of Sydney — the whole alternative thing. The lamas were due in Southern Queensland in August. It was the first time they had been out of Nepal. I decided I'd definitely do the meditation course again. I did that, in September, in Diamond Valley. Same course as in Nepal, but different in an Australian environment. The food was good and healthy. I don't function very well in the cold, and it had been

cold in Nepal. Even though September was a bit chilly in
Diamond Valley, it was pleasant. It was getting into spring,
camp fires, boiling billies over the fire at night, a little more
talking with other people. So somehow the course seemed
more integrated. Also, as it was my second time, it wasn't
so strange or intense.

From that course, some land and money was donated
to start a permanent centre, the Chenreizig Institute, in
Australia. One of the nuns who came with the lamas stayed
behind to get it off the ground, and was the first director.
We stayed on after the course to help. I had nowhere to go,
and I liked the idea of having something happening here
in Australia. That was a pleasant time. We'd eat together,
and have some meditation in the morning. In the night,
we'd discuss one of the chapters of the Lam Rim: a basic
text of the Gelugpa sect. During the day, we'd work on the
property. When we finished, we came down to Sydney and
spent Christmas with parents.

After that time, I somehow lost touch with Chenreizig,
which was the centre of Buddhism in Australia at that
time. Eventually I settled near Grafton, on a lovely property
on the banks of a river. I stayed there for three years,
trying to live some kind of alternative lifestyle but basically
just hanging about. It was a pretty lazy time. Doing some
sound mixing for a friend's rock and roll band, reading,
meditating, doing Tai Chi and macrobiotic cooking. Then
the band broke up, in late '78. Towards mid '79, another
band was coming together, with a few of the same guys
who were old friends of mine. I was thinking about doing
a mixing job for that band as well, but not sure of the
lifestyle involved — late nights, lots of booze and dope.
Around that time, I got a call from Yeshe Kadro (YK),
the director of Chenreizig, saying that the lamas were
coming again in September. They were giving two courses,
one on meditation and one on tantra. I decided that I
wanted to do them. I don't know that it was a conscious

decision to get back into Buddhism, but it was some kind of dissatisfaction with the lifestyle I was leading. I wasn't really going anywhere spiritually. YK said that if I helped with the preparation for the course, they would support me until the course time.

That was a full on period, lots of people building to get the place ready for the lamas. It was their first visit in three years. I had some building skills, so when I got there YK gave me some plans and said we want the house built there. It was a bit of a shock, but with the help of a couple of other guys we had it finished in time for the lamas. I developed a role as an organiser — it's my personality to step into control. YK appreciated the help, and we got along well. Gradually I became more involved in the organisational side of Chenreizig, and that somehow tied me into the place.

Then I did the course with Lama Yeshe. It was the first major tantric[5] initiation I had taken. I took it with the idea that I wanted to have some kind of daily commitment to tie me in more strongly. I had avoided tantric teachings prior to that because I didn't feel that I could keep the daily commitments. Tantra was good for me. Christianity always has rules, but, with tantra, you don't impose things on yourself. You take what is happening and use it, being in the middle of the experience rather than trying to put it outside yourself. For example, from a Christian point of view, the way you deal with anger is to say that you shouldn't feel angry — it's a sin. As a Buddhist, in the heat of the anger, I try to redirect the energy, to cool it out. I try to make the mind calm and quiet by breathing. I don't have many situations now where I lose control with people — it's more likely to happen with inanimate objects. Once I've calmed myself down and no longer want to smash the thing, I start looking at what's gone on, analysing it. The inanimate thing doesn't work. At one time, it was working well for me, the next time it's not. It hasn't changed, it's just my attitude. So I try to change my attitude, and see the uselessness of anger, and how it burns up one's positive karma, rather than just saying I shouldn't be angry, and forcing the energy down.

Towards the end of the course, I went to Lama with three other friends, and for the first time asked him if he would be my teacher, my guru. He said, I already am. We said, yes Lama, but we have never formally requested it before. He said he was delighted. I felt a mixture of emotion and awe for him. For some time, I had had a thing with him where he would always be there when I needed to see him. During '76, when I went up to Diamond Valley, there were a lot of people there, and it was difficult to see him. I was out walking somewhere, and there he was, and we had a chat. My connection with him continued like that, right through. He taught the whole tantra course himself, and I found his teaching amazing, so clear. His English was good, and he had a skilful way of interpreting Buddhist teachings, and presenting them in a way that was palatable for a Westerner.

I decided that I wanted to help at the centre. I had no commitments so I could say, I don't care what I'm doing, but I'll hang around and do what I can for the place. YK was happy with the idea, and I became involved in trying to make money for Chenreizig. Our first idea was to build a spec. house and sell it. It wasn't very successful, because we were pretty amateurish. The reality of a group like that is that everyone is gung-ho at the beginning, but working over twelve months we tended to lose sight of the goal. Fortunately we sold the house and made a little, nothing like the projected profit. For the next year, I imported goods from Hong Kong, Nepal and Delhi and sold them in conjunction with the centre which had started in Melbourne.

There was no lama at Chenreizig in that period, although There were some monks and nuns. There were meditations, practices and discussions but I was becoming

immersed in working for the place. It was a good thing to
be doing. By your work for the centre, you help people
by making the dharma available to them. Up until that
time in my life, I had been not so much self-centred as
self-involved. Although I was married, we only mixed with
our little circle, and tended to avoid getting involved in
large group activities. Living at Chenreizig, with all its
residents, eating in a communal kitchen, working with the
people there was as much a lesson for my mind as any kind
of formal teaching. But, I had to draw on the teachings to
deal with day to day living. It's all right to have in your
prayers and meditations the thought of working for the
benefit of all sentient beings. However, you may wish that
the sentient beings were not the particular ones around
you at the time. You have to bring that aspiration down to
dealing with the people you are with, rather than having it
as a goal that is easy to recite in the mornings.

Those couple of years were difficult. When a centre is
new, there is a lot to be worked out. Particularly in those
days, going through the transisition from the love and
peace era. If a centre is going to survive, as Lama says, until
the next Buddha comes, you have to be organised. There
were two factions, those who wanted that, and those who
didn't.

In '82 I went back to the East for the first dharma
celebrations. Lama Yeshe's idea was to get students and
sangha from all over the world together in India for a
couple of concentrated periods to have teachings from
different high lamas. It was a wonderful six weeks. I lived in
a little hut in Bodh Gaya and walked up in the mornings to
the stupa where Jonathan Landau was leading meditations
for lay people. Then I had the morning free to do some
practice in my room. After lunch there would be initiations
and teachings until eleven o'clock at night. A few meetings
in the mornings to discuss dharma in the West, and FPMT
affairs.

Towards the end of that period, YK decided that it was time for a change in direction. A few names for a new director of Chenreizig had been given to Lama. YK had been hassling me to do it, because I had been working fairly closely with her and it would be an easy transition. It was at a picnic that Lama asked me who was going to take over Chenreizig. I'd been hedging on it until that very moment but when he asked me to do it I made the decision. I said that I could do it.

By that time, I was coming to understand that I was not the sort of person to become a monk. I don't have a desire to renounce the world, to withdraw physically from it. I have some understanding that the path to happiness isn't through worldly success or the accumulation of wordly goods. My path at this stage in my life is one of trying to work for the dharma on a mundane level, maintaining some personal practice and integrating that with my life. Being the director of Chenreizig fitted in with that concept of my path. I remember thinking at the beginning of my time, no matter how bad this job gets, I'll hang in for three years. This is going to be the hardest three years in my life, but it's exactly what I need. I have seen what YK went through running a voluntary organisation where people live. Everyone has their own idea of how things should be. It's not like Bodh Gaya where people come and get involved in the teachings and then go home. I didn't get along perfectly with all the people there, although some of them I still consider as close family. So I could see it wasn't going to be easy.

I remember it as a period of hard work rather than hard dharma. I received a small allowance, fifty dollars a week, food and lodging. I had some money saved, which I was depleting. The director is responsible for everything — the accounting system, policies, resident issues, work group periods, organising courses, finances. There was a committee, and people looked after different areas, but I was involved with each of the people and each of the areas. For a lot of that time, I was also regional coordinator of the other Australian centres in Adelaide, Bendigo, Melbourne and later Sydney. I dealt with our international office on current decisions and policy. Overall, it was a time of consolidation for Chenreizig, getting systems into place, finishing off buildings, trying to make plans for the future, getting resident policy sorted out. A lot of my job was dealing with people's problems. After meditation, there would quite often be someone on the doorstep with a problem.

I was always in a situation of compromise. You have an overview of something you are trying to create — your understanding of what Lama's vision for that facility is, and the policy from the organisation on centres. But then you have to reconcile that with what is existing at the time, particularly on a personal level. The place is full of people who have varying degrees of understanding of what the place is about, Lama's vision of the place, and the policy of the international organisation. Some new people have never met Lama. To them, it's a nice community in the country where there are Buddhist teachings. There are others who are old students, whose main concern is the practice. They are not very interested in organisation. There are others who have family problems. Your decisions affect all these people to different degrees.

It's an incredible job from a spiritual point of view, because it stretches you beyond your limits. You are not making a decision that someone implements and that is it. It's not like being a politician, although there are those kind of skills involved, and it's not like being an arbitrator, although there is some of that involved too. It's like trying to steer a huge unwieldly thing through a mass of people without harming anyone. You have to weigh up the long term development of the place against the immediate needs of the people. At the same time, you have to be aware of your feelings towards these people and how that influences your decisions. There were some heated arguments at community meetings. Many people saw what I was doing as a threat to them, so I got some heavy personal attacks.

Spiritually, on a really earthy level, that period was an incredible development for me. It made me more confident, more outgoing, more able to deal with people. Before I moved back to Chenreizig, my main way of dealing with conflicts was to remove myself from them. Now, if there's a problem, I'm much more able to deal with it. I can make a decision, understanding that although it may not be perfect, something has to be done. That extends very much now into my personal life.

From '79 Lama went to America on tours, and Rinpoche came here. I started to develop an affinity with him. In certain practices, you visualise your guru, and I always used to wonder if it was Lama or Rinpoche, because they were inseparable. I had always done courses with both of them, and Lama is Rinpoche's teacher. Somehow my relationship with Rinpoche changed from what it had been at that first course in Kopan. At that time Rinpoche was an austere skinny little monk who sat bolt upright and looked about to fly off to the moon. Lama was a big rolling mother figure, warm and wonderful. I found Rinpoche awe inspiring and unapproachable, and Lama kind and soft, someone who made everyone laugh. Over the years, their roles reversed. By the end, I was scared of Lama. There were certain things I was reluctant to tell him. I could tell Rinpoche anything — he oozed compassion. Lama died in '84. It wasn't a shock because he had been sick for a long time. He should have been dead years before. It was just through his own power that he managed to keep himself alive. Sometimes he'd look like death, so grey and sick. Then he would do a short retreat, and he'd come back looking wonderful. He had a lot of power over his own body. When he died,

I was concerned for the organisation, because Lama had a real way of touching people. I had no doubts about Rinpoche's ability to take over. I thought he'd just change his manifestation, and become less of an austere retiring monk, and take on a more involved role. He has done that, incredibly skilfully.

At the end of my three years as director, Rinpoche told me that he thought it would be good if I did something different. By that time, he had taken over from Lama as my guru, and the head of the organisation who appointed or replaced directors. I asked if there were some difficulty. He just explained that karma changes — and sometimes it's good to do something else. He said that it looked highly beneficial for me to work for Wisdom[6] and that I should work it out with Nick[7]. I told Nick I didn't want to live in London, but I didn't care what else I did. He said it would be good if I ran the operation in Australia and made it more professional. Someone had been doing it for a while, but only part time. So I tidied up at Chenreizig and moved to Sydney in '85.

I started off knowing nothing about the publishing industry. I had a good friend in publishing who was and is an invaluable advisor. To support myself, I set up a small cleaning business which I worked at for a few hours each day to pay for rent, food and living. I've developed Wisdom to the point now where it's turning over almost $50 000 a year. Last year, Nick asked me to try to get it to a point where I could work full time for Wisdom. We made a deal where I would get some wages and a percentage of the profit. Since then, I have cut back on my cleaning so all that I do now is a few hours in the evening to supplement my income.

It's wonderful to be working with my own energy rather than trying to make decisions with a committee where you have to convince everyone before you can take a step. In Australia and New Zealand, I am Wisdom: I import the books, I do all the promotion, and I sell them, though now I have a representative who travels for me. I'm about to move into publishing transcripts of Lama's teachings in a little booklet form. I like working with books. I have a strong affinity for them, and I have confidence in their quality. It's a continuation of what I was doing at Chenreizig, trying to create a facility to make dharma available to people. Rinpoche said in one of his teachings that the best thing you can do is to practise and become enlightened. If you can't do that, then it's good to teach, and, if you can't do that, then it's good to work for the dharma. That's the level I feel I'm at.

Overall, the effect of my spiritual practice over the years is that my view of the world now includes other people. The main emphasis of Tibetan Buddhism is Bodhicitta, developing the wish to be enlightened for the benefit of all sentient beings. I certainly don't have the Bodhicitta mind, but my mind has expanded fractionally to consider other people, to see that whatever I do impacts on them. Tibetan Buddhism has given me a purpose, a meaning in life. I don't feel that I am wandering around lost. I feel that I am heading in a direction, albeit slowly. I have a goal, and things I can do to move closer to it. Catholicism never offered me a method. Tibetan Buddhism has methods — it has ways for dealing with any situations. I may not know all the techniques, but I'm convinced they are there. I started off, as I did with everything that I looked at when I was searching, a little sceptical. But I found that it's an unbelievable system — it all holds together so well.

Rinpoche is my guru. I would do whatever he asked, even if I didn't want to. But he wouldn't give a command, just like that. I have confidence in him. With a certain level of spiritual development comes an ability to understand karma, to see the workings of things, the directions of the energies. When you take on a teacher, they say certain things will be good, and you understand and do them.

There are other things they say will be good to do, and because you don't understand, you don't do them. Some time down the track, it turns out it would have been good to have done them. I've both accepted advice, and had it turn out well, and not been able to do what was offered, and seen that it would have been better to have done so. That has happened enough now for me to give Rinpoche the benefit of the doubt.

My first course at Kopan, and the first tantric course with Lama Yeshe in '79 were like jolts. They created big changes in my life. From then on it's been much more subtle. It's much more an ongoing thing. If I do a retreat, I come out thinking that I notice a change. I am clearer, less caught up, less involved. Living in Sydney, I am caught up in restaurants, making money, music. I notice after just one meditation session of an hour and a half in the morning that my mind is clearer, the delusions have receded a bit and I have created a little space for myself.

My daily practice is getting my commitments done. That takes about an hour and a half. Commitments mean practices that I have undertaken to do in initiations[8] — reciting mantras and prayers and meditating. When there is enough time, I do a little concentration meditation, focussing on my breath or my mind. And I work with my mind through the day. The bustle and hustle of Sydney make it a good environment for maintaining a daily practice, trying to develop equanimity of mind, working with the practice of thought transformation — dealing with a situation by changing your own mind and not worrying so much about who's right and who's wrong. I enjoy Sydney. The noise and the pollution don't bother me. I was at Chenreizig recently for a few days. I found it refreshing to be there, but I couldn't go back unless I had something to do.

Some people think that in order to be involved seriously in spiritual practice you need to be alone. Obviously that's true for a monk or a nun, but otherwise it varies from person to person. I was married for almost ten years, and then we decided to go separate ways. I had a few passing involvements. Then I made a conscious decision to be in a relationship, because I believed it was better for my practice. When I'm alone, I tend to be efficient and a little cold. Being with another person forces me to consider them. Living with them, you are constantly confronted with the need for patience and understanding. I imagine it's like having children, although that terrifies me so far. I would find it extremely difficult to be with someone who is not into dharma. I have to have that commonality. When you make a long term commitment it can bring a lot of growth on an interpersonal level.

You could say that religion is the opium of the people — it puts everything in place for you and numbs the mind. The reverse is actually true. If you are really practising, you are forced to face issues and deal with them, rather than just saying that it is God's will or some other platitude. For people without any kind of practice, or any kind of view beyond this life, life must be extremely difficult. You are constantly dealing with situations, and you need the ability to step back and get a large picture. I don't know how people go on from one thing to the next without some kind of understanding of what they are doing, and without an ability to look into their emotions and the difficulties they have to face.

1 Boudnath is the site of a large stupa (memorial shrine to the Buddha), just outside Kathmandu. It is the home of a large Tibetan community, and of several Tibetan monasteries.

2 Kopan is a monastery/teaching institute near Boudnath established by Lama Zopa, Rinpoche, and Lama Yeshe, two Tibetan lamas (teachers). Both Nepalese and Western students of Tibetan Buddhism are taught there.

3   Rinpoche is an honorific term used in Tibetan Buddhism to describe the reincarnation of a lama who has died: such a being is said to bring the attainment of his predecessor into this life, and therefore to be especially spiritually developed.

4   Bodhicitta: the thought of attaining perfection in order to be qualified to benefit others.

5   tantra: profound teachings given by the Buddha, utilising sound, symbols, imagination and subtle energy, to attain enlightenment quickly.

6   Wisdom Publications publishes and distributes spiritual literature, principally books on Tibetan Buddhism.

7   Nick Rebush at that time was an Australian ordained in the Tibetan tradition and in charge of Wisdom Publications.

8   Initiation: transmission of energy from a qualified master, enabling the meditator to meditate on a particular deity, with the aim of energising in oneself the qualities the deity embodies.

John Cleary

'In my mid-thirties, I began to think that I had done something fundamentally wrong on a personal level. I went through three years of intense personal misery. Options were closing off — children. I begin to think, my God, what is going to happen to me? But you work through that. It's the old twenty-third psalm — you walk through the valley of death, and keep pushing through. You accept that ultimately all that matters in your life is the benefit you have been to those immediately around you.'

Born in 1948, John Cleary has been involved with the Salvation Army since the age of nine. Inspired by the Army's radical tradition, John feels that spirituality cannot be divorced from the world: religion should always provide a critique of society, and spiritual commitment should always lead to altruistic social action. At some considerable personal sacrifice, John combines a full time job for the ABC, where he is President of the Staff Association and a member of the Board of Directors, with a private life oriented to helping others within the Salvation Army context. His reformist politics and anti-authoritarian views place John on the boundaries of the Army, where he feels 'the capacity for change is greatest', and he can contribute best. His story is notable also for his awareness of the problem of suffering and his wide perspective on spiritual traditions other than his own.

———————— ✳✳✳ ————————

My family had no formal religious connections. My home life was fairly happy, a little different in that my father was a commercial traveller, away in the country for five or six days a week. I was at home with my mother and grandmother so I didn't have a strong father role model. I was christened in an Anglican church, but revolted against Anglicanism when I was five. I wouldn't go back to the place, I hated it. I ran into some kids who were six years old, and happened to have connections with the Salvation Army. I used to go along with them occasionally, but my first contact with any sort of spirituality came when a guy who was in the Salvation Army approached me, and asked me if I wanted to learn to play a musical instrument. I was eight. I tried for a while, and found it a bit hard, so I let it go. He approached me again a year later. I was just a kid who went to their Sunday School — I was not too heavily involved.

When I was about seven, we moved out of Carlton to Pascoe Vale, several miles away. It meant leaving all the kids I'd started to go to school with, but my connection with the Salvation Army remained because it was after school. I could get on the tram and go and learn to play. That was terribly important. At that time, when you are just learning to make friends, if you get cut off from them it's pretty devastating. What I gained out of that was a sense of the importance of relationships.

An organisation like the Salvation Army provides you with not only a moral but a social framework. The social framework can be all embracing, and helps you to grow up. The moral framework is generous. It focusses on what you are doing for other people. It's an altruistic view of the world: the world is not about you fulfilling yourself, but about having obligations to society. There is a strong element of sacrifice in religion, a giving of oneself to something for no necessary personal reward. This view, developed at that time, has coloured an enormous amount of what I've done since. I also gained from being part of an organisation which had emerged in the middle of the nineteenth century as a strong critic of society. The Army was involved in radical law reform over child labour, child prostitution and exploitation of workers in factories. Working in the East End of London, it came up with the same sort of analysis as Marx, at about the same time. Its agitation intuitively went towards a military style, and they saw their military organisations almost as a vanguard of the proletariat.

The local Salvation Army church that I attended in Brunswick had been one of the biggest centres in Australia, but, during the period I was there, it diminished in size. Brunswick had been a strong working-class area from the 1880s to the 1950s. When European migrants moved in there was less interest in the Salvation Army. At the same time the local Army had a musical combination that was world renowned. Before World War II its band leader had won the ABC Composer of the Year award. During the war he and the band enlisted as non-combatants. The Salvation Army was pacifist and encouraged its people to join as stretcher bearers and medical orderlies. The band joined up as one group, and when the Japanese hit Rabaul they were all taken prisoner and put on a hospital ship. The ship was torpedoed by the Americans and the band members were all killed. So this one little church community had faced the death of all its significant men. I came in after that but the women were still there. So it was in the air. So you had to come to terms with a religion which didn't necessarily make people happy.

Through my teens, the Salvation Army offered me the opportunity to travel interstate, to go to conferences, talk

to people and experience music. One of the great vehicles
of spiritual communion for the individual is the ability
to make music in a group. The Salvation Army intuitively
preserves that, and it's extraordinarily powerful. I play tuba
and trombone, and I fiddle around on the clarinet. I was
still playing with good musical combinations until a year
ago, when pressures of work meant I had to stop.

My mother and father didn't like my involvement with
the Salvation Army. My father was a professional drinker
for a living, a salesman, and he found the Salvation Army's
teetotalism hard to handle. In my HSC year I was strongly
influenced by a teacher who saw that I had potential.
He took a group of us to all the major theatrical events
in Melbourne and this opened up a new world for me.
When I left school I went to La Trobe University and
majored in politics and philosophy. There were only a few
hundred students in those days, and immense intellectual
ferment. Because there were no university societies, we
had to create them. If people wanted to talk about
religion there were no holds barred. It was all open and
dynamic. I had come from a narrow Protestant background
and found myself dialoguing with Catholics, Jews and
Buddhists. Another important development was political
radicalisation. I got mixed up with anti-Vietnam protests,
not because it was fashionable to do so but because
the radical tradition of the Salvation Army led me to be
conscientiously opposed to the war.

My religious beliefs were formed and tested during this
period. Religion provides a sense of common coherence
for the individual and that coherence has to be applicable
to the world at large. A lot of religion today is totally
self-oriented and ultimately that is destructive to the world
and the environment. One of the problems with New
Age religions is that they tend to be so focussed on the
personal that they entirely miss the dimension of the
other. The great religious traditions must always provide

a critique of society. A totally personalised belief is of no value at all. What continues to impress me about the Judeo-Christian tradition is the strength of its historical revelation. At one level, it's philosophical, but it is rooted in an historical tradition that relates to the world. When the Old Testament prophets talked about social justice, they weren't telling a little parable, they were talking about real life — you don't rob widows and orphans. Their religion grew out of practical situations, and their experience of God was related to history — God acts through people. There is a sense of the transcending, and a sense that the transcending can be known.

University almost led me to break completely with the Salvation Army. I helped form an organisation, 'Christians for Peace'. I was helping carry a banner at one of the Moratorium demonstrations. As we passed the Salvation Army headquarters for Southern Australia I walked over to the headquarters to hand out 'Christians Against the Vietnam War' brochures. I was met by the most unmitigated hostility from people I knew well. It wasn't the hostility of aggression, it was cold steel. It was a moment of catharsis. I realised that my belief systems couldn't be tied to institutions. Institutions are devices for preserving beliefs, and they are fallible. Most of them preserve the outward form and lose the substance. We have no other way of operating: if we are going to preserve knowledge, we have to have institutions. I see their enormous value, yet I see that they must always be open to radical restructuring.

After university I lived with a group of students connected with the Salvation Army who were at teachers college or university. We formed a Salvation Army ginger group, and I became known as a *bête-noire*. We worked to push a reformist platform through the local Salvation Army institutions. We put out a satirical magazine with cartoons that people found more offensive than the articles. We weren't trying to change structures fundamentally, we were

trying to make people see that there was another way. The
Army bands were playing music that was thirty years out of
date but to get them to recognise that rock and roll had
been around for fifteen years was hard. The generation
of the sixties was really dislocated. I was finding a way
through it, spiritually and intellectually, but so many kids
weren't. A lot of them weren't because they were sitting
at the Salvation Army playing in the bands, singing in the
choirs, doing work on the streets, yet having immense
inner struggles because they couldn't relate their personal
faith to their institutional faith. Great droves of them
were leaving. In the late sixties and early seventies, all
churches went through an exodus of young people who
found church life totally irrelevant, because the structures
were inflexible. We were committed to cleaning up the
structures.

I spent a number of years travelling and working
overseas before returning to Melbourne where I worked
in Welfare and got back in touch with the Brunswick
Salvation Army Church. In 1979, in a way that made me
think there are moments of divine intervention in my life,
I heard about a position coming up in the Religious Affairs
Department of the ABC. I applied, got the job, and took
up my appointment in 1980. I walked into an organisation
in a state of crisis. I spent the first two years of the job
in Perth, and got involved with the local union which had
been bitterly factionalised. I did two years as Vice-President
and at the next election, with the ABC going through a
critical time with budget cuts, I became Federal President.
Because of my church background, I was acceptable to
both the left and the right factions and so, for the first time
in many years, the union went to an election with a joint
position. I'm now in my second term as Federal President.
From there, I was recently elected to the Board of Directors
of the ABC.

I'm not married. My faith is central to me, and informs

my view of the world. That has meant that I have been less concerned than other people my age about settling down and getting married. I always had a fundamental belief that, if the centre was right, the fringes would take care of themselves. That has meant that there have been times when I have been extremely lonely, but the core of my belief has sustained me. It was a conscious decision on my part. My lifestyle is not conducive to me giving much care or attention to a family. I was aware of the decisions that I was making, but it is sometimes hard to see how far down the line you've compromised yourself. In my mid-thirties, I began to think that I had done something fundamentally wrong on a personal level. I went through three years of intense personal misery. Options were closing off — children. I began to think, my God, what is going to happen to me? But you work through that. It's the old twenty-third psalm — you walk through the valley of death, and keep pushing through. You accept that ultimately all that matters in your life is the benefit you have been to those immediately around you. Everybody dies, and the impression they make personally and the memory of what they have contributed, will die very quickly. If you are of no benefit, then your life has no meaning, because you are only defined in relationship to your anonymous contribution to the flow of history.

It worries me that people in search of spiritual fulfilment, and this applies to both conservative Christians and New Agers, are pursuing self-interest at an incredible rate. On the conservative Christian side you get this prosperity gospel. If you have Jesus in your heart, and do the right thing, and pay your 10 per cent to the church every week, God will reward you. The extreme version of New Age religion is exactly the same. What matters is personal fulfilment, so I will design a religion to suit my personal needs. It doesn't matter if it's intellectually shallow or if it has no relationship to the real world. In the late eighties, both new and old religion have been captured by materialism. But, for every action, there's a reaction, and there is now a re-emergence of social conscience in the major religious traditions. This will be helped by the environmental crisis. The big spiritual question for the rest of this century is the survival of the planet. This issue will bring science and religion together over the next decades. I don't mean that all religion is going to become one, because there are ethical insights unique to each religion which are, at times, incompatible. What there will be is a loose federation of understanding which will generate the moral drive to force the public and government bureaucracy to realise that they have been on the wrong track. The planet cannot stand the pace of current economic development.

The Salvation Army keeps me in touch with the real world. The ABC and union politics are cultural ghettos and the upper reaches of the Board of Directors is even worse. Salvation Army members are, in their daily occupations, ordinary people. They can give you a healthy view of how important or unimportant the particular intellectual currents that you're running with are. They also constantly remind me of the fact that spirituality is a very profound thing for a substantial majority of people. You can use the Salvation Army as your local church, and turn up on Sunday, go to a meeting and go home, that's fine. But there are a number of other options. One of them is 'soldiership'. That means putting on a uniform, and signing a declaration to give a percentage of your time and money to the Salvation Army.

Until a year ago, I was involved as a principal planner with the local Salvation Army band in Sydney. That consumed an enormous amount of my time. On Sundays, I would play in the band for the church service, teach a group of kids how to play instruments, be out with the band at a hospital or old people's home giving a concert.

In the evening there was fellowship tea and then evening service finished about nine. I would be there from 10.30 am till 9 pm every Sunday, plus two nights a week for rehearsals with the band.

Because of my union work, and work with the ABC, I tend now to use the Salvation Army as my local church. These days, I'm in the fortunate position of knowing the current head of, and a number of key individuals in, the Salvation Army. This makes it possible for me to work for change in a very small way. There needs to be change. The Army needs to be far less authoritarian. Its great beauty is its military structure, which provides a way of mobilising in emergencies which no other Christian organisation can match. When the Salvation Army delivers aid, there is no middleman, so the aid goes directly to the recipient. The servicing cost of any Salvation Army project is very low — three to five per cent compared to twenty-five per cent in other institutions where they have to employ middlemen. The trouble is that the military structure leads to rigidity. It's a matter of finding a way to get over that, because otherwise it will die.

The reason I stay a member, even though at times I find it profoundly discomforting, is so that I can provide a little kick in the direction of positive change. I would find being a member of a larger church personally comfortable, but I would have less opportunity to be of benefit. Unless you put yourself on the boundary, on the cutting edge of any situation, you are not doing your bit. That's where the capacity for change is greatest. My membership doesn't affect my work. My commitment to the Salvation Army is consistent with a view of myself that I've thought through which is consistent with the Salvation Army, work and the union. In practical ways, it informs it. Being a member of a small denomination puts me in a very good position as a religious journalist. I am not seen by any one of the major players as a threat to their position. As a journalist, what I've gained out of my membership is an understanding of human suffering, the dangers and benefits of organisations. It's also given me something to test my spiritual development against, to see whether my belief in God was contingent on an institution, or was something that related to myself and my view of the world. I've broken away from the institutions, and see my spiritual dynamic as not coming from them, or from my family, but as growing within me on two thousand years of tradition. It's something I came to myself, at the age of nineteen or twenty, and it's still growing. I find myself becoming aware of what people have been saying since the first Jewish scribes wrote the Bible. I'm a big kid, I get excited about new things. I love knowing that I don't know, and applying myself to something and seeing where it fits coherently into my vision of the world.

I would find it difficult to live without having a period every day where I do absolutely nothing for at least an hour. No matter what pressure I am under I retain that ability to cut off, to pull the shutters down. It's at those times that I come to terms with myself. When there is a danger of going over the edge, that sense of being in touch with the infinite gives you a sense of perspective. Sometimes I read — I read enormously — spiritual literature, the Bible, historical literature, sometimes I listen to music. Prayer is something that I engage in as an act of meditative reflection, morning and night. It happens without fail two or three times a day, it's so much a part of me. I have had that hour more often since I've been living by myself because I can order my life. I'm a very privileged person — I don't think I would have that as a parent. The great weakness of the Salvation Army is its lack of a reflective tradition. It doesn't have one — it's pro-active. I've come out of that tradition, and I'm moving towards a more reflective, cerebral one. It's like the difference between a revivalist meeting and a High Anglican service.

The revivalist meeting has all the emotional experiential dimensions, but they are totally incomprehensible to a High Anglican. The High Anglican service has two thousand years of religious tradition informing every act of the Mass. The whole architecture of God and theology is there, but the other traditions are incomprehensible to them.

Orthodox Christianity still provides for me the most coherent set of intellectual and spiritual guidelines for life. It's terribly unfashionable but it works. The problem with it today is that it's become institutionally hidebound. But that's the institution, it's not the vitality of what Christ said. What He said is immensely powerful, and man can't get away from that. Christianity has a meditative tradition, albeit undernourished, it has a mystical tradition, it has a social activist tradition and it has a way of coming to terms with the world. That first chapter in Genesis sets out God's relationship to man, and man's relationshp with the environment. It's that coherence, that ability of a religion to bring together the intellectual, the spiritual and the social, and to focus on a coherent point, which is at once far away in the distance at the end of my existence, and right here at the centre of me as a human being, that convinces me of its power.

The suffering of others is something for which you have compassion, and act to change. Coming to terms with suffering in yourself — only the individual can do. I haven't suffered very much. Whether you are happy or sad is something that you decide internally. Whether you are content within yourself, is ultimately contingent on nothing other than the operation of your brain. What gives me the strength to say that is knowing that my life has a purpose beyond this sheer physical existence. If I didn't have that understanding, then I wouldn't be able to make the choice to be content. That purpose is to recognise that there is something beyond, a point in the distance on which everything focuses, and that my only useful function is to be of benefit to those around me, whether that means giving a present to my nephew on his birthday, or impacting on the future of the ABC, or helping its employees through the union. We all have only limited opportunities. Maybe we only get one or two significant ones in our lives. If we don't take advantage of them, we are not participating in the infinite, because we only touch the infinite by participating in life.

Traditional Christian doctrine comes to terms with the suffering of mankind by saying that the moment free will operates there is the possibility of suffering. One has to accept the existence of evil the moment one accepts the existence of free will. Love is the ony force in the universe, and what determines whether it is good or evil is the use to which it is put. If it is directed towards self it becomes evil — whether it's expressed in selfish nationalism or free market economics. Ultimately love directed towards the self is destructive of the planet and of the universe. To come to terms with natural disasters like earthquakes and the suffering they generate, you have to bring in some concept of the order that underpins the cosmos. You have to accept that evolutionary processes are operating on a physical and a biological level, and that they involve life and death. What profoundly impresses me is that there is an underlying sense of security about the universe. That doesn't mean that it's not all going to end with a big bang. It does mean that there is, to use a Biblical allusion, 'underneath the everlasting arms' an immense well of support. Some people call it the river of history, some people call it other things, but whether you like it or not, you are part of it.

Bibliography

Religion and Spirituality in Australia

Bouma Gary D. and Dixon, Beverly *The Religious Factor in Australian Life* (MARC, Australia, Melbourne, 1986).

Brady, V. A. *Crucible of Prophets: Australians and the Question of God* (Theological Explorations, Sydney, 1981).

Campion, Edmund *The Rockchoppers* (Penguin, Melbourne, 1982). *Australian Catholics* (Penguin, Melbourne, 1988).

Collins, Paul *Mixed Blessings: John Paul II and the Church of the Eighties* (Penguin, Melbourne, 1986).

Gillman Ian (ed) *Many Faiths, One Nation* (William Collins, Sydney, 1988).

Harris, Dorothy, Hynd, Douglas and Millikan, David (ed) *The Shape of Belief* Christianity in Australia Today (Lancer, Homebush, Sydney, 1982).

Mol, Hans *The Faith of Australians* (Allen and Unwin, Sydney, 1985).

Nelson, Kate and Nelson, Dominica *Sweet Mothers, Sweet Maids* (Penguin, Melbourne, 1986).

O'Farrell, Patrick *The Catholic Church and Community: an Australian History* (University of New South Wales Press, Kensington, 1985).

Eastern Religions and the Human Potential Movement

Anthony, Dick, Ecker, Bruce and Wilber Ken (ed) *Spiritual Choices: The Problem of Recognising Authentic Paths to Inner Transformation* (Paragon House Publishers, New York, 1987).

Claxton, Guy (ed) *Beyond Therapy: The Impact of Eastern Religions on Psychological Theory and Practice* (Wisdom Publications, London, 1986).

Naranjo, Claudio *The One Quest* (Wildwood House, London, 1974).

Welwood, John (ed) *Awakening the Heart: East/West Approaches to Psychotherapy and the Healing Relationship* (Shambhala, Colorado, 1983).

Women and Spirituality

Franklin, Margaret Ann (ed) *The Force of the Feminine* (Allen and Unwin, Sydney, 1986).

Franklin, Margaret Ann and Jones, Ruth Sturmey (ed) *Opening the Cage* (Allen and Unwin, Sydney, 1987).

Friedman, Lenore *Meetings with Remarkable Women: Buddhist Teachers in America* (Shambhala, Boston, 1987).

King, Petrea *Quest for Life* (Equinox Press, Sydney, 1988).

Meadow, Mary Jo and Rayburn Carole A. (ed) *A Time to Weep, A Time to Sing: Faith Journeys of Women Scholars of Religion* (Winston Press, Minneapolis, 1985).

Spretnak, Charlene (ed) *The Politics of Women's Spirituality* (Anchor Press, New York, 1982).

DATE DUE